MOON

D1253234

PITTSBURGH

EMILY KING

Contents

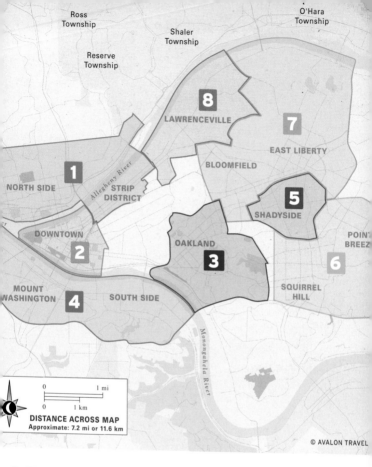

Maps

SIGHTS

3	Randyland	35	St. Stanislaus Kostka Church
7	National Aviary	45	Wigle Whiskey
25	Andy Warhol Museum		
28	St. Patrick Church		

RESTAURANTS

1	Wilson's Bar-B-Q	34	Pamela's Diner
5	Nicky's Thai Kitchen	36	DeLuca's Restaurant
10	Max's Allegheny Tavern	38	La Prima Espresso Company
13	Penn Brewery	41	Bar Marco
27	Gaucho Parrilla Argentina	44	Kelly O's
29	Primanti Brothers	46	Klavon's Ice Cream Parlor
31	Kaya	47	Salem's Market and Grill
33	Smallman Galley		

© AVALON TRAVEL

TROY HILL

47

46

Wigle
45 Whiskey

St. Stanislaus
Kostka Church 35
44   43

34
33   42
32   41
31
40
39
STRIP   29   38
DISTRICT   30   37
27   36
26
EAST BUSWAY   BIGELOW BLVD

SMALLMAN ST   28 St. Patrick
Church

BEDFORD
DWELLINGS

SEE MAP 3

0   250 yds

0   250 m

DISTANCE ACROSS MAP
Approximate: 2.7 mi or 4.3 km

COLWELL ST
OUR WAY

CENTRE AVE

9TH AVE
WATSON ST
FORBES AVE
GIBBON ST
LOCUST ST

DUQUESNE   BLUFF
UNIVERSITY

BLVD OF THE ALLIES

SEE MAP 4

NIGHTLIFE

| 26 | Real Luck Cafe | 43 | Mullany's |
| 42 | The Beerhive | | Harp and Fiddle |

ARTS AND CULTURE

2	Mattress Factory	14	Carnegie Science
8	Children's Museum of Pittsburgh		Center and Highmark SportsWorks
9	New Hazlett Theater		
11	Photo Antiquities Museum of Photographic History		

SPORTS AND ACTIVITIES

15	Pittsburgh Steelers	22	PNC Park Tours
16	Pitt Panthers Football	23	Pittsburgh Pirates
17	North Shore Riverfront Park	24	Kayak Pittsburgh
18	Three Rivers Heritage Trail		

SHOPS

| 30 | Strip District | 39 | Hot Haute Hot |
| 37 | Lucy's Handmade Clothing | 40 | Loom Exquisite Textiles |

HOTELS

4	The Parador	20	Hyatt Place Pittsburgh— North Shore
6	The Inn on the Mexican War Streets	21	Residence Inn North Shore
12	The Priory		

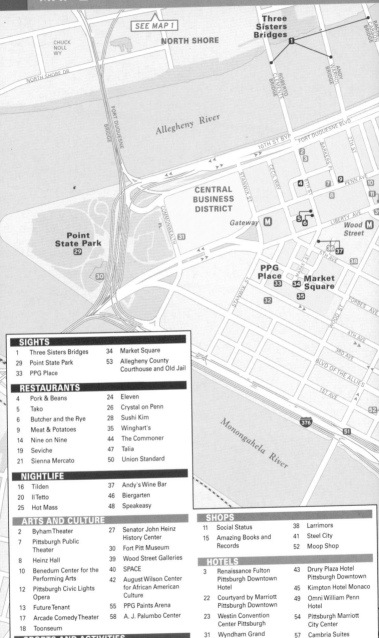

SEE MAP 1

NORTH SHORE

CHUCK NOLL WY

NORTH SHORE DR

FORT DUQUESNE BRIDGE

Three Sisters Bridges

RACHEL CARSON BRIDGE

ROBERTO CLEMENTE BRIDGE

ANDY WARHOL BRIDGE

Allegheny River

10TH ST BYP   FORT DUQUESNE BLVD

BARKERS PL

11TH ST

STANWIX ST

CECIL WAY

7TH ST

PENN AVE

CENTRAL BUSINESS DISTRICT

Gateway M

LIBERTY AVE

Wood Street M

COMMONWEALTH PL

FT PL

5TH AVE

Point State Park

PPG Place

Market Square

STANWIX ST

MARKET ST

FORBES AVE

4TH AVE

3RD AVE

BLVD OF THE ALLIES

1ST AVE

Monongahela River

376

SIGHTS
1	Three Sisters Bridges	34	Market Square
29	Point State Park	53	Allegheny County Courthouse and Old Jail
33	PPG Place		

RESTAURANTS
4	Pork & Beans	24	Eleven
5	Tako	26	Crystal on Penn
6	Butcher and the Rye	28	Sushi Kim
9	Meat & Potatoes	35	Winghart's
13	Nine on Nine	44	The Commoner
19	Seviche	47	Talia
21	Sienna Mercato	50	Union Standard

NIGHTLIFE
16	Tilden	37	Andy's Wine Bar
20	Il Tetto	46	Biergarten
25	Hot Mass	48	Speakeasy

ARTS AND CULTURE
2	Byham Theater	27	Senator John Heinz History Center
7	Pittsburgh Public Theater	30	Fort Pitt Museum
8	Heinz Hall	39	Wood Street Galleries
10	Benedum Center for the Performing Arts	40	SPACE
12	Pittsburgh Civic Lights Opera	42	August Wilson Center for African American Culture
13	Future Tenant	55	PPG Paints Arena
17	Arcade Comedy Theater	58	A. J. Palumbo Center
18	Toonseum		

SPORTS AND ACTIVITIES
32	Ice Rink at PPG Place	56	Pittsburgh Penguins
51	Eliza Furnace Trail		

SHOPS
11	Social Status	38	Larrimors
15	Amazing Books and Records	41	Steel City
		52	Moop Shop

HOTELS
3	Renaissance Fulton Pittsburgh Downtown Hotel	43	Drury Plaza Hotel Pittsburgh Downtown
22	Courtyard by Marriott Pittsburgh Downtown	45	Kimpton Hotel Monaco
23	Westin Convention Center Pittsburgh	49	Omni William Penn Hotel
31	Wyndham Grand Pittsburgh Downtown	54	Pittsburgh Marriott City Center
36	Fairmont Pittsburgh	57	Cambria Suites Pittsburgh at PPG Paints Arena

SEE MAP 1

SMALLMAN ST

27
28
24
26
25

MULBERRY WAY

PENN AVE

9TH ST

GARRISON PL

FRENCH ST

21
20
22
19
23

10TH ST

LIBERTY AVE

13

PENN AVE

14

EXCHANGE WY

15 16 17 18

12

42

BEDFORD AVE

CRAWFORD ST

WYLIE AVE

11TH AVE

40

STRAWBERRY WY

41

43

6TH AVE

WILLIAM PENN PL

44

45 46

47

SMITHFIELD ST

OLIVER AVE

48

50

49

Steel
Plaza
M

WASHINGTON PL

CENTRE AVE

57

CHERRY WAY

GRANT ST

53

Allegheny County
Courthouse and Old Jail

CROSSTOWN BLVD RAMP

54

55 56

COLWELL ST

OUR WAY

5TH AVE

WATSON ST

FORBES AVE

58

GIBBON ST

MAGEE ST

STEVENSON ST

3RD AVE

BLVD OF THE ALLIES

LOCUST ST

ARMSTRONG TUNL

DUQUESNE UNL

UNIVERSITY

BLUFF

M First
Avenue

BLVD OF THE ALLIES

SEE MAP 3

SEE MAP 4

0   200 yds

0   200 m

DISTANCE ACROSS MAP
Approximate: 1.6 mi or 2.6 km

© AVALON TRAVEL

West Penn Park

BIGELOW BLVD

BEDFORD
DWELLINGS

SEE MAP 8

WEBSTER AVE

WYLIE AVE

MIDDLE HILL

ELBA ST

CENTRE AVE

BRACKENRIDGE ST

UNIVERSITY
OF
PITTSBURGH

ALLEQUIPPA ST

TERRACE
VILLAGE

DARRAGH ST

TERRACE ST

OAK HILL DR

ECKSTEIN PL

WEST OAKLAND

CHESTERFIELD ST

SEE MAP 1

CARLOW
UNIVERSITY

5TH AVE

MAGEE-WOMEN'S
HOSPITAL OF
UPMC

CRAFT AVE

GALE ST

2ND AVE

SIGHTS

4 Soldiers & Sailors Memorial Hall & Museum
15 Cathedral of Learning
16 Stephen Foster Memorial
24 Carnegie Museum of Natural History
25 Carnegie Museum of Art
27 Carnegie Mellon University
31 Phipps Conservatory and Botanical Gardens

RESTAURANTS

2 Legume
9 Dave & Andy's
10 Fuel and Fuddle
12 The Original Hot Dog Shop
20 Lulu's Noodles
21 Ali Baba
28 Spice Island Tea House
30 Mad Mex

NIGHTLIFE

11 Peter's Pub
13 Hemingway's
18 KBOX Karaoke House

ARTS AND CULTURE

7 Pittsburgh Playhouse
26 Carnegie Music Hall

SPORTS AND ACTIVITIES

3 Pitt Panthers Basketball
32 Schenley Park Skating Rink
33 Schenley Park

SHOPS

14 The University Store on Fifth
17 Snowlion Imports
19 Irish Design Center
22 Caliban Bookshop
23 Phantom of the Attic Comics
29 Iron City Bikes

HOTELS

1 Residence Inn Pittsburgh University/ Medical Center
5 Wyndham Pittsburgh University Center
6 Hampton Inn University Center
8 Hilton Garden Inn Pittsburgh University Place

0   200 yds

0   200 m

DISTANCE ACROSS MAP
Approximate: 2.2 mi or 3.5 km

2ND AVE

PENN LINCOLN PKWY

LAWN ST

HAMLET ST

JONCAIRE ST

2ND AVE

TECHNOLOGY CENTER

Monongahela River

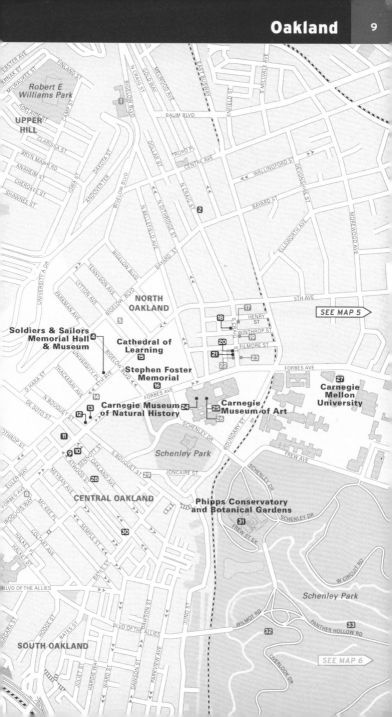

Robert E Williams Park

UPPER HILL

NORTH OAKLAND

Soldiers & Sailors Memorial Hall & Museum

Cathedral of Learning

Stephen Foster Memorial

Carnegie Museum of Natural History

Carnegie Museum of Art

Carnegie Mellon University

CENTRAL OAKLAND

Schenley Park

Phipps Conservatory and Botanical Gardens

Schenley Park

SOUTH OAKLAND

SEE MAP 5

SEE MAP 6

Duquesne
Incline

CENTRAL
BUSINESS
DISTRICT

SEE MAP 2

BLVD OF THE ALLIES

PLYMOUTH ST

GRANDVIEW AVE

W STATION
SQUARE DR

W CARSON ST

Grandview
Avenue Vista

376

Station
Square

BIGHAM ST

MERRIMAC ST

WABASH ST

Monongahela
Incline

W SYCAMORE ST

LIBERTY BRG

376

SOUTH SHORE

P.J. MCARDLE ROWY

SHILOH ST

WYOMING ST

BOGGS AVE

MOUNT WASHINGTON

Emerald
View
Park

LIBERTY TUNL

E WARRINGTON AVE

LIBERTY TUNL

BELTZHOOVER AVE

BAUSMAN ST

SIGHTS
1	Duquesne Incline	13	Station Square
5	Grandview Avenue Vista	14	Monongahela Incline

RESTAURANTS
2	Monterey Bay Fish Grotto	31	Café du Jour
3	Grandview Saloon & Coal Hill Steakhouse	38	Beehive Coffeehouse
		42	Mike and Tonys
4	LeMont Restaurant	48	Cambod-ican Kitchen
11	Grand Concourse	49	The Milk Shake Factory
15	Shiloh Grill	52	Fat Head's Saloon
18	La Tavola	54	Carmella's Plates and Pints
21	Nadine's		
22	Big Dog Coffee	61	Mallorca
25	Hofbräuhaus Pittsburgh	62	The Library

NIGHTLIFE
6	Bigham Tavern	43	Local Bar + Kitchen
16	The Summit	44	Diesel
17	Redbeard's	45	Skybar
20	Over the Bar Bicycle Café	47	Rex Theatre
		50	Jimmy D's
30	Bar 11	51	Jekyl and Hyde
32	Club Café	53	Piper's Pub
33	Jack's Bar	56	Smokin' Joe's
34	The Urban Tap	57	Tiki Lounge
36	The Smiling Moose	58	Acacia
37	Dee's Café		

ARTS AND CULTURE
35	City Theatre

SPORTS AND ACTIVITIES
7	Pittsburgh Riverhounds	19	Emerald View Park
9	Just Ducky Tours	23	The Pittsburgh Tour Company Double Decker Tours
10	Segway Pittsburgh		
12	Pittsburgh History and Landmarks Foundation Tours	29	Oliver Bath House

MURIEL ST

BINGHAM ST

BINGHAM ST

E CARSON ST

S 11TH ST

S 12TH ST

S 13TH ST

Armstrong
Field

BRADISH ST

ENON WY

BREED ST

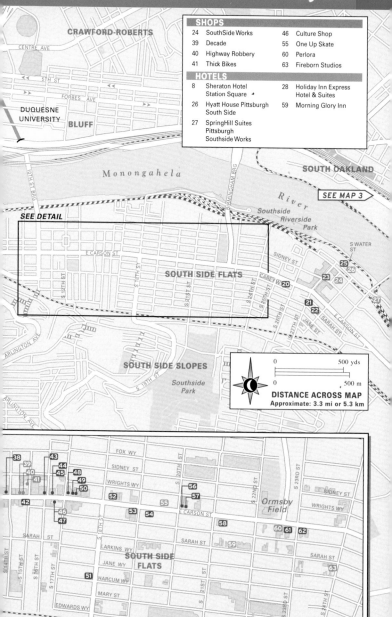

SHOPS

24	SouthSide Works	46	Culture Shop
39	Decade	55	One Up Skate
40	Highway Robbery	60	Perlora
41	Thick Bikes	63	Fireborn Studios

HOTELS

8	Sheraton Hotel Station Square	28	Holiday Inn Express Hotel & Suites
26	Hyatt House Pittsburgh South Side	59	Morning Glory Inn
27	SpringHill Suites Pittsburgh Southside Works		

CRAWFORD-ROBERTS

CENTRE AVE

5TH ST

FORBES AVE

DUQUESNE UNIVERSITY

BLUFF

10TH ST BRG

M o n o n g a h e l a

BIRMINGHAM BRG

SOUTH OAKLAND

R i v e r

SEE MAP 3

Southside Riverside Park

SEE DETAIL

E CARSON ST

SIDNEY ST

S WATER ST

S 12TH ST

S 17TH ST

S 21ST ST

SOUTH SIDE FLATS

S 24TH ST

S 25TH ST

CAREY W 20

SIDNEY ST

25

23

24

21

22

E CARSON ST

S 27TH ST

JANE ST

SARAH ST

ARLINGTON AVE

ARLINGTON AVE

SOUTH SIDE SLOPES

S 18TH ST

Southside Park

0   500 yds
0   500 m

DISTANCE ACROSS MAP
Approximate: 3.3 mi or 5.3 km

FOX WY

S 20TH ST

38

39

43

44

45

48

40

41

49

50

SIDNEY ST

WRIGHTS WY

S 22ND ST

S 23RD ST

SIDNEY ST

56

57

Ormsby Field

WRIGHTS WY

42

52

55

E CARSON ST

53

54

58

S 15TH ST

S 16TH ST

S 17TH ST

46

47

SARAH ST

SOUTH SIDE FLATS

LARKINS WY

JANE WY

SARAH ST

60 61 62

S 21ST ST

S 24TH ST

SARAH ST

63

51

HARCUM WY

MARY ST

EDWARDS WY

S 23RD ST

59

SEE MAP 7

S AIKEN AVE

VINTAGE WAY

S GRAHAM ST

EAST BUSWAY

6

7

5

Morrow
Park

CENTRE AVE

ELLSWORTH AVE

FELIX WAY

4

S GRAHAM ST

S AIKEN AVE

CLAYBOURNE ST

POTTER ST

EAST BUSWAY

SUMMERLEA ST

2

3

MARYLAND AVE

ALDER ST

COLLEGE AVE

HOLDEN ST

ELMER ST

IVY ST

SHADYSIDE

MEDICAL
CENTER

**Roslyn
Place**

1

ELLSWORTH AVE

MYRTLE WAY

S NEGLEY AVE

ROSARY WAY

ELWOOD ST

S AIKEN AVE

COPELAND ST

TELEPHONE WAY

TELEGRAPH WAY

ELMER ST

BELLEFONTE ST

CULLODEN WAY

FILBERT ST

URN WY

IVY ST

30

23

24

25

26

17

15

16

18

WALNUT

29

14

13

22

27

28

20

21

19

COMET WAY

HOWE ST

SEE MAP 3

PEMBROKE PL

KENTUCKY AVE

BELLEFONTE ST

IVY ST

S NEGLEY AVE

S AIKEN AVE

ST JAMES ST

5TH AVE

35

MAPLE HEIGHTS RD

34

5TH AVE

36

WILKINS AVE

DUNMOYLE ST

WARWICK TER

KIPLING RD

WIGHTMAN ST

0   500 yds

0   500 m

DISTANCE ACROSS MAP
Approximate: 4.2 mi or 6.9 km

© AVALON TRAVEL

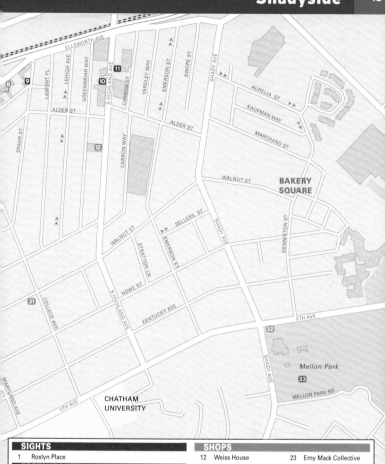

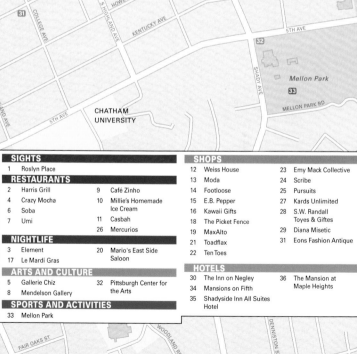

SIGHTS

1 Roslyn Place

RESTAURANTS

2 Harris Grill
4 Crazy Mocha
6 Soba
7 Umi
9 Café Zinho
10 Millie's Homemade Ice Cream
11 Casbah
26 Mercurios

NIGHTLIFE

3 Element
17 Le Mardi Gras
20 Mario's East Side Saloon

ARTS AND CULTURE

5 Gallerie Chiz
8 Mendelson Gallery
32 Pittsburgh Center for the Arts

SPORTS AND ACTIVITIES

33 Mellon Park

SHOPS

12 Weiss House
13 Moda
14 Footloose
15 E.B. Pepper
16 Kawaii Gifts
18 The Picket Fence
19 MaxAlto
21 Toadflax
22 TenToes
23 Emy Mack Collective
24 Scribe
25 Pursuits
27 Kards Unlimited
28 S.W. Randall Toyes & Giftes
29 Diana Misetic
31 Eons Fashion Antique

HOTELS

30 The Inn on Negley
34 Mansions on Fifth
35 Shadyside Inn All Suites Hotel
36 The Mansion at Maple Heights

SEE MAP 6

DISTANCE ACROSS MAP
Approximate: 1.9 mi or 3.0 km

0   500 yds
0   500 m

GETTYSBURG ST

1
2

REYNOLDS ST

EDGERTON AVE

HASTINGS ST

S LINDEN AVE

S DALLAS AVE

WILLARD ST

BEECHWOOD BLVD

DENNISTON ST

SHADY AVE

KINSMAN RD

WOODWELL ST

RIDGEVILLE ST

SEVERN ST

SEE MAP 3

WILKINS AVE

SOLWAY ST

NORTHUMBERLAND ST

WOODMONT ST

DALZELL PL

FERREE ST

AYLESBORO AVE

AYLESBORO AVE

SQUIRREL
HILL

DENNISTON ST

BEECHWOOD BLVD

Smithfield
East End
Cemetery

S DALLAS AVE

American
Jewish
Museum

11

8
9 10

21

SHADY AVE

FORBES AVE

12

19
20

22

MURRAY AVE

DARLINGTON RD

BARTLETT ST

SHAW AVE

23

BEECHWOOD BLVD

SQUIRREL HILL
SOUTH

BEACON ST

13

HOBART ST

14

DOUGLAS ST

SHADY AVE

15

MURRAY AVE

16

PHILLIPS AVE

Davis Parklet

Frick Park

NICHOLSON ST

ELDRIDGE ST

WALDRON ST

CROMBIE ST

FRICK PARK ACCESS RD W

NICHOLSON ST

FORWARD AVE

MAEBURN RD

SHADY AVE

17

FORWARD AVE

BEECHWOOD BLVD

18

ALDERSON ST

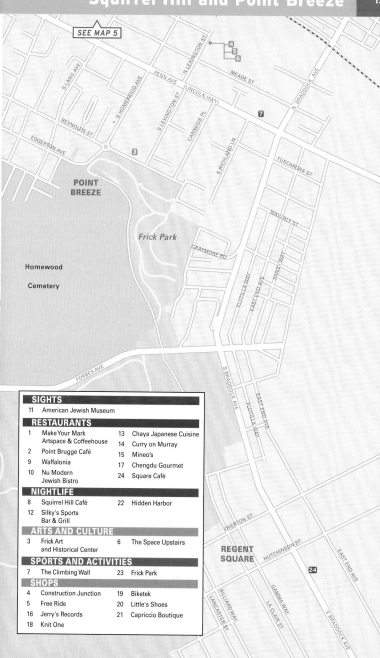

SEE MAP 5

POINT
BREEZE

Frick Park

Homewood

Cemetery

REGENT
SQUARE

© AVALON TRAVEL

SIGHTS
11   American Jewish Museum

RESTAURANTS
1   Make Your Mark
      Artspace & Coffeehouse
2   Point Brugge Café
9   Waffalonia
10   Nu Modern
      Jewish Bistro
13   Chaya Japanese Cuisine
14   Curry on Murray
15   Mineo's
17   Chengdu Gourmet
24   Square Café

NIGHTLIFE
8   Squirrel Hill Café
12   Silky's Sports
      Bar & Grill
22   Hidden Harbor

ARTS AND CULTURE
3   Frick Art
      and Historical Center
6   The Space Upstairs

SPORTS AND ACTIVITIES
7   The Climbing Wall
23   Frick Park

SHOPS
4   Construction Junction
5   Free Ride
16   Jerry's Records
18   Knit One
19   Biketek
20   Little's Shoes
21   Capriccio Boutique

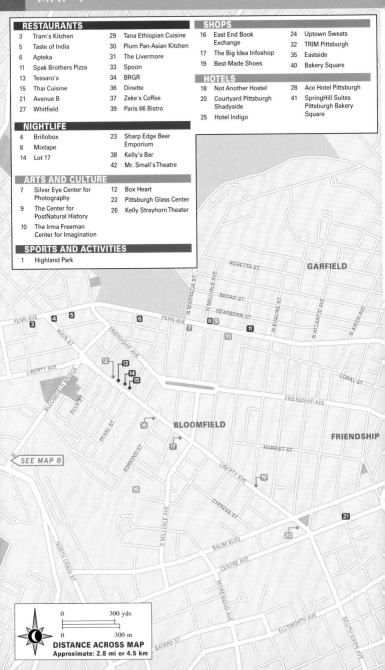

RESTAURANTS

3	Tram's Kitchen
5	Taste of India
6	Apteka
11	Spak Brothers Pizza
13	Tessaro's
15	Thai Cuisine
21	Avenue B
27	Whitfield
29	Tana Ethiopian Cuisine
30	Plum Pan-Asian Kitchen
31	The Livermore
33	Spoon
34	BRGR
36	Dinette
37	Zeke's Coffee
39	Paris 66 Bistro

NIGHTLIFE

4	Brillobox
8	Mixtape
14	Lot 17
23	Sharp Edge Beer Emporium
38	Kelly's Bar
42	Mr. Small's Theatre

ARTS AND CULTURE

7	Silver Eye Center for Photography
9	The Center for PostNatural History
10	The Irma Freeman Center for Imagination
12	Box Heart
22	Pittsburgh Glass Center
26	Kelly Strayhorn Theater

SPORTS AND ACTIVITIES

1	Highland Park

SHOPS

16	East End Book Exchange
17	The Big Idea Infoshop
19	Best-Made Shoes
24	Uptown Sweats
32	TRIM Pittsburgh
35	Eastside
40	Bakery Square

HOTELS

18	Not Another Hostel
20	Courtyard Pittsburgh Shadyside
25	Hotel Indigo
28	Ace Hotel Pittsburgh
41	SpringHill Suites Pittsburgh Bakery Square

SEE MAP 8

DISTANCE ACROSS MAP
Approximate: 2.8 mi or 4.5 km

0 — 300 yds
0 — 300 m

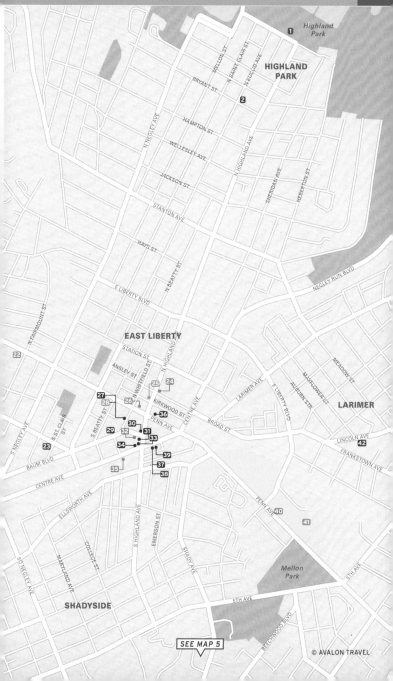

Highland
Park

**HIGHLAND
PARK**

MELLON ST
N SAINT CLAIR ST
N EUCLID AVE

BRYANT ST

2

HAMPTON ST

N NEGLEY AVE

WELLESLEY AVE

N HIGHLAND AVE

SHERIDAN AVE

HEBERTON ST

JACKSON ST

STANTON AVE

HAYS ST

N BEATTY ST

E LIBERTY BLVD

NEGLEY RUN BLVD

EAST LIBERTY

N FAIRMOUNT ST

STATION ST

ANSLEY ST

N WHITFIELD ST

N HIGHLAND

LARIMER AVE

MEADOW ST

MAYFLOWER ST

AUBURN STR

LARIMER

22

25 24

27
28

26

KIRKWOOD ST

CENTRE AVE

E LIBERTY BLVD

S ST CLAIR ST

S BEATTY ST

36

BROAD ST

LINCOLN AVE

42

S NEGLEY AVE

23

29

32
30
31
33
34

PENN AVE

FRANKSTOWN AVE

BAUM BLVD

39

CENTRE AVE

35

37
38

ELLSWORTH AVE

S HIGHLAND AVE

EMERSON ST

SHADY AVE

PENN AVE 40

41

SO NEGLEY AVE

N MARYLAND AVE

COLLEGE ST

Mellon
Park

5TH AVE

SHADYSIDE

5TH AVE

BEECHWOOD BLVD

SEE MAP 5

© AVALON TRAVEL

28

7
8
9

10

51ST ST

BUTLER ST
11
12
13
14
15

49TH ST

48TH ST

CARNEGIE ST

KEYSTONE ST

HOLMES ST

STANTON AVE

A l l e g h e n y   R i v e r

47TH ST

HATFIELD ST

PLUMMER ST

BUTLER ST

**Allegheny
Cemetery**

16

17
18
19

44TH ST

20

21
22

*Leslie
Recreation
Center*

23

46TH ST

45TH ST

40TH ST BRIDGE

WILLOW ST

43RD ST

41ST ST   FOSTER ST

25
26

BUTLER ST

24

27

28

44TH ST

40TH ST

29

30

31

DAVISON ST

MAIN ST

42ND ST

FISK ST

34
35

32
33

36

*Arsenal
Park*

47

38
37
39

40

41

42

37TH ST

38TH ST

39TH ST

SMALLMAN ST

BUTLER ST

43
44

48

MAIN ST

CHARLOTTE ST

45

PENN AVE

MINTWOOD ST

HOWLEY ST

*Bloomfield
Playground*

46

PENN AVE

LIGONIER ST

DENNY ST

49

LIBERTY AVE

BLOOMFIELD BRIDGE

To
50 The Copacetic Comics Company
and
51 Gooski's

SIGHTS
16 Allegheny Cemetery

RESTAURANTS
3 Pusadee's Garden
4 Cure
17 La Gourmandine
22 Banh Mi and Ti
27 The Vandal
29 Smoke
32 Coca Café
35 Piccolo Forno
36 Franktuary
39 Umami
41 Espresso a Mano
43 Morcilla
45 Senti

NIGHTLIFE
5 Allegheny Wine Mixer
12 Blue Moon
15 Spirit
19 The Goldmark
20 Cattivo
21 New Amsterdam
26 Industry Public House
28 Hambone's
31 Belvedere's Ultra-Dive
34 Grapparia
37 Round Corner Cantina
48 Arsenal Cider House
49 Church Brew Works
51 Gooski's

ARTS AND CULTURE
46 The Clemente Museum

SPORTS AND ACTIVITIES
24 Arsenal Bowling Lanes
47 Arsenal Park

SHOPS
1 Calligramme
2 Nine Stories
6 Glitter and Grit
7 16:62 Design Zone
8 Von Walter and Funk
9 City Grows
10 Thriftique
11 Who New?
13 Vestis
14 The Gilded Girl Beauty Emporium
18 No. 14
23 Mid-Atlantic Mercantile
25 Gallery on 43rd Street
30 Wildcard
33 Kinsman
38 Toll Gate Revival
40 Pavement
42 Brambler Boutique
44 Asian Influences
50 The Copacetic Comics Company

Allegheny Cemetery

0   200 yds
0   200 m

DISTANCE ACROSS MAP
Approximate: 2.0 mi or 3.2 km

© AVALON TRAVEL

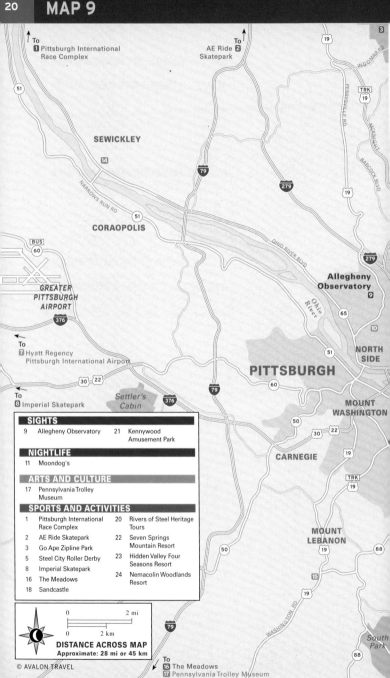

To **1** Pittsburgh International Race Complex

To **2** AE Ride Skatepark

3

19

INGOMAR RD

51

PERRYSVILLE RD

TRK 19

MCKNIGHT RD

BABCOCK BLVD

SEWICKLEY

14

79

279

NARROWS RUN RD

OHIO RIVER BLVD

51

CORAOPOLIS

BUS 60

279

GREATER PITTSBURGH AIRPORT

376

Ohio River

Allegheny Observatory 9

65

10

51

NORTH SIDE

To **7** Hyatt Regency Pittsburgh International Airport

PITTSBURGH

60

30 22

To **8** Imperial Skatepark

Settler's Cabin

376

79

50

MOUNT WASHINGTON

30 22

19

CARNEGIE

TRK 19

MOUNT LEBANON

50

19

88

15

88

WASHINGTON RD

South Park

19

79

To **16** The Meadows
17 Pennsylvania Trolley Museum

SIGHTS

9	Allegheny Observatory
21	Kennywood Amusement Park

NIGHTLIFE

11	Moondog's

ARTS AND CULTURE

17	Pennsylvania Trolley Museum

SPORTS AND ACTIVITIES

1	Pittsburgh International Race Complex	20	Rivers of Steel Heritage Tours
2	AE Ride Skatepark	22	Seven Springs Mountain Resort
3	Go Ape Zipline Park	23	Hidden Valley Four Seasons Resort
5	Steel City Roller Derby	24	Nemacolin Woodlands Resort
8	Imperial Skatepark		
16	The Meadows		
18	Sandcastle		

---

0 —————— 2 mi

0 —————— 2 km

DISTANCE ACROSS MAP
Approximate: 28 mi or 45 km

© AVALON TRAVEL

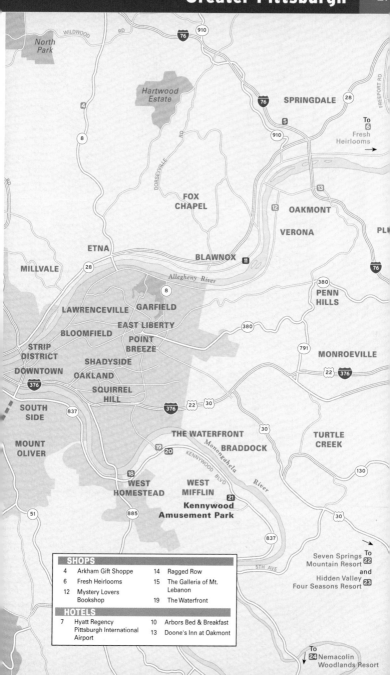

SHOPS
4 Arkham Gift Shoppe
6 Fresh Heirlooms
12 Mystery Lovers
   Bookshop

14 Ragged Row
15 The Galleria of Mt.
   Lebanon
19 The Waterfront

HOTELS
7 Hyatt Regency
   Pittsburgh International
   Airport

10 Arbors Bed & Breakfast
13 Doone's Inn at Oakmont

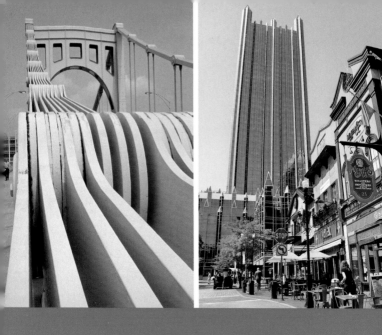

Pittsburgh

Hardworking. Industrial. Practical. These are the terms that have identified Pittsburgh since its days as a steel town. Nicknamed "The Gateway to the West," the city's location at the confluence of the Allegheny and Monongahela Rivers and the head of the Ohio River made it an ideal location for trade and commerce.

A word that better identifies today's Pittsburgh is reinvention. New arrivals are drawn here by its top universities, technological advances, and pioneering medicine. It's a city on the rise, recognized as much for its cutting-edge art, its food scene, and its tech startups as it is for its champion sports teams. Abandoned warehouses from the bygone industrial era have been converted into galleries, hip eateries, and upscale boutiques.

What hasn't changed are its people. Defined by a rich history of immigration, they have never lost their hard-working, humble spirit. The city is a patchwork of colorful, multicultural neighborhoods, no two of them alike. To really understand the heart of the 'Burgh, roam the streets of Bloomfield at Little Italy Days, wander the Strip District's iconic fish market, and browse the upscale boutiques in Shadyside.

At their core, Pittsburghers are still practical and down-to-earth, but they are, above all, friendly. Walk into any neighborhood bar and someone is guaranteed to invite you to pull up a stool, enjoy an I.C. Light, and talk about the latest Pirates or Steelers game. One thing hasn't changed: You'll be welcomed here.

Clockwise from top left: Andy Warhol Bridge; PPG Place in downtown Pittsburgh; Duquesne Incline; Pittsburgh at night.

Planning Your Trip

Neighborhoods

Strip District

Don't be put off by its gritty exterior: The Strip District holds a lot of surprises. A **formerly industrial** area filled with warehouses and loft buildings, the Strip District plays two separate but important roles in the life of the city. During the day, the area is visited largely for its produce dealers and **ethnic restaurants,** which line the parallel thoroughfares of **Penn Avenue** and **Smallman Street.** But once night falls, club-goers fill the district's **bars** and **dance clubs** in full force.

North Side

Situated just across the Allegheny River from downtown, the majority of the North Side's main attractions can be found in the area known as the North Shore, which is spread out alongside the river. The North Shore is the perfect destination for a breathtaking view of the city skyline or to catch a ball game. The **Pirates** and the **Steelers** have been battling it out on their respective fields for years, although the North Shore is also home to the **Andy Warhol Museum** and the **Carnegie Science Center.** Head a bit farther into the heart of the North Side to visit can't-miss attractions like the **National Aviary,** the **Children's Museum of Pittsburgh,** and the **Mattress Factory.**

Downtown

Also known as the **Golden Triangle,** Pittsburgh's downtown is where you'll find the **Cultural District,** which offers Broadway-style entertainment and the occasional concert. Downtown is also home to its fair share of highly regarded eateries, contemporary art galleries, and a few museums, the largest by far being the **August Wilson Center for African American Culture.** Following a massive renovation, the grandeur of **Point State Park** has grown even more awe-inspiring. Downtown is also where you'll find the bus and train stations, the Welcome Pittsburgh visitors center, and probably your hotel.

Oakland

Oakland is the **academic center** of Pittsburgh, with a selection of **museums, libraries,** and **universities.** It's also a lively neighborhood with a great selection of restaurants and bars. **Carnegie Mellon University** and the **University of Pittsburgh** are the best known of Oakland's institutions of higher learning. The main branch of the **Carnegie Library** can be found here, along with the **Carnegie Museums of Art and Natural History,** behind which you'll find the urban playground of **Schenley Park. Forbes Avenue,** the neighborhood's main drag, is home to dozens of retail outlets, bars, and ethnic eateries.

South Side

One of Pittsburgh's most eclectic and interesting areas, the South Side stretches along the Monongahela River from **Station Square** to **SouthSide Works**, a former steel mill turned shopping mall. **East Carson Street**, alternately referred to as Pittsburgh's Bourbon Street and the country's longest uninterrupted stretch of bars, runs the length of the district. Vintage clothing stores, art galleries, cafés, and ethnic eateries can also be found there.

Mount Washington

Sitting atop the city's South Side, Mount Washington exists in the mind of the average Pittsburgher for two reasons only: the breathtaking views along **Grandview Avenue,** which every visitor to the city should see, and the expensive eateries of **Restaurant Row.** Near to the **Monongahela Incline,** which ferries its passengers from Station Square to Mount Washington's peak, is the mini commercial district of **Shiloh Street.**

Shadyside

Just east of Oakland, Shadyside is one of the city's most **prestigious** and image-conscious neighborhoods. **Walnut Street** forms the area's commercial core; you'll find both big-name and **boutique shopping** and a near-steady stream of pedestrian traffic. Running parallel to Walnut Street is **Ellsworth Avenue,** where many of Shadyside's better bars and restaurants can be found. In between are rows of restored Victorian mansions and modern apartments.

Squirrel Hill and Point Breeze

Home to one of the largest Jewish communities in the Mid-Atlantic region, Squirrel Hill begins at the eastern end of Carnegie Mellon University. Its two major thoroughfares, **Forbes Avenue** and **Murray Avenue**, offer grocers, movie theaters, synagogues, kosher eateries, and cafés.

PNC Park and downtown

Phipps Conservatory and Botanical Gardens

On the opposite side of Frick Park, Point Breeze and the small district of **Regent Square** are Squirrel Hill's somewhat **upscale** neighbors to the east. Although largely residential, both areas have small commercial strips. Split between the two neighborhoods is **Frick Park**, a sprawling oasis and retreat from city life.

Bloomfield and East Liberty

Also known as Pittsburgh's **Little Italy**, the East End neighborhood of Bloomfield is a tightly knit residential community and a popular **shopping district. Liberty Avenue**, the neighborhood's heart and soul, is home to a charming medley of boutiques, cafés, and restaurants.

Nearby are East Liberty and **Garfield**, both neighborhoods in transition. Garfield is notable primarily for the art galleries and cafés that run the length of **Penn Avenue**, while East Liberty is home to a wide variety of popular **bars, restaurants,** and **boutiques.**

Lawrenceville

Lawrenceville, one of Pittsburgh's largest neighborhoods, is also arguably Pittsburgh's hippest place to hang out, due to its many **galleries, trendy restaurants,** and cool **boutiques** along **Butler Street**. The neighborhood stretches along the river from the Strip District to Morningside.

Greater Pittsburgh

The outlying suburbs and small towns of Greater Pittsburgh have much to offer the curious traveler, from the high-end retail district of **Sewickley** to the historical settlement of **Old Economy Village**. Another highlight is the retro, family-friendly **Kennywood Amusement Park.**

MassMutual Pittsburgh Ice Rink at PPG Place

When to Go

Choosing the perfect time to visit is really nothing more than a matter of personal inclination. When snow falls, the **winter season** (late December to early April) is absolutely gorgeous, yet the months of January and February can be unbearably cold; even native Pittsburghers tend to hibernate during this time of the year.

Pittsburgh's **summers** are often scorching hot and dripping with humidity, although this is also the season when the city comes alive with the most dynamism and excitement. What's more, a score of important festivals and events take place during the summer.

Spring and **fall** are both ideal seasons to visit Pittsburgh. Fall is especially lovely, complete with leaf-peeping opportunities and pleasant weather, with days that are cool but not cold and evenings that might best be described as light-jacket weather: sharp and brisk.

view from Mount Washington

The Two-Day Best of Pittsburgh

Although a thorough exploration of Pittsburgh and its environs would require at least a week, the city is compact enough that its most important sights and activities can be experienced easily in two days. The following itinerary assumes a Saturday-morning arrival in Pittsburgh; with the exception of a visit to the Strip District, which is at its best on Saturday mornings, the following activities can easily be shuffled around at will.

Day 1

▶ Start your visit with an early-morning trip to the **Strip District.** Stop by **Pamela's Diner** for breakfast and then join the throngs of shoppers searching for kitschy souvenirs along **Penn Avenue.**

▶ Spend an hour or two at the **Senator John Heinz History Center,** and browse in the gift shop on your way out; you're unlikely to find a better selection of books about Pittsburgh anywhere else in the city. If the weather is cooperating, treat yourself to a trip up **Mount Washington** on the **Duquesne Incline**—there's a gift shop and small museum in the upper-level station—and then to one of the best views of the city along **Grandview Avenue.** The eastward walk along Grandview is one of the nicest strolls in town. Continue on for just under a mile, pausing to enjoy the view from the large lookout platforms, to reach the **Monongahela Incline,** which you can ride back down to street level. Upon reaching the bottom, you'll see **Station Square** just ahead—it's a perfect pit stop for coffee or lunch. Should you find yourself in the mood for fine dining, head to Station Square's historical **Grand Concourse.**

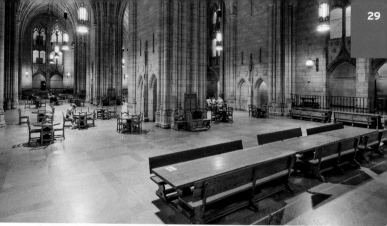

the Cathedral of Learning in Oakland

▶ Afterward, make your way down **East Carson Street** toward the South Side Flats for a bit of late-afternoon shopping. Indulge in authentic Spanish cuisine at **Mallorca,** where fresh seafood and original recipes are the stars—try the paella.

▶ Head back to the heart of the South Side Flats and end your day with a nightcap. Relax with a margarita on the rooftop deck at **Local Bar + Kitchen,** which also serves good pub grub.

Day 2

▶ Weekend brunch at trendy **Bar Marco** is a good way to start your day. But if you're only in the mood for a latte, wander over to **La Prima Espresso** instead and belly up to the coffee bar.

▶ When it's time to start moving again, take a long and leisurely stroll through **downtown** and into **Point State Park,** stopping off at the **ToonSeum** along the way. After you've seen the Point State Park fountain, use the pedestrian walkway on the Fort Duquesne Bridge to cross over the **Allegheny River** and into the section of the North Side known as the North Shore.

▶ Head to the nearby **Andy Warhol Museum,** the largest single-artist museum in the United States. The Warhol has a great gift shop and a surprisingly good basement café, a great choice for lunch.

▶ Next, head to the **National Aviary** in West Park, the only nonprofit bird zoo in the country. Spend the rest of the afternoon exploring the **Oakland** neighborhood. Take a self-guided tour of the **Nationality Rooms** in the **Cathedral of Learning.** All this exploration will leave you hungry, so stop by **Fuel and Fuddle** for their filling lunch options

Andy Warhol Bridge, one of the Three Sisters Bridges

and excellent sweet potato fries. If the sun is shining, visit **Schenley Park** and its **Phipps Conservatory and Botanical Gardens.**

▶ For dinner, head back downtown. Take a cab if the weather is chilly, or if you're still on the North Side, go by foot across one of the **Three Sisters Bridges.** Your dining destination is **Meat & Potatoes,** a gastro-pub that dishes out simple but excellent American fare and legendary Prohibition-era cocktails.

▶ After dinner, take in a show in the **Cultural District.** Pick up a free copy of the *Pittsburgh City Paper* to see what's going on. If nothing grabs your interest or you'd prefer a less expensive and more intimate entertainment option, head back to the South Side via taxi and stop in at **Club Café,** which usually offers two pop or folk concerts nightly. (Ask your cabbie to take the 10th Street Bridge from downtown, which can also be crossed on foot.)

Pittsburgh on a Budget

Schenley Park

Operating on a shoestring budget? You've come to the right city. Budget living is practically a religion in some quarters of Pittsburgh, where a night on the town costs as little as $20 and a day exploring the urban jungle can be had for almost nothing at all. For both year-round and seasonal cheapskate suggestions, visit www.livingpittsburgh.com.

Sightseeing

For budget sightseeing, take a self-guided tour of the **Nationality Rooms** inside Pitt's **Cathedral of Learning.** After exploring the nearby **Schenley Park,** stroll the length of the **Three Rivers Heritage Trail** on the North Shore, which has lately turned into something of an outdoor sculpture garden. And don't worry about public transit: As long as you stick to the four stops within the Golden Triangle itself and the two North Shore stops, rides on the city's light rail, known locally as the T, are always free.

Food

Due to its dead-broke student population, Oakland is replete with restaurants serving half-priced food after 11pm. Try **Fuel and Fuddle** for American pub grub or **Mad Mex** for huge, toothsome burritos. And many of the food stalls in Oakland's **Schenley Plaza** are dirt cheap, yet of surprisingly high quality.

Shopping

For budget souvenir shopping, make the scene on **Penn Avenue** in the Strip District, where everything from unlicensed Steelers T-shirts to Peruvian finger puppets is on offer. Downtown parking is free on Sundays.

The Arts

During summer, **free movies** are screened outdoors in seven different parks, including Schenley Park in Oakland and Grandview Park in Mount Washington. For movie listings and times, call **Cinema in the Park** (412/422-6426). **Mattress Factory** offers half-price admission on Tuesday, while admission to the **Andy Warhol Museum** is half off on Friday 5pm-10pm. Entrance to the **Center for PostNatural History** in Garfield is always free. **Gallery Crawl,** the quarterly art walk put on by the Cultural District, is also free.

Recreation

Kayak Pittsburgh offers fantastic ways to experience the city from a duck's-eye view; kayaks, canoes, and even hydrobikes and stand-up paddle boards can be rented for roughly $16-19 an hour. The **Pittsburgh History and Landmarks Foundation** (www.phlf.org) offers scores of free walking tours.

Cool and Quirky in the 'Burgh

As you walk around Pittsburgh, you may notice some downright weird stuff. This is a town full of quirks—and locals are proud of it!

- **Dinosaurs—everywhere.** As you visit different neighborhoods around the city, you may notice a strange trend. There are dinosaur statues in the most unexpected places. In 2003, the Carnegie Museum of Natural History asked for artists to create colorful dinosaur statues and then auctioned them off to create awareness of the museum's impressive collection of dinosaur fossils. Look for Dolly Dollarasaurus on the corner of Penn and Braddock Avenues and a Mr. Rogers dinosaur in South Side.

Dinosaurs are everywhere in Pittsburgh.

- **Fries on salad.** If you're visiting Pittsburgh and simultaneously watching your waistline, take caution while ordering a salad. A traditional Pittsburgh salad is mounded with hot, crispy French fries. Don't forget the ranch dressing!

- **Steps, steps, and more steps.** Before you opt to take the stairs, know what you're getting into. Pittsburgh has more public steps than any city in the world: 712 sets, to be exact. That adds up to 44,645 steps.

- **The protractor mystery.** When's the last time you used one? In Pittsburgh, chances are you'll see them more than the average person. Around 2011, protractors started showing up all over the city, glued to road signs, stuck to mailboxes, and many other places. Why? The mystery has never been solved.

- **Livestreaming a grave.** Pittsburgh has an obsession with pop art icon Andy Warhol. After all, he was born here, and the Andy Warhol Museum, the largest museum dedicated to a single artist, is in the North Side. The most offbeat dedication to the artist is an ongoing livestream of his gravesite (www.warhol.com/andy-warhols-life/figment).

- **An app for odors.** Smell PGH is a smartphone app that lets you report weird smells in the 'Burgh. It's a project of the CMU Community Robotics, Education and Technology Empowerment Lab. Bad smells are often a red flag for air pollution, so it's a cool tool for those concerned about the environment.

Sights

Highlights

★ **Best Offbeat Museum:** Pay your respects to the iconic artist by visiting the unexpected and quirky **Andy Warhol Museum,** the largest space dedicated to a single artist in the United States (page 38).

★ **Best Photo Op:** Pittsburgh's three rivers, the Allegheny, Monongahela, and Youghiogheny, converge at **Point State Park** (page 40). ·

★ **Best Bridges:** Pittsburgh is known for its bridges—and the bright yellow **Three Sisters Bridges** are arguably the most dazzling of them all (page 42).

★ **Most Collegiate:** Spend an afternoon exploring the **Cathedral of Learning** on the University of Pittsburgh's campus, where students study in the hidden arches and gather for classes in the famous Nationality Rooms (page 45).

★ **Best Place to Take a Nature Break:** Get away from the bustle of the city and revel in nature at **Phipps Conservatory and Botanical Gardens** (page 47).

★ **Only in Pittsburgh:** The **Duquesne and Monongahela Inclines** are Pittsburgh trademarks that everyone has to ride at least once. Take the funicular up and down Mount Washington, enjoying the clacking of the wooden tracks and the views of the city (page 49).

★ **Best View:** Tourists and locals alike flock to the **Grandview Avenue Vista** on Mount Washington to glimpse one of America's most stunning views (page 50).

Before beginning your exploration of the hilly and often-circuitous city of Pittsburgh, consider this: Even locals joke about how easy it is to get hopelessly lost on the town's twisting and turning roads.

Visitors get easily frustrated by this seemingly nonsensical tangle of roads. Pittsburgh's topography consists of steep hills, deep valleys, and three rivers—the Allegheny, the Monongahela, and the Ohio—all of which weave their way in and out of Pittsburgh's multihued quilt of neighborhoods.

Spending a day in the downtown area may put you in the center of the city, but it will show you only a fraction of what Pittsburgh is all about. Be sure to make time to explore the outlying neighborhoods. Take at least a day to explore Pittsburgh's eastern neighborhoods, like Oakland, Shadyside, Squirrel Hill, Lawrenceville, and Bloomfield. You'll find posh shops on tree-lined Walnut Street in Shadyside, historical architecture and ethnic eateries near the University of Pittsburgh campus in Oakland, and hipster hangouts and boutiques in Lawrenceville. This section of the city is also ripe with sprawling city parks, like Frick Park and Schenley Park.

South Side is a great place to experience at night. Take one of the inclines to the top of Mount Washington for a stunning view of the city lights. Head north of town for the day for a ball game. The North Shore is home to Heinz Field and PNC Park, home of the Steelers, University of Pittsburgh Panthers, and Pittsburgh Pirates. If you're coming from downtown, make the trek across the river via one of the Three Sisters bridges.

This is just a sampling of the possible adventures you can have, whether you are a sports fanatic, an art aficionado, or a parent looking for ways to entertain the kids.

Previous: fountain in Point State Park; Duquesne Incline.

Clockwise from top left: an owl at the National Aviary; Wigle Whiskey; the Andy Warhol Museum.

Strip District

Map 1

ST. PATRICK CHURCH

Known to area residents as Old St. Patrick's, St. Patrick Church was Pittsburgh's first Catholic parish. And while the church building itself wasn't constructed until 1936, the parish was founded way back in 1808 by a group of Irish immigrants. This most likely explains the structure's stone tower, built to resemble the towers of Irish monasteries in medieval times.

Old St. Patrick's has something of a national reputation; it's one of the few churches in the world to house a replica of the famous **Holy Stairs,** which represent the number of steps Jesus climbed on the day Pontius Pilate condemned him to death. Visitors may climb the 28 steps during normal church hours, except during the noon hour on Mondays and Thursdays, when Mass is held. Do keep in mind, however, that ascending the steps must be done on one's knees. (Walking *down* the steps is allowed.)

MAP 1: 1711 Liberty Ave., 412/471-4767, www.saintsinthestrip.org; 8am-3:30pm daily (see website for weekly Mass schedule)

ST. STANISLAUS KOSTKA CHURCH

St. Stanislaus Kostka was consecrated in the summer of 1892 and was built using a blend of Romanesque and Baroque styles, with Byzantine influences. It can easily be spotted from blocks away, thanks to its front-facing **Great Rose Window,** which symbolizes God and the rays of the sun. The church is also home to a number of Munich-style stained-glass windows; experts have proclaimed them to be some of the finest examples of their kind in the country. Especially impressive are the church's paintings, such as those found in the semi-dome over the main altar.

MAP 1: 57 21st St., 412/471-4767, www.saintsinthestrip.org; 8am-3:30pm daily (see website for weekly Mass schedule)

WIGLE WHISKEY

In the 1790s, George Washington's administration introduced a whiskey tax, but many distillers in Western Pennsylvania bridled at this. Some, like Philip Wigle, scuffled with tax collectors, which eventually ignited the Whiskey Rebellion, a brief skirmish between the protesting distillers and troops led by President Washington himself. Wigle was sentenced to hang for treason but was pardoned by Washington, and Pittsburgh went on to create the finest whiskey in America.

Wigle Whiskey, named after that unknowing pioneer, opened to the public in 2012 and quickly started racking up awards. In 2015 and 2016, Wigle was the most awarded craft whiskey distillery in the United States by the American Craft Spirits Association. The distillery sticks to the traditional way of making whiskey: with a copper pot and local ingredients.

The one-hour **tour** (Sat., $20-25, advance reservations required) starts with a cocktail. Throughout the tour, visitors are given liquor samples to sip as they learn how the various whiskeys distilled here are created. Wigle strongly prefers that tour-goers be 21 or older. Those under the age of 12 are not allowed on the tour.

Wigle's tasting room offers the chance to sample their wares in the form of cocktails or flights in an urban industrial setting. An on-site gift shop sells Wigle beverages and other souvenirs.

MAP 1: 2401 Smallman St., 412/224-2827, www.wiglewhiskey.com; tasting room 11am-6pm Mon., 10am-6pm Tues.-Sat., 10am-4pm Sun.

North Side   Map 1

★ ANDY WARHOL MUSEUM

As the country's largest museum dedicated to a single artist, the Andy Warhol Museum is a particularly unique feather in Pittsburgh's cap. To explore the building properly, start on the top floor, where temporary exhibitions are generally held. As you work your way down, you'll encounter pieces both obscure (Jesus punching bags, oxidation paintings made of urine) and familiar (Campbell's soup cans, Brillo boxes). Don't miss *Silver Clouds,* a room where metallic balloons float freely. A theater that regularly screens films by and about Warhol and his entourage is on the ground level. The basement holds a café and the city's only vintage photo booth. An archival collection housing thousands of pieces of Warhol's personal ephemera is also on-site.

MAP 1: 117 Sandusky St., 412/237-8300, www.warhol.org; 10am-5pm Tues.-Thurs. and Sat.-Sun., 10am-10pm Fri.; $20 adults, $10 seniors, students, and children, free for children 2 and under

NATIONAL AVIARY

The North Side is home to the National Aviary, one of the most important bird zoos in the country. The aviary houses more than 600 exotic birds of over 200 species—many of them endangered. The zoo offers an immersive experience, in which visitors can walk among the birds, which are mostly unrestricted. (Just don't forget to shut the doors behind you!)

See birds from all over the world in their own environment, flying tree to tree, splashing in water, and seeking out food. Represented regions include grasslands, tropical rainforest, and wetlands. Just a few of the types of birds you'll see are the bald eagle, burrowing owl, rainbow lorikeet, roseate spoonbill, and the scissor-tailed flycatcher. Other residents of the aviary include two-toed sloths and a flock of African penguins.

Appealing to adults and children alike, the aviary offers exciting live shows ($5), feedings (free), and interactive encounters ($40-150) daily. At the especially popular lorikeet feeding, you can line up to offer a cup of nectar to the colorful birds, who willingly perch on your arms. The aviary also offers occasional VIP animal encounters ($300 and up).

MAP 1: 700 Arch St., 412/323-7235, www.aviary.org; 10am-5pm daily; $15 adults, $14 seniors and children

RANDYLAND

Pittsburgh native Randy Gilson has spent the years since 1995 transforming his three-story home into what is commonly referred to as the most colorful building in the city. Indeed, stumbling across this improbably cheerful parcel of land, which sits in the heart of the North Side, is certainly one of Pittsburgh's happiest surprises. The house itself is coated in primary colors and covered in murals, vintage signs, and random tchotchkes of all sorts, including a handmade 3-D map of the North Side. Over the years, Gilson has also painstakingly applied his creative touch to a roughly 30-block area around his home, a process that has resulted in more than 800 Day-Glo street gardens and 50 vegetable gardens cropping up around the neighborhood.

MAP 1: 1501 Arch St., 412/342-8152; free, donations welcome

Downtown

Map 2

ALLEGHENY COUNTY COURTHOUSE AND OLD JAIL

Designed in 1883 by the much-imitated architect Henry Hobson Richardson, the Allegheny County Courthouse is one of downtown's most recognizable and historic sights. Construction of the complex cost approximately $2.25 million, not a particularly small sum in the late 19th century. Today, the courthouse is a decent location for a midday picnic; anyone is welcome to join the nine-to-fivers who gather around the outdoor fountain in the courtyard.

Locals frequently refer to the building's most interesting feature, an arching stone bridge, as the **Bridge of Sighs.** This bridge connects the courthouse to the adjoining jail, which is no longer in operation.

It's possible to enter the courthouse to look around, although you must pass through a metal detector first. A model of the courthouse complex is on display on the second floor. The granite structure is impossible to miss—just keep your eyes peeled for the ancient-looking block building that sticks out among Grant Street's modern skyscrapers.

MAP 2: 436 Grant St., 412/350-4636; 8:30am-4:30pm Mon.-Fri.; free

MARKET SQUARE

Market Square is a slice of Italy in Pittsburgh. This great little city square, originally the seat of the city government, was inspired by Italian piazzas. It contains cafés and restaurants with outdoor seating, making it a great spot for enjoying lunch alfresco on a warm day.

One highly recommended activity for Market Square is people watching. Grab a drink from **Nicholas Coffee** (try their flavored roasts of the day, like

Won't You Be My Neighbor?

It's not really that surprising that a city that prides itself on being down to earth and neighborly is home to the most famous neighbor of all: **Mr. Rogers.**

Fred Rogers was born and raised in Western Pennsylvania and built his television career in Pittsburgh, after a brief stint with NBC in New York City. His interest in television was sparked by his distaste for it. He wanted to find a way to use the technology for educational purposes.

Rogers began working on a children's show, manipulating puppets, creating characters, and even developing his own character, complete with that iconic sweater and pair of sneakers. In 1968, *Mister Rogers' Neighborhood* went on the air, to the delight of children everywhere, and Mr. Rogers became a household name. *Mister Rogers' Neighborhood* ran for 895 episodes; the last episode aired in 2001.

Fred Rogers died in January 2003, just several months after being diagnosed with stomach cancer, and not long after his retirement. His death hit Pittsburgh hard, and the entire front page of the *Pittsburgh Post-Gazette* was dedicated to his memory. His public memorial was attended by more than 2,700 people. Speakers such as Teresa Heinz Kerry, philanthropist Elsie Hillman, PBS president Pat Mitchell, and *The Very Hungry Caterpillar* author-illustrator Eric Carle spoke of his dedication to the enrichment of children, his love of music, and his goodness.

Almond Joy), pull up a chair in the square, and watch the people milling around. Count the Steelers jerseys if you'd like. Or check out one of Market Square's delectable restaurants. If it's your first time in Pittsburgh, you have to go to **Primanti Bros.** (2 South Market Sq., 412/261-1599, www.primanti-bros.com). Or try **Il Pizzaiolo** (8 Market Sq., 412/575-5858, www.pizzaio-loprimo.com) or **The Original Oyster House** (20 Market Sq., 412/566-7925, www.originaloysterhousepittsburgh.com).

MAP 2: Bordered by Stanwix St., Wood St., 4th Ave., and 5th Ave., www.marketsquarepgh.com

★ POINT STATE PARK

Point State Park is probably the most recognizable Pittsburgh landmark. It sits smack in the center of the city's skyline, housing the iconic fountain that festoons the front of almost every Pittsburgh postcard. The triangular slice of green juts into the middle of the conjoining three rivers, welcoming all to the fair city.

Point State Park, known just as The Point to the locals, is a 36-acre city park in downtown Pittsburgh, at the joining of the Allegheny, Monongahela, and Youghiogheny Rivers. This strategic position made the city a travel and trade hub throughout history, as well as the site of some bloody battles, including the French and Indian War. Explore more of the region's military history while you're at Point State Park by visiting **Fort Pitt Museum** (101 Commonwealth Pl., Point State Park, 412/281-9284,

Though Mr. Rogers is gone, his spirit is very much alive in Pittsburgh. Here are a few ways you can visit the legendary neighbor:

- Visit the largest collection of original items from the *Mister Rogers' Neighborhood* set at the **Senator John Heinz History Center** (page 122). Check out his sweater and sneakers, Mr. McFeely's tricycle, and even the original living room set.

- The **Children's Museum of Pittsburgh** (page 116) is home to *Daniel Tiger's Neighborhood: A Grr-ific Exhibit,* an interactive space that's based on the cartoon *Daniel Tiger's Neighborhood*—which itself is based on Rogers's original show. Head up to the Nursery exhibit to see some of the original puppets on display, like King Friday XIII, Queen Sarah Saturday, and Daniel Striped Tiger.

- In 2009, the **Fred Rogers Memorial Statue** was erected on the North Shore riverfront. The 10-foot statue depicts Rogers tying his sneakers, just as he did at the beginning of every episode of the show. It's a great place to snap a photo or to sit at Mr. Rogers's feet and watch the river flow by.

www.heinzhistorycenter.org; 10am-5pm daily; $8 adults, $4.50 children ages 6-17, $7 seniors).

Point State Park comes alive in the spring and summer months, when people flock to the park and children dance around the fountain to cool off in the spray. On hot summer days, boaters drop anchor around The Point, creating one giant floating party. The park is also the official host of events like the Three Rivers Arts Festival and EQT Three Rivers Regatta, as well as many races.

MAP 2: 101 Commonwealth Pl., 412/471-0235, www.pointstatepark.com; sunrise-11pm daily; free

PPG PLACE

Completed in 1984 and designed by the legendary architect Philip Johnson, PPG Place is the most noticeable and modern complex (some would say postmodern) within the Golden Triangle. Wander toward Market Square to separately view the six structures of PPG Place, or simply look skyward as you approach: PPG's massive tower, covered in a reflective glass skin, rises skyward. At its top are jagged spires with triangular tips. The remaining five buildings, while of a much smaller stature, are also covered in glass and sport Gothic spires; in total, there are 231 spires in the complex.

Perhaps the most exciting (and most interactive) feature is the glass covering the facade: Because of the way the angled plates of glass reflect upon each other and upon the gritty scene of urban Pittsburgh surrounding them, the images in the structure's reflections make for incredible photographs.

Each winter, the plaza between 3rd Avenue and 4th Avenue transforms into a popular ice-skating rink, the **MassMutual Pittsburgh Ice Rink at PPG Place** (mid-Nov.-late Feb.; $8 adults, $7 seniors and children, $4 skate rental).

MAP 2: 2 PPG Pl., www.ppgplace.com

★ THREE SISTERS BRIDGES

No trio of bridges means more to the city than those known collectively as the Three Sisters. And because all three are identically designed and painted a rather striking shade of yellow known as Aztec gold, it's likely that these bridges are the first you'll notice when exploring the Golden Triangle. The Three Sisters are the only identical trio of side-by-side bridges in the world. They were also the very first self-anchored suspension spans built in the United States.

Today known as the **Roberto Clemente Bridge** (formerly the 6th Street Bridge, built in 1928), the **Andy Warhol Bridge** (formerly the 7th Street Bridge, built in 1926), and the **Rachel Carson Bridge** (formerly the 9th Street Bridge, built in 1927), all three bridges cross the Allegheny River to reach the North Side.

The Andy Warhol Bridge was renamed on March 18, 2005. It earned its new name as part of a 10th anniversary celebration for the Andy Warhol Museum, which sits just steps from the north end of the bridge.

The Roberto Clemente gained its new name on April 8, 1999, the day after a ground-breaking ceremony took place on the bridge's northern end for PNC Park, which became the new home of the Pittsburgh baseball club two years later (Clemente was a legendary Pirate who played from 1955 until his death in a plane crash in 1972).

The Rachel Carson Bridge was renamed on April 22, 2006, after the pioneering environmentalist who authored the classic tome *Silent Spring* and remains known as one of Southwestern Pennsylvania's most influential natives.

MAP 2: Roberto Clemente Bridge: 6th St. between Federal St. and Fort Duquesne Blvd.; Andy Warhol Bridge: 7th St. between Sandusky St. and Fort Duquesne Blvd.; Rachel Carson Bridge: 9th St. between Anderson St. and Fort Duquesne Blvd.; www.pghbridges.com

Clockwise from top left: Point State Park; Allegheny County Courthouse; PPG Place.

Pittsburgh's Cultural District

Pittsburgh has always had different reputations, first as a hardworking steel manufacturing hub, then (and still) as a rough-and-tumble sports town. But the city has also come into its own as a place of arts and culture.

A 14-square-block area of the Golden Triangle bordered by the Allegheny River, 10th Street, Stanwix Street, and Liberty Avenue, the **Cultural District** (http://culturaldistrict.org) is anchored by theaters, art galleries, and chic restaurants and bars. The district's theaters, with their glowing marquees, host world-class acts from the Pittsburgh Symphony Orchestra to Chris Rock and everyone in between. Four times a year, traipse through the dozens of niche galleries as you sip complimentary wine and beer at the free **Gallery Crawl** (page 120) put on by the Pittsburgh Cultural Trust.

The Cultural District is rich in history. The historic building that houses the **Benedum Center for the Performing Arts** (page 122) was built in 1928. In the 1960s, the landmark **Heinz Hall** (page 125) was purchased by H. J. Heinz for the Pittsburgh Symphony Orchestra. In 1984, the Pittsburgh Cultural Trust was formed to revitalize the blocks of the Penn-Liberty Avenue corridor in order to form today's Cultural District.

The Cultural District has not been immune to Pittsburgh's restaurant boom either. Many of the world-class chefs that have migrated to Pittsburgh have picked the Cultural District as their home. The Cultural District's location certainly has its perks: The hungry after-show crowd needs a place to eat, and the ball parks are just a quick walk across the bridge. Instead of being the place to go to catch a show, the Cultural District has just become the place to go.

Oakland

Map 3

CARNEGIE MELLON UNIVERSITY

Carnegie Mellon University was founded by Andrew Carnegie, one of the world's most famous philanthropists, in 1900. Today, the university is considered a worldwide leader in the fields of robotics and computer engineering and, to a lesser extent, in fine arts and business administration. Beginning in 1937 with physics professor Clinton Davisson, 15 graduates or faculty members of Carnegie Mellon have been awarded the Nobel Prize.

In total, CMU has seven colleges and schools, and since the campus is relatively small and quite walkable, a stroll across the grounds shouldn't take much longer than a half hour. Visitors interested in computer technology might want to stroll the halls of Carnegie Mellon's **School of Computer Science** (www.cs.cmu.edu); its graduate program has been ranked the top such program in the country by *U.S. News & World Report*. The university's **Robotics Institute** (www.ri.cmu.edu) is also notable. Founded in 1979, it's the largest college research facility of its type in the United States, and its faculty, students, and the innovations of both frequently appear in the local and national press.

MAP 3: 5000 Forbes Ave., 412/268-2000, www.cmu.edu

CARNEGIE MUSEUM OF ART

When Andrew Carnegie conceived of the Carnegie Museum of Art in the 1880s, he envisioned a collection of "the Old Masters of tomorrow." The city's premiere and largest modern art museum also houses a notable collection of post-Impressionist paintings, European and American decorative arts, and late-19th-century American art. The Hall of Sculpture features Greek and Roman reproductions. Check the website for visiting exhibitions from around the world. Your admission also gets you into the Carnegie Museum of Natural History, in the same building.

MAP 3: 4400 Forbes Ave., 412/622-3131, www.cmoa.org; 10am-5pm Tues.-Wed. and Fri.-Sat., 10am-8pm Thurs., noon-5pm Sun.; $20 adults, $15 seniors, $12 students and children 3-18

CARNEGIE MUSEUM OF NATURAL HISTORY

This natural history museum is ranked as one of the top five of its kind in the United States. Visitors come to check out the world's largest collection of Jurassic-era dinosaur bones and the world's first specimen of a *T. rex*. In the jaw-dropping Hall of Minerals and Gems, a dimly lit gallery, spotlights bounce off of sparkling jewels in glass cases. Don't miss the Fluorescence and Phosphorescence Room, an amazing exhibit lit only by the natural glow of these fascinating minerals. Other major exhibits include Polar World, which houses a life-size igloo, and the Hall of Ancient Egypt, where you can see a real mummy and its sarcophagus. Your admission also gets you into the adjoining Carnegie Museum of Art.

MAP 3: 4400 Forbes Ave., 412/622-3131, www.carnegiemnh.org; 10am-5pm Tues.-Wed. and Fri.-Sat., 10am-8pm Thurs., noon-5pm Sun.; $20 adults, $15 seniors, $12 students and children 3-18

★ CATHEDRAL OF LEARNING

When you drive down Forbes Avenue, into the heart of Oakland, an odd sight rises up to greet you: a towering limestone structure that looks like it's from another era and perhaps another continent. This is the 42-story Cathedral of Learning. The Gothic Revival skyscraper was commissioned in 1921, and the 535-foot-tall structure remains one of the tallest educational buildings in the world.

The Cathedral of Learning is owned by the University of Pittsburgh, so it's primarily made up of classrooms, offices, and study areas. However, the building is open to the public and visitors can check out the classrooms that are not in use. (The levels above the 36th floor are not accessible to the public.) Inside is the four-story Commons Room with plenty of tables, cozy corners, and hidden nooks that are perfect for studying.

Possibly the most famous feature of the building is the ring of classrooms around the first floor called the **Nationality Rooms,** each of which is authentically decorated to represent a different country. Though many of the rooms are used for classes, you can tour them on your own or as part of a **guided tour** (412/624-6001, www.nationalityrooms.pitt.edu; adults $4, children 6-18 $2). Guided tours are for groups of 10 or more and must be reserved two weeks in advance.

Clockwise from top left: Phipps Conservatory in Schenley Park; the Cathedral of Learning; the Carnegie Museum of Natural History.

There are always people milling around the building, especially during the busy study times before midterms and finals, but it's easy to find a quiet space of your own. The building is much emptier on weekends, when classes are not in session. The interiors of the classrooms are well-lit and airier than the rest of the building.

MAP 3: 4200 5th Ave., 412/624-4141, www.pitt.edu; 24 hours daily, Nationality Rooms generally 9:30am-2:30pm Mon.-Sat., 11am-2:30pm Sun.; free

★ PHIPPS CONSERVATORY AND BOTANICAL GARDENS

One of the best places to relax in the city is at the Phipps Conservatory and Botanical Gardens, located in Schenley Park. The conservatory, which features 14 rooms of gardens, remains a prime example of Victorian greenhouse architecture.

Spend a morning or afternoon meandering through the giant glass Victorian-style greenhouse. Each room will take you to a different climate and type of plant life. One room features hundreds of types of delicate orchids. Another room is warm and dry, with desert succulents and huge, decades-old cacti. In the spring, you can visit the butterfly gardens and sniff gardenias while butterflies perch on your shoulders. Spot pieces by renowned glass artist Dale Chihuly placed throughout the gardens. The multilevel Tropical Forest exhibit allows visitors to explore a tropical region for themselves, passing waterfalls and examining flora native to the featured region.

Phipps boasts a silver-level LEED certification, which deems it one of the greenest facilities in the world. Its greenhouse was the first building in the world to be certified at a platinum level.

MAP 3: 1 Schenley Park, 412/622-6914, www.phipps.conservatory.org; 9:30am-5pm Sat.-Thurs., 9:30am-10pm Fri.; $18 adults, $17 seniors and students, $12 children 2-18

SOLDIERS & SAILORS MEMORIAL HALL & MUSEUM

This is the largest memorial in the United States dedicated to veterans and service personnel of all branches of the military. The hall is right in the middle of the University of Pittsburgh's campus. Inside, exhibits span from the Civil War to present day. The Hall of Valor honors over 600 Pennsylvania veterans who went above and beyond the call of duty. The building also houses an auditorium and banquet hall, which are used for special events.

MAP 3: 4141 5th Ave., 412/621-4253, www.soldiersandsailorshall.org; 10am-4pm Mon.-Sat.; $10 adults, $5 seniors and children 5-13

STEPHEN FOSTER MEMORIAL

Stephen Collins Foster was born in the Lawrenceville neighborhood of Pittsburgh in 1826 and is considered by many to be the first professional American composer. His songs include famous tunes such as "Camptown Races," "Oh! Susanna," "My Old Kentucky Home," and many more. This complex at the University of Pittsburgh is dedicated to Foster's life and legacy.

The building contains the **Stephen Foster Memorial Museum**

(9am-4pm Mon.-Wed. and Fri., noon-8pm Thurs.; free), a performing arts center, and the Stephen Foster Archives, the largest collection of documents and other artifacts related to Foster's life and works. The museum was originally envisioned as a shrine to Foster. It contains a series of stained-glass windows depicting scenes from famous Foster songs. **Private tours** ($5 adults, $2.50 seniors and children) of the museum are available with advance reservations.

The University of Pittsburgh uses the building's two theaters for its Department of Theater Arts program's performances. A separate wing contains the archives, including manuscripts, examples of recordings, books, memorabilia, and instruments, including one of Foster's pianos.

The building itself mimics the Gothic Revival style of the adjacent Cathedral of Learning, and was built with the same limestone—not surprising, given that it was designed by the same architect.

MAP 3: 4301 Forbes Ave., 412/624-4100, www.pitt.edu

South Side

Map 4

STATION SQUARE

Once the site of the historic Pittsburgh and Lake Erie Railroad Complex and Pittsburgh Railroad Station, Station Square today houses shops and restaurants. Though its days of rail transport are over, the original aesthetic remains and the freight house and concourse area are still intact.

Station Square is a destination for locals and visitors year-round. The building contains specialty shops, a few upscale restaurants, and several chain restaurants. You won't find too many of the new trendy spots like you will downtown or in Lawrenceville, but you will find old standby chains like Houlihan's, The Melting Pot, and Bar Louie's. Check out the Pittsburgh classic, the Grand Concourse, and the adjoining seafood spot, Gandy Dancer Saloon.

Don't forget to check out the patio area between restaurants on the upper deck. The dancing water fountains will keep the kids entertained while you take in the gorgeous views of the city from across the river.

MAP 4: Carson St. at the Smithfield Street Bridge, www.stationsquare.com; 10am-9pm Mon.-Sat., noon-5pm Sun., individual merchant hours may vary

Climbing the South Side Slopes

From a distance, the South Side Slopes resemble a European village built into a hillside. And you'd almost be right, because that's where a lot of its residents originate from. The original settlers of the South Side were mostly factory workers with roots in Germany, Ireland, Poland, Lithuania, and Ukraine. Today, its residents are still a tight-knit community holding onto its roots, evident in the equal numbers of bars and churches dedicated to these ethnicities. The South Side Slopes are a great place to visit, whether you want to experience a traditional Pittsburgh neighborhood or build up your calf muscles.

Because many of this small neighborhood's hills are steeply graded, it's home to approximately 70 sets of stairways, many of which act as sidewalks along the steep roads. Each year, the **South Side Slopes Neighborhood Association** (www.southsideslopes.org) hosts **StepTrek,** where neighbors and visitors climb the neighborhood's 5,447 steps.

A popular way to see the best of the slopes is by taking the **Church Route,** which travels up 15th Street past several historical churches. You'll go through South Side Park, climb 379 steps, then descend 441 steps. Find the full route online at the South Side Slopes Neighborhood Association's website.

One of the best views from the slopes is at the **Mission Street steps,** between Oakley Street and Barry Street. From here, you can see an expansive view of downtown Pittsburgh and the South Side Flats. Another good spot is at the top of **Yard Way** off of Pius Street. **South Side Park** also offers views of the Pittsburgh skyline, along with hiking trails, an orchard, and baseball fields.

Mount Washington

Map 4

★ DUQUESNE AND MONONGAHELA INCLINES

The best way to view the Pittsburgh skyline is the same way Pittsburghers have been doing it since the 1800s: in one of its two hillside cable cars. Every day of the year, these century-old cable cars climb up and down Mount Washington, carrying passengers over clacking wooden tracks. If that's not enough to make you shaky, the sheer height and steep grades (over 30 degrees!) will. The Duquesne and Monongahela Inclines are two of the few remaining funiculars in the country.

The 794-foot-long Duquesne Incline was originally built to carry cargo up and down Mount Washington, but eventually it was used to transport passengers. The incline was almost closed in the 1960s, but a fundraising operation brought it back to life. Its elevation is 400 feet and it has a 30.5-degree grade.

The 635-foot-long Monongahela Incline is the oldest continuously operating funicular in the United States and was built with the purpose of carrying passengers. It has an elevation of 367 feet and a 35-degree grade.

The ride is not for the faint of heart. While the cars are completely safe and impeccably maintained, it's hard to ignore the reality that you're being lowered down the side of a mountain by a rope and pulley system. Both inclines afford magnificent views. If you're feeling up for a jaunt, take one incline up, make the one-mile walk to the other (the stunning views will make it go quickly), and ride back down.

The inclines are a great and convenient way to get around the city. They also serve as part of the daily commute for many Pittsburghers.

MAP 4: Duquesne Incline: 1197 W. Carson St. and 1220 Grandview Ave., 412/381-1665, www.duquesneincline.org, 5:30am-12:45am Mon.-Sat., 7am-12:45am Sun.; Monongahela Incline: Carson St. at Smithfield Street Bridge, 412/442-2000, www. portauthority.org, 5:30am-12:45am Mon.-Sat., 8:45am-midnight Sun.; $2.50 each way with ConnectCard, $2.75 cash

★ GRANDVIEW AVENUE VISTA

If you want that perfect shot of Pittsburgh, this is where to get it. The view from Mount Washington's Grandview Avenue has gained the reputation as one of the most beautiful vistas in America. You can reach the top of Mount Washington by car (you may see a few bumper stickers reading "This car climbed Mount Washington" around the city) or by taking the Duquesne or Monongahela Inclines.

On a nice day, visitors flock to Grandview Avenue, but even lifetime Pittsburghers still admit to being in awe of the magnificent view. Visit on any Saturday in the summer and you're sure to see wedding parties having their photos taken in front of the iconic view.

All along Grandview Avenue, **circular viewing decks** (which resemble flattened mushrooms) jut out over the cliff, allowing for the best viewing experience. Take a stroll along the street or grab a meal at one of the fine dining establishments along **Restaurant Row** (Grandview Ave. between Sweetbriar St. and Meridian St.), all of which offer seats with the best view in the city. Street parking on Grandview is plentiful.

MAP 4: Grandview Ave. between Shaler St. and Bigham St.

Shadyside   Map 5

ROSLYN PLACE

This 250-foot-long narrow street doesn't look like much, except that it's the only wooden street left in the city and one of only a few left in the entire world.

Roslyn Place was built in 1914. It took six months for five men to cut the 26,000 wooden blocks that make up the street. In 1985, the city considered paving Roslyn Place, but residents convinced the city to restore the road, which was showing its age after years of exposure to traffic, weather, and rock salt. Today, a few homeowners on Roslyn Place even perform their own on-the-spot repairs when the road needs it.

MAP 5: Roslyn Pl., off Ellsworth Ave.

Squirrel Hill and Point Breeze

Map 6

AMERICAN JEWISH MUSEUM

Housed inside the Jewish Community Center of Pittsburgh is the incredible American Jewish Museum, a collection of contemporary Jewish art. The museum does not have a permanent collection but hosts several exhibitions throughout the year. Though the museum emphasizes works from the Pittsburgh Jewish community, its focus has expanded to showcase artists from all over the country and world. The artists and themes featured are very diverse. A previous exhibition displayed the drawings of an artist who was a guard during the Nuremberg Trials after World War II. Another exhibit, called BubbeWisdom, featured the quilts of a Jewish grandmother who expresses her views on politics, culture, and women's issues through her quilt-making. Because there is usually only one exhibit at a time, you may only need an hour to see everything here.

The Jewish Community Center (JCC) is a social center, recreational clubhouse, and educational hub that caters to the area's Jewish community as well as welcoming non-Jewish members. The JCC has been around since 1895.

MAP 6: 5738 Forbes Ave., 412/521-8010, www.jccpgh.org; 5:30am-9:30pm Mon.-Thurs., 5:30am-6pm Fri., 8am-6pm Sat.-Sun.

Lawrenceville

Map 8

ALLEGHENY CEMETERY

Not many people think of a cemetery as a place to relax, exercise, and enjoy nature, but Allegheny Cemetery is just that. This historic burial ground encompasses 300 acres and over 15 miles of roadways in the Lawrenceville neighborhood. More than 124,000 people have been buried here, from pioneers of early Pittsburgh to steel mill workers. Built into a hillside, Allegheny Cemetery is modeled after Mount Auburn Cemetery in Cambridge, the nation's first rural cemetery. The goal of the landscaping is to make the cemetery feel more like a park, with gently winding walkways, planned clusters of trees, and stunning river views.

Cemetery buffs can easily spend a day traipsing through the hilly cemetery, spotting the stones of early Pittsburgh politicians and industrialists. Composer Stephen Foster ("Oh! Susanna," "My Old Kentucky Home") is undoubtedly the cemetery's most recognizable name; difficult-to-follow signs point the way to his grave, which can be found in Section 21, Lot 30. Other Allegheny Cemetery notables include Don Brockett (Chef Brockett of *Mister Rogers' Neighborhood*), Thomas Mellon, and General Alexander Hays.

But even if you're more interested in the living, it's still a great place to visit. Amateur photographers will find plenty of willing subjects, from the curious deer that roam the grounds to the immaculate carved monuments at every turn.

MAP 8: 4734 Butler St., 412/682-1624, www.alleghenycemetery.com; 7am-5pm daily Sept.-Apr., 7am-8pm daily May, 7am-7pm daily June-Aug.; free

Greater Pittsburgh   Map 9

ALLEGHENY OBSERVATORY

Who could guess that just a few miles outside of downtown Pittsburgh, nestled in the hills of Riverview Park, is one of the most important astronomical research institutions in the world? The Allegheny Observatory is a part of the University of Pittsburgh. In the latter half of the 19th century, astronomer Samuel Langley used the observatory to help create a synchronized time schedule for U.S. and Canadian railroads. The current work of the observatory focuses on the search for extrasolar planets using photometry, or the measure of the brightness of stars.

The Allegheny Observatory is an example of Classic Revival style. Its decor symbolizes the unity of art and science, with a depiction of the Greek muse of astronomy, Urania, set in stained glass. The L-shaped building contains a library, lecture hall, labs, offices, and three telescope enclosures. Two of the enclosures are for research only, but the third is available to the public and university students.

Free guided tours of the observatory are offered from April through October. Advance reservations are required. The highlight of the tour is a stop at the 13-inch Fitz-Clark refractor, through which visitors may view any number of celestial wonders, assuming the night sky is clear. The tour also includes a short film and a walking tour of the building. Because of the private research going on at the observatory, visitors can tour the facilities only during the designated tour times.

MAP 9: 159 Riverview Ave., Riverview Park, 412/321-2400, www.pitt.edu/~aobsvtry; tours 8pm-10pm Thurs.-Fri. May-Aug., 8pm-10pm Fri. Apr. and Sept.-Oct.; free, by reservation only

KENNYWOOD AMUSEMENT PARK

Built in 1898, Kennywood is not your typical modern amusement park. Thanks to its rich history and historic wooden roller coasters, it's one of only two amusement parks designated a National Historic Landmark. A decent number of classic rides are still in operation—like the paddleboats, the bumper cars, and the merry-go-round—lending the park its sense of nostalgia.

If you're a thrill-seeker, don't be turned off by the park's old-fashioned appeal; Kennywood still delivers some serious rides. There are six roller coasters, including the Phantom's Revenge, with a maximum drop exceeding 200 feet. Not thrilling enough? Try bungee-jumping on the Skycoaster.

Commissioned for the 1926 Sesquicentennial Exposition, the park's Grand Carousel is gorgeous, and its organ music is the backdrop to so many Pittsburghers' memories. Try your luck to get the tiger or the lion, the only two non-horse animals on the carousel.

The park is large and full of rides and games, so many visitors spend a full day at the park. During the summer, Kennywood gets packed, so expect long lines at the most popular rides. If you don't want to spend a full day, consider coming in the evening when the bright lights of the park make for a nostalgic and romantic setting.

MAP 9: 4800 Kennywood Blvd., West Mifflin, 412/461-0500, www.kennywood.com; 10:30am-10pm daily Memorial Day-Labor Day; $42-49 adults, $27-30 children under 46 inches, $20-23 seniors

Restaurants

While hunting down especially refined dining options was once an uphill battle in Pittsburgh, the city has become something of a foodie's paradise in recent years.

As farm-to-fork cuisine has been embraced here, local chefs have shown a real knack for sneaking in just a hint of the Steel City's feel-good comfort food. This is a town where both salads and sandwiches are frequently served with French fries on top, and where the double-carb concoction known as a pierogi—a pasta dumpling filled with mashed potatoes and cheese—is considered something of a delicacy.

Pittsburgh is rich in ethnic eateries, and not only of the Italian and eastern European varieties. Master sushi chefs now call Pittsburgh home, and throughout the East End, locals gorge themselves at affordable Thai, Vietnamese, Indian, Ethiopian, and Filipino restaurants. It's easy to find contemporary cuisine in just about any neighborhood that's seen recent development, particularly downtown, Lawrenceville, and East Liberty.

Perhaps the smartest manner in which to approach Pittsburgh's culinary bonanza is to think of each neighborhood as a separate and unique dining experience: Bloomfield for Italian and comfort food restaurants, Oakland for ethnic and late-night bites, Mount Washington or downtown for romantic fine dining. And on the South Side, you can always head to a bar after dinner if it's not quite time for the evening to end.

Previous: Meat & Potatoes; Klavon's Ice Cream Parlor.

Highlights

★ **Most Authentic Pittsburgh Dining Experience:** Yes, Pittsburghers really do eat sandwiches with French fries inside. Join the locals at the original **Primanti Bros.** and try one for yourself (page 57).

★ **Best Italian Feast:** Sometimes you just crave a big plate of pasta. **Bar Marco** meets your needs with homemade pasta and gnocchi dishes (page 60).

★ **Best-Kept Secret:** It may not look like much, but **Salem's Market and Grill** serves some of the most authentic and delicious Middle Eastern dishes in the city (page 60).

★ **Best Local Coffee: La Prima Espresso** roasts their own small batches of organic beans (page 62).

★ **Most Creative Tacos: Täkō** takes Mexican street food to a new level with exotic ingredients and inventive recipes (page 65).

★ **Best First Date Restaurant:** South Side's **Carmella's Plates and Pints** sets the scene with dim lighting and a roaring wood stove; plus you can calm your nerves with one of their 76 varieties of bourbon (page 70).

★ **Best After-the-Bar Bites:** Finish up your night at **Mike and Tony's Gyros,** where the gyros are hefty enough to soak up any remaining booze in your belly (page 71).

★ **Best Asian Cuisine:** Chef Wei Zhu serves up authentic spicy Sichuan dishes at **Chengdu Gourmet** (page 77).

★ **Celebration of the City's Past: Apteka** is a nod to Pittsburgh's Polish roots, with a vegan twist (page 85).

★ **Best Brunch:** Head to **Coca Café** for the goat-cheese-stuffed French toast, creative omelets, or eggs Bennie (page 88).

Strip District

Map 1

DINERS AND DELIS
DELUCA'S DINER 💲💲

A truly rough-around-the-edges diner in the finest greasy spoon tradition, DeLuca's has held legendary status among Pittsburgh's breakfast aficionados for eons; this is the place to bring an out-of-town visitor who wants to experience the *real* Steel City. The huge menu is exactly what you'd expect: massive plates full of eggs, bacon, and buttered toast. For something a bit different, try the fruit-filled pancakes; a regular order is so large you may not be able to finish it in one sitting. Customer favorites include eggs Benedict, the waffle sundae, and their perfectly crisp and greasy home fries. But be prepared to wait, as the line to get in is usually out the door on busy mornings.

MAP 1: 2015 Penn Ave., 412/566-2195, www.delucastripdistrict.com; 6:30am-2:30pm Mon.-Fri., 6am-3pm Sat., 7am-3pm Sun.

PAMELA'S DINER 💲💲

Pamela's pancakes are so legendary that after indulging in them on one of his campaign stops, President Obama invited the owners of the diner to the White House to make the crepe-like thin pancakes for the first couple and 80 military veterans on Memorial Day. Besides their unique pancakes, Pamela's has tons of other breakfast plates that will cure the worst of hangovers, like the Tex-Mex Omelet (chorizo, cheddar, salsa and guacamole piled inside an omelet) or Croissant French Toast (croissants soaked in cinnamon-vanilla egg batter and topped with caramel sauce and nuts). There are five other locations throughout the city and suburbs. Don't forget to bring cash, as none of the Pamela's locations accept credit cards.

MAP 1: 60 21st St., 412/281-6366, www.pamelasdiner.com; 7am-3pm Mon.-Sat., 8am-3pm Sun.

★ PRIMANTI BROS. 💲

Much more than just a restaurant, the original Primanti Bros. location in the Strip is a destination, a tourist attraction, and a staple of Pittsburgh's history. The rumors you've heard are true: A huge pile of French fries and (sometimes) a fried egg go *inside* the sandwich, which is already stacked sky-high with coleslaw and your choice of artery-clogging meat (roast beef and pastrami are favorites). Add a pop (soda) onto your order, and the combination will soak up even the worst hangover. This sit-down restaurant has the feel of a neighborhood bar. There are several other locations in the city, and more in the suburbs, so you've got few excuses to miss this venerable Pittsburgh institution.

MAP 1: 46 18th St., 412/263-2142, www.primantibros.com; 24 hours daily

Top Breakfast Spots

A great diner breakfast has to tick off several boxes. It needs to be greasy, portions need to be big, and the coffee should be bottomless. Plus, the regulars should be constantly defending it as the best spot in town. Though Pittsburgh has plenty of trendy upscale restaurants, if we're going out to breakfast we prefer simple, filling meals, preferably served in a hole-in-the-wall. These spots, which fulfill all the above requirements, are arguably the greatest places to grab breakfast:

- **DeLuca's Diner** (page 57)

- **Pamela's Diner** (page 57)

- **Kelly O's** (page 58)

- **Nadine's** (page 70)

KELLY O'S ❸

Kelly O's is DeLuca's fiercest competitor, and legions of fans on both sides argue which one is better. Kelly O's focuses on fast service, hearty portions, and something you won't find at very many other diners: freshly squeezed orange juice. One of its claims to fame is that it was featured on Food Network's *Diners, Drive-ins and Dives*. For the most part, they serve up traditional diner fare like hearty stuffed omelets and decadent pancakes, but several "fancier" items like the crab Benedict and the crab and asparagus omelet may satisfy more refined appetites. You'll find regional favorites like corned beef hash, and the toast is from Mancini's, one of Pittsburgh's favorite bakeries.

MAP 1: 100 24th St., 412/232-3447, www.kellyos.com, 5am-3pm Mon.-Sat., 7am-3pm Sun.

NEW AMERICAN
SMALLMAN GALLEY ❸❸

Smallman Galley introduces a new dining concept to the Pittsburgh restaurant scene. The Strip District restaurant is considered a "chef incubator," where up-and-coming local chefs get to run their own restaurant for a period of 18 months, without the risk of owning a stand-alone business. The 200-seat dining hall gives diners the opportunity to choose from four different "restaurants" with their own inventive menus. Each chef cooks at a "micro-kitchen" out in the open, so diners can watch their food being prepared. Rather than ordering from a waiter, diners visit each stall, then select from whichever menu most appeals to them.

MAP 1: 54 21st St., 412/281-0949, www.smallmangalley.com; 11am-9pm Tues.-Thurs., 11am-10pm Fri., 10am-10pm Sat., 10am-3pm Sun.

Clockwise from top left: Bar Marco, known for simple Italian-inspired dishes and top wines; delicious food at Pamela's Diner; the famed Primanti Bros.

CARIBBEAN
KAYA 〇〇

An island paradise in the heart of the Strip's warehouse district, Kaya represents the Caribbean arm of the local Big Burrito restaurant group. This is certainly Pittsburgh's premiere locale for Jamaican jerk chicken and Cuban sandwiches, and the menu changes daily, so dining often feels like a culinary adventure. The clientele leans toward the young, beautiful, and trust-funded, and the happy hour is a scene unto itself; saddle up for tropical island drinks or a martini.

MAP 1: 2000 Smallman St., 412/261-6565, www.bigburrito.com/kaya; 11:30am-10pm Mon.-Wed., 11:30am-11pm Thurs.-Sat., 11am-9pm Sun.

ITALIAN
★ BAR MARCO 〇〇〇

Given the Bar Marco's reputation as one of the best restaurants in Pittsburgh, food prices are surprisingly affordable, though you will want to order lots of "start" and "follow" plates (appetizers and entrées) to share. Begin with charcuterie, then order main dishes like mac-and-cheese with rosemary and peppers or squash and sweet sausage. Punch bowl social hours and the Sunday brunch are especially popular with local hipster types.

MAP 1: 2216 Penn Ave., 412/471-1900, www.barmarcopgh.com; 5pm-11pm Tues.-Fri., 10am-3pm and 5pm-11pm Sat.

LATIN AMERICAN
GAUCHO PARRILLA ARGENTINA 〇〇

Pittsburgh's first Argentinian wood-fired grill is simply a mouthwatering experience for local carnivores. The staff is highly knowledgeable and friendly, and that's a big plus, as you may need some assistance and recommendations during your first couple of visits. Don't get too full on appetizers, as the meats are the real menu highlights—most are served à la carte with a selection of condiments for just $3 each—sauces include *chimichurri*, *pimentón*, *ajo*, and the like. Though it's BYOB, there's no corkage fee.

MAP 1: 1601 Penn Ave., 412/709-6622, www.eatgaucho.com; 11am-9pm Tues.-Thurs., 11am-10pm Fri.-Sat.

MIDDLE EASTERN
★ SALEM'S MARKET AND GRILL 〇

Salem's is a gem in the Strip District that is easy to pass up unless you know what it's all about. Salem's started as a halal butcher in Oakland, but demand for their homemade curries grew so much that they expanded to a giant no-frills restaurant in the Strip. Salem's serves some of the freshest and best-sourced meat in the 'Burgh, all processed to halal specifications. But instead of boasting about it in an overpriced, trendy way, Salem's serves up their delicacies cafeteria-style in Styrofoam containers. Diners from all walks of life eat together, from blue-collar workers on break to international students and Middle Eastern expats craving a taste from home.

MAP 1: 2923 Penn Ave., 412-235-7828, 9am-8pm Mon.-Sat., 10am-6pm Sun.

Meals on Wheels

Some of the best bites in Pittsburgh aren't found in brick and mortar restaurants but on four wheels. The **food truck revolution** certainly hasn't skipped Pittsburgh, and more chefs are taking to the streets and making their menus accessible to people all over the 'Burgh. The best way to find your truck of choice is by following it on social media to see where it's parked. Here are a few of the most famous mobile eateries.

· **Blue Sparrow** (Twitter and Instagram @BlueSparrowPgh) dishes up global street food made from scratch with fresh local ingredients. Think kimchi grilled cheese, tikka masala taco, and a ramen burger, all over-the-top delicious.

· With a serious brick pizza oven hitched to the back of a truck, **Driftwood Oven** (Twitter and Instagram @DriftwoodOven) brings their mobile pizza shop all around town. The pizza's base is a sourdough crust, and the toppings range from tried and true mozzarella to unique ingredients like crispy kale.

· You'll easily recognize **Mac and Gold** (Twitter and Instagram @macandgoldtruck) by its bright yellow truck. As the name suggests, they serve up gourmet mac-and-cheese, like the Polish Hill Mac (with kielbasa, cabbage, onion, and potato) or the roasted butternut squash and prosciutto mac. You can throw in extras like asparagus, bacon, and even crab.

· The **PGH Taco Truck** (Twitter and Instagram @PghTacoTruck) serves up one of the most food-truck-friendly dishes: tacos. They serve a menu of goodies including jalapeno and cider-braised pork tacos and General Tso chicken tacos.

· **Burgh Bites** (Twitter and Instagram @BurghBitesCart) offers sandwiches, torts (seasoned tortilla chips piled high with toppings), and gourmet hot dogs. Try the Rastafarian (Jamaican jerk chicken, corn/mango salsa, chili pepper aioli, and greens on a grilled pita), and don't miss the perfect dill potato salad.

RESTAURANTS
STRIP DISTRICT

DESSERT
KLAVON'S ICE CREAM PARLOR ❸

This art deco drugstore and ice cream shop is the real deal. It opened way back in 1925, and all the trimmings are original, including the marble soda fountain and its attendant swivel stools, which are designed to look like soda bottle caps. Along with the regular assortment of sundaes and banana splits, Klavon's also stocks a wide array of old-school candy and even boasts a sandwich and soup menu for the sugar-phobic.

MAP 1: 2801 Penn Ave., 412-434/0451, www.klavonsicecream.com; 11am-9pm Mon.-Thurs., 11am-11pm Fri.-Sat., noon-8pm Sun. mid-Mar.-Sept., 11am-7pm Mon. and Wed.-Thurs., 11am-9pm Fri.-Sat., noon-8pm Sun. Oct.-mid-Mar.

COFFEE
★ LA PRIMA ESPRESSO $

Some call La Prima the most authentic espresso shop in Pittsburgh, and if you show up during the morning rush, you'll see why. Clusters of middle-aged men gather around the front counter with espresso and Italian-language newspapers, and the baristas busily craft specialty drinks with speed and skill. Even drip coffee is something special; there's almost always a Central American fair-trade or shade-grown selection on offer.

MAP 1: 205 21st St., 412/281-1922, www.laprima.com; 6am-4pm Mon.-Wed., 6am-5pm Thurs., 7am-4pm Sun.

North Side   Map 1

ASIAN
NICKY'S THAI KITCHEN $$

Decidedly Pittsburgh's most lauded Thai joint, Nicky's Thai combines a cozy date-night atmosphere with traditional Thai cuisine. The restaurant features a bar with wine, sake, cocktails, and beer, but you're welcome to BYOB with a corkage fee. Nicky's consistently racks up the restaurant awards, including "Best Thai" from *Pittsburgh Magazine* several years in a row. You can't go wrong with their spicy and comforting curries, or you could try something slightly more exotic like *gaprow lad kao*—ground meat of your choice, garlic, pepper, and basil topped with a fried egg and served over rice. There are additional locations downtown (903 Penn Ave., 412/471-8424) and in North Hills (1026 Mt. Nebo Rd., 412/438-8424).

MAP 1: 856 Western Ave., 412/321-8424, www.nickysthaikitchen.com; 11:30am-3pm and 5pm-9pm Mon.-Thurs., 11:30am-3pm and 5pm-10pm Fri.-Sat., 5pm-9pm Sun.

BARBECUE
WILSON'S BAR-B-Q $$

Wilson's Bar-B-Q has long been lauded as absolutely top-notch Southern pit barbecue. "Genuine" is probably the best word to describe the place: Most everyone takes the award-winning chicken and pork ribs to go, and the shop itself is utilitarian at best. But no matter, as the delectable meat at Wilson's simply falls off the bone and melts in your mouth—the result of a wood-fired grill and a family sauce recipe handed down from former-slave ancestors, according to employees.

MAP 1: 700 N. Taylor Ave., 412/322-7427; noon-8pm Mon.-Sat.

GERMAN
MAX'S ALLEGHENY TAVERN $$

Max's Allegheny Tavern is really more of a local institution than a simple German restaurant. Anyone with eastern European grandparents will definitely recognize the traditional decor and menu full of comfort foods, such as schnitzel, bratwurst, and that tangy and warm potato salad. The history of Max's serves as a microcosm for the history of the North Side neighborhood where the restaurant is located, and both staff and owners will be more than happy to share it with you.

MAP 1: 537 Suismon St., 412/231-1899, www.maxsalleghenytavern.com; 11am-10pm Mon.-Thurs., 11am-11pm Fri.-Sat., 9:30am-9pm Sun.

PENN BREWERY ⑤⑤

The Penn Brewery isn't your average brewpub. The interior is designed to resemble a Deutschland mead hall, and if you time your visit right, you might catch a lederhosen-clad German band entertaining on the outdoor patio. Dinners are heavy, authentic, and artery clogging; imagine steak drenched in dark beer sauce or tender beef sirloin rolls stuffed with bacon, and you'll start to get the idea. A few vegetarian entrées and sandwiches are available.

MAP 1: 800 Vinial St., 412/237-9402, www.pennbrew.com; 11am-10pm Mon.-Thurs., 11am-11pm Fri.-Sat., 11am-9pm Sun.

Downtown

Map 2

CLASSIC AMERICAN
PORK & BEANS ⑤⑤

Head here for slabs of expertly smoked, fall-off-the-bone meats piled high on old-school, cafeteria-style lunch trays. Pair your choice of meat with savory and gut-busting sides like Truck Stop Poutine (tater tots, hot sticks, redeye gravy, and cheese curds) or house-made pork rinds topped with manchego cheese, Tajín seasoning, and chipotle remoulade. Enjoy your hearty meal surrounded by old metal tobacco advertisements and neon signs. Their superstar team includes Richard Deshantz, who also owns Butcher and the Rye and Täkō, and Keith Fuller, so it's no surprise that Pork & Beans has been so successful.

MAP 2: 136 6th St., 412/338-1876, www.porkandbeanspgh.com; 4pm-10pm Mon., 11:30am-2pm and 4pm-10pm Tues.-Thurs., 11:30am-2pm and 4pm-11pm Fri.-Sat., noon-6pm Sun.

WINGHART'S ⑤⑤

Take the all-American burger, use only the freshest meat, and pile it high with gourmet toppings: This is the modus operandi at Winghart's. They're so serious about freshness that you won't find a microwave or even a freezer on the premises. Every menu item is made in-house, down to the white truffle fries and homemade pierogi. But the burgers are the real shining star. Try The Shipwreck (with arugula, white truffle aioli, caramelized onions, and bacon) or The Necessity (Swiss cheese, house-made honey mustard, barbecue sauce, mushrooms and jalapenos). The vibe here is industrial, with lots of rough wood and metal accents, all lit by softly glowing Edison bulbs. It's a great spot for a casual lunch or romantic date night.

MAP 2: 5 Market Sq., 412/434-5600, http://winghartburgers.com; 11am-midnight Mon.-Thurs., 11am-2am Fri., noon-2am Sat., noon-midnight Sun.

Clockwise from top left: La Prima Espresso; Täkō; Butcher and the Rye.

NEW AMERICAN
★ TÄKŌ ⬤⬤⬤

The success of Täkō has been immediate and enduring: There's nothing quite like it in the city. *Tako* is the Japanese word for octopus, which is reflected in their top menu option, the Täkō taco, a fat grilled octopus tentacle with aioli, greens, and pickled red onion. If you're not quite adventurous enough for that, you might enjoy their other inventive tacos, like the Korean taco or tacos *al pastor*. Can't decide? Get the Big Board, where you can choose six pairs of tacos for $75. The atmosphere might not be the best for a first date: It's dark, loud, and decorated with neon lights and bizarre knickknacks, more like an acid trip than a romantic setting.

MAP 2: 214 6th St., 412/471-8256, www.takopgh.com; 5pm-11pm Mon.-Thurs., 5pm-midnight Fri.-Sat., 3pm-9pm Sun.

BUTCHER AND THE RYE ⬤⬤⬤

Operated by the same team responsible for downtown's runaway dining success Meat & Potatoes, the two-story Butcher and the Rye features two dining rooms serving artisan-quality meat- and fish-based entrées with ingredients sourced from local farms. And while the big draw is the 400-strong bourbon and rye menu (craft cocktails are also offered), the interior design and ambience are just as impressive. Think midcentury upper-crust hunting lodge, complete with antique wallpaper, taxidermied critters, and lamps made of faux antlers.

MAP 2: 212 6th St., 412/391-2752, www.butcherandtherye.com; 5pm-11pm Tues.-Thurs., 5pm-midnight Fri.-Sat.

THE COMMONER ⬤⬤⬤

Self-described as a "modern American tavern," The Commoner is casual but upscale, with a large industrial-style setting, sitting below street level in downtown's Hotel Monaco. Thanks to its rejection of the trend of artfully arranged bite-sized dinner portions, you'll leave Commoner satisfied, if not in a food coma. Expect creative takes on classic comfort food, like crab and corn fritters with watercress and chive aioli or Buffalo Cottage Pie, with ground buffalo, peas, carrots, gravy, and whipped potatoes.

MAP 2: 458 Strawberry Way, 412/230-4800, www.bthecommonerpgh.com; 6:30am-10:30am, 11am-3pm, and 4pm-11pm Mon.-Thurs., 6:30am-10:30am, 11am-3pm, and 4pm-midnight Fri., 7:30am-3pm and 4pm-midnight Sat., 7:30am-3pm and 4pm-10pm Sun.

ELEVEN ⬤⬤⬤

The aptly named Eleven (it's the 11th creation of the Big Burrito restaurant group) has become a particularly strong cornerstone of the fine contemporary dining scene in Pittsburgh. The philosophy is contemporary, too: As a serious adherent to the slow food movement, chef Greg Alauzen takes pains to include seasonal, regional ingredients in most dishes. But it's the gracefully prepared plates that truly make dining here a high-art experience.

MAP 2: 1150 Smallman St., 412/201-5656, www.elevenck.com; 11:30am-10pm Mon.-Fri., 5pm-11pm Sat., 11am-9pm Sun.

MEAT & POTATOES 🄢🄢🄢

This hotshot gastropub in the Cultural District has been getting all-around rave reviews since first opening its doors in 2011, and for good reason: The menu centers around simple, fuss-free, and utterly delicious preparations of meat, potatoes, and veggies. Portions are quite generous, and the Prohibition-era cocktails are already a citywide legend. Young creatives and professionals flock to this contemporary space after the business day ends.

MAP 2: 649 Penn Ave., 412/325-7007, www.meatandpotatoespgh.com; 5pm-11pm Mon.-Thurs., 5pm-midnight Fri.-Sat., 10:30am-2pm and 5pm-10pm Sun.

UNION STANDARD 🄢🄢🄢

Union Standard's focus on local ingredients is reflected in their constantly changing menu, which celebrates the culinary traditions of the American Northwest, Mid-Atlantic, and Appalachian areas. At this fashionable yet relaxed spot, choose from upscale eats like crispy squash blossoms, cider steamed clams, and ancho braised beef short rib. A big draw for Union Standard is their raw bar, which features a selection of Jonah crab claws, Wellfleet oysters, and Chesapeake littleneck clams.

MAP 2: 524 William Penn Pl., 412/281-0738, www.unionstandardpgh.com; 11am-2pm and 5pm-10pm Mon.-Thurs., 11am-2pm and 5pm-11pm Fri., 5pm-11pm Sat.

NINE ON NINE 🄢🄢

This downtown restaurant features an exciting American fusion menu in a fresh setting—a great place for happy hour bites or a four-course dinner. The quality and creativity are evident in dishes like Lamb Lollipops and Vegan English Sweet Pea Gnocchi, with surprisingly affordable prices. They also feature an impressive wine list. Save room for dessert, because the patisseries menu is seriously impressive.

MAP 2: 900 Penn Ave., 412/338-6463, www.nineonninepgh.com; 5pm-10pm Mon.-Thurs., 5pm-11pm Fri.-Sat.

SIENNA MERCATO 🄢🄢

Sienna Mercato is three restaurants in one: Emporio, Mezzo and Il Tetto. First floor Emporio offers a comfort-food heavy menu of build-your-own meatballs and savory poutine (add the pork belly to make it extra indulgent). The dining area here can feel crowded, but on nice days they open the garage-door wall for open-air dining. Mezzo, on the second floor, has a more romantic vibe, and offers charcuterie, wine pairings, and wood-fired pizza. Head up to the rooftop bar, Il Tetto, for after dinner drinks.

MAP 2: 942 Penn Ave., 412/281-2810, www.siennamercato.com; Emporio: 11am-10pm Sun.-Tues., 11am-midnight Wed.-Sat.; Mezzo: 5pm-10pm Mon.-Thurs., 5pm-11pm Fri., 4pm-11pm Sat., 4pm-10pm Sun.

ASIAN
SUSHI KIM 🄢🄢

Tucked away on a battered stretch of Penn Avenue between downtown and the Strip, Sushi Kim is a local diamond in the rough: The decor exists somewhere between Asian pop culture and hipster kitsch, and the entrée list is split evenly between traditional Japanese and Korean dishes—about **67** 40 in all. But most come for the sushi, which is some of the best in the Strip. Particularly amusing are the massive sushi boats, a sort of combo platter for the young-at-heart fresh-fish lover.

MAP 2: 1241 Penn Ave., 412/281-9956; 11:30am-9:30pm Tues.-Thurs., 11:30am-10pm Fri.-Sat., noon-9pm Sun.

GREEK
CRYSTAL ON PENN $

Famously featured on the Food Network show *Diners, Drive-ins and Dives*, Crystal is the place to go in the 'Burgh for a mix of traditional Lebanese cuisine mixed with American classics. Crystal is cozy but no-frills, and easy to miss if you aren't looking for it. Where else can you get wings and beer and then authentic lamb kebabs for an entrée? Guy Fieri's favorite dish? The stuffed grape leaves.

MAP 2: 1211 Penn Ave., 412/434-0480; 11am-9pm Tues.-Thurs., 11am-10pm Fri., 10am-10pm Sat., 10am-3pm Sun.

RESTAURANTS DOWNTOWN

ITALIAN
TALIA CUCINA AND ROSTICCERIA $$$

Opened in 2017, Talia is a newcomer to the Pittsburgh restaurant scene, but with executive chef Steve Lanzilotti behind the helm, the restaurant is already filling a void with its roasted meats. The showpiece of the kitchen is a five-figure rotisserie custom made in France, which is responsible for turning out rib eye, *porchetta* (pork roast), and roasted chicken. They also serve fresh pastas, like squid ink *gemelli* with sea urchin saffron cream and ricotta cheese gnocchi with brisket and San Marzano chili sauce. The dining space is chic and understated, with high-backed booths and darks walls decorated with commissioned art.

MAP 2: 425 6th Ave., 412/456-8214, www.taliapgh.com; 11am-3pm and 5pm-10pm Mon.-Thurs., 11am-3pm and 5pm-11pm Fri., 4pm-11pm Sat.

LATIN AMERICAN
SEVICHE $$

Seviche is one of the more adventurous restaurants to have popped up during the Cultural District's foodie renaissance. Quality seafood is offered in a variety of different preparations, and a seafood bar features seven different versions of the eponymous dish, in addition to a full menu of other Latin American goodies, such as empanadas, tostadas, and *croquetas* (fritters).

MAP 2: 930 Penn Ave., 412/697-3120, www.seviche.com; 4pm-10pm Mon.-Thurs., 4pm-11pm Fri.-Sat.

Oakland

Map 3

CLASSIC AMERICAN

FUEL AND FUDDLE $

A popular college eatery centered around the dual themes of bar food and good beer, Fuel and Fuddle is the perfect place to eat when you can't quite decide what you're in the mood for. The menu consists of large plates of pub grub and finger foods such as chicken wings, Thai skewers, jack cheese quesadillas, and nacho plates. Beer specials change daily.

MAP 3: 212 Oakland Ave., 412/682-3473, www.fuelandfuddle.com; 11am-2am daily

THE ORIGINAL HOT DOG SHOP $

Much more than just a corner hot dog and pizza shop, "The O," as it's known locally, is nothing less than a Pittsburgh institution. Opened in 1960, it's probably safe to say that anyone who's ever spent time in the nearby Pitt dorms has a story to tell about the place. The all-natural dogs are world class, but most come for the ridiculously large baskets of cheese fries, or the cheap pizzas, or at least a six-pack. The O is always at its best after dark, when they're crowded and chaotic.

MAP 3: 3901 Forbes Ave., 412/621-7388, www.theoriginalhotdogshop.com; 10am-10pm Sun.-Wed., 10am-2am Thurs.-Sat.

NEW AMERICAN

LEGUME $$$

At Legume, the staff does the majority of its food processing in-house, including whole-animal butchery, vegetable canning, and grinding grain, so the menu changes a bit each day. You're quite likely, though, to find an even mixture of creatively prepared pastas, meats, fish, and vegetables at this white-tablecloth restaurant, all of it gathered from small area farmers and food purveyors and artisans. Plates are always true works of art, and you'll never come across anything processed or otherwise prepared through industrial means.

MAP 3: 214 N. Craig St., 412/621-2700, www.legumebistro.com; 5pm-9pm Mon.-Thurs., 5pm-9:30pm Fri.-Sat.

ASIAN

SPICE ISLAND TEA HOUSE $$

A pan-Asian legend that for eons now has been introducing Oakland's college community to Indonesian, Burmese, Thai, Cambodian, and Filipino food, Spice Island Tea House is one of the area's few can't-miss institutions. With the charming mismatched furniture and thatched-roof vibe, even a bad meal would still be fun—but nearly every Spice Island entrée is a crowd pleaser.

MAP 3: 253 Atwood St., 412/687-8821, www.spiceislandteahouse.com; 11:30am-8:45pm Mon.-Thurs., 11:30am-9:45pm Fri.-Sat.

LULU'S NOODLES $

Living somewhere in between cafeteria-style casual dining and chic urban café, Lulu's Noodles is a favorite destination for budget-conscious Pitt and CMU undergrads looking for good value in a stylish setting. Portion sizes are generous, too: Order a noodle dish—the Singapore rice noodles are a good bet—and you'll have a tough time cleaning your plate. The noodle soups are also recommended, and Lulu's is well known for its bubble tea.

MAP 3: 400 S. Craig St., 412/687-7777; 11am-8:45pm Sun.-Thurs., 11am-9:45pm Fri.-Sat.

MEXICAN
MAD MEX $$

For lovers of quality Tex-Mex and massive food portions, it doesn't get much better than Mad Mex, a locally based restaurant-and-bar chain. The menu is an inventive collection of burritos, enchiladas, and quesadillas with a twist: portobello mushrooms inside, say, or tofu or chickpea chili. If it's the truly sublime you're after, go with the Dance Marathon Burrito (spinach, portobellos, and marinated chicken) or the Kristy's Big Sister's Red Velvet Burrito, complete with *pico de gallo* (fresh salsa) and zucchini inside. There are other locations in the suburbs and towns surrounding the city.

MAP 3: 370 Atwood St., 412/681-5656, www.madmex.com; 11am-1am daily

MIDDLE EASTERN
ALI BABA $$

Ali Baba is the Steel City's preeminent Middle Eastern deal. It's been "the best Middle Eastern restaurant in Pittsburgh" according to *Pittsburgh Magazine* multiple times. With higher prices and a classy atmosphere, this isn't exactly a college dive, although Pitt and CMU types are almost always in attendance. Food-wise, it's tough to go wrong, although the shish kebab dinner is particularly inviting, as is the *sheik el-mahshi* (roasted eggplant with seasoned lamb). The baklava is an especially agreeable dessert; be aware that the BYO policy extends to wine only.

MAP 3: 404 S. Craig St., 412/682-2829; 11:30am-2:30pm and 4:30pm-9:45pm Mon.-Fri., 4:30pm-9:45pm Sat.-Sun.

DESSERT
DAVE & ANDY'S $

Without a doubt, this non-chain store is the finest purveyor of ice cream in Pittsburgh. The confections at Dave & Andy's are good for a reason: Ice cream is made the old-fashioned way, with wooden churns and rock salt. The result? Fresh, perfectly creamy ice cream offered in a regularly rotating selection of flavors. Ask for yours in a homemade waffle cone (also made fresh in-house), which includes a handful of M&Ms that plug up the hole at the bottom.

MAP 3: 207 Atwood St., 412/681-9906; 11:30am-10pm Mon.-Fri., noon-10pm Sat.-Sun.

South Side

Map 4

DINERS
NADINE'S $

If you find yourself still in the South Side after a night of barhopping, head directly to Nadine's for sustenance. The family-owned diner has been around since 2001 and feeding the hungry masses of long time locals as well as hungry college students that live in the area. Besides typical breakfast platters, omelets and pancakes, Nadine's puts together a satisfying breakfast sandwich served on a bagel or English muffin. The breakfast hoagie, piled high with fried egg, meats, cheese, plus lettuce and tomato, is served on a giant hoagie roll.

MAP 4: 19 S. 27th St., 412/481-1793, www.nadinesbar.com; 6am-4am Mon.-Fri., 9am-4pm Sat., 10am-4pm Sun.

CLASSIC AMERICAN
FAT HEAD'S SALOON $$

Fat Head's is easily one of the South Side's best bar and grill joints. Fat Head's has three dozen or so imports and craft brews on tap, but pick up a menu between pints and you'll find that Fat Head's has much more than just alcohol on offer: in short, a pub-grub-on-steroids menu featuring mostly burgers, sandwiches, and the massive (and massively popular) "headwiches." Diners watching their waistlines, in other words, will want to proceed to Fat Head's with extreme prejudice.

MAP 4: 1805 E. Carson St., 412/431-7433, www.fatheads.com; 11am-midnight Mon.-Thurs., 11am-1am Fri.-Sat., 11am-11pm Sun.

NEW AMERICAN
★ CARMELLA'S PLATES AND PINTS $$

Carmella's might be the perfect date spot in Pittsburgh. Dimly lit, with a wood-fired stove crackling in the center of the dining room, it's upscale but casual, without the pretension of some of the trendier downtown digs. The array of big game mounted on the walls interspersed with a kitschy collection of salt and pepper shakers will surely be an ice-breaker. Start your meal with infused liquor cocktails (they stock more than 170 bourbons and scotches) and move on to duck confit tacos, bison burgers, or veal Bolognese.

MAP 4: 1908 E. Carson St., 412/918-1215, www.carmellasplatesandpints.com; 5pm-10pm Mon.-Thurs., 5pm-11pm Fri., 11am-3pm and 5pm-11pm Sat., 5pm-11pm Sun.

THE LIBRARY $$

Bibliophiles will nerd out over this literary-themed restaurant. The tabletops are decoupaged with book pages and the menus are printed inside old book covers. Though the dishes are creatively titled (a beer-battered cod sandwich called the Moby Dick, the Julius Caesar salad), the food is pretty ordinary. Despite the fun motif, the owners could have done more to extend it: The walls are mostly bare and the furniture has seen better days. But if you want a solid meal at an affordable price, you won't be disappointed.

MAP 4: 2302 E. Carson St., 412/381-0517, www.thelibrary-pgh.com; 4pm-2am daily

ASIAN
CAMBOD-ICAN KITCHEN ⊙

Originally a legendary street food cart that fed the hungry barhopping masses of East Carson Street, Cambod-ican Kitchen—now reinvented as a sit-down restaurant—has returned to Pittsburgh after a nearly three-year hiatus. Cambod-ican purists need not fret, however—the original Cat on a Stick (chicken shish kebab) is still for sale. So too is a wonderfully adventurous menu of fried noodles and wontons, curry rolls, and fresh spring rolls.

MAP 4: 1701 E. Carson St., 412/381-6199, www.cambodicankitchen.com; 6pm-5am Tues.-Sat.

FRENCH
CAFÉ DU JOUR ⊙⊙

In a city where contemporary dining always seems to revolve around dishes from the old country, Café du Jour stands out with its contemporary twists on old favorites. Don't be afraid to let the servers guide your choices, as some are wont to do; after all, everything from the portobello soup to the cheese plates to the *cassoulet* (French stew) is simply stunning. If the weather's right, you'll want to make reservations for a patio seat.

MAP 4: 1107 E. Carson St., 412/488-9695, www.cafedujourpgh.com; 11am-3pm and 5pm-10pm Tues.-Sat.

GERMAN
HOFBRÄUHAUS PITTSBURGH ⊙⊙

Despite its location in the SouthSide Works shopping center, Hofbräuhaus manages to feel like an authentic Munich beer hall. There are long tables in the main hall where you can dine, European-style, with perfect strangers. Beer brewed on the premises adheres strictly to the Bavarian beer purity law. And there's an abundance of live music, as well as an incredibly hearty menu of bona fide Bavarian delicacies. Don't forget to visit the outdoor beer garden, with its fantastic views.

MAP 4: 2705 S. Water St., 412/224-2328, www.hofbrauhauspittsburgh.com; 11am-11pm Mon.-Wed., 11am-midnight Thurs., 11am-2am Fri.-Sat., noon-11pm Sun.

GREEK
★ MIKE AND TONY'S GYROS ⊙

Mike and Tony's is the ultimate after-bar treat or hangover cure. A mainstay in the South Side for years, its convenient location near the bars and its reputation for the best gyro in Pittsburgh make it popular and packed both late night and at more traditional mealtimes. The restaurant is a hole-in-the-wall, but the aroma of gyro meat roasting on a spit in front of your eyes distracts you from the less than spectacular surroundings. Of course, the most popular dish is a fat gyro dripping with delectable homemade gyro sauce and wrapped in foil, but Mike and Tony's also serves up other

Greek plates and treats, like the sticky and decadent baklava. There's also a location downtown.

MAP 4: 1414 E. Carson St., 412/431-2299, www.mikeandtonysgyros.com; 11am-10:30pm Mon., 11am-3am Tues.-Sat., 11am-midnight Sun.

SEAFOOD
GRAND CONCOURSE $$$

Located in the concourse of the old P&LE Railway station, and with seating for 500, the Grand Concourse is quite accurately known as one of Pittsburgh's most elegant and stately places in which to dine. The somewhat timid menu is largely seafood based; typical entrées include lobster ravioli, coconut shrimp, and Maryland crab cakes. For a slightly more informal experience, ask to be seated in the Gandy Dancer Bar, where oysters and clams can be ordered alongside old-style cocktails. Sunday brunch is quite an occasion, though more casual than evening dinner hours.

MAP 4: 100 W. Station Square Dr., 412/261-1717, www.grandconcourserestaurant.com; 11am-10pm Mon.-Thurs., 11am-11pm Fri.-Sat., 9am-9pm Sun.

SPANISH
MALLORCA $$$

A traditional Spanish restaurant in the finest white-tablecloth style, Mallorca offers a premiere dining experience that is simply unequaled elsewhere in the city. Families and young couples on dates crowd the gated outdoor terrace or the often-packed dining room to gorge on Spanish- and Mediterranean-style seafood dishes or the exotic house specialties: roast suckling pig, say, or even goat. Diners often find themselves lingering to nosh, sample, and sip for hours.

MAP 4: 2228 E. Carson St., 412/488-1818, www.mallorcarestaurantpgh.com; 11:30am-10:30pm Mon.-Thurs., 11:30am-11:30pm Fri.-Sat., noon-10pm Sun.

DESSERT
THE MILK SHAKE FACTORY $

While this author admittedly has something of a mild ice cream addiction, just about everyone loves the old-fashioned, hand-spun milkshakes at this South Side gem. The Milk Shake Factory is something of a candy shop and ice cream shop all in one, so you might as well plan to indulge, picking up some chocolates from Edward Marc Chocolatier while you're there. Fifty-five smooth and creamy ice cream flavors await, along with the best chocolate confections in town.

MAP 4: 1705 E. Carson St., 412/488-1808, www.themilkshakefactory.com; 11am-10pm Sun.-Thurs., 11am-11pm Fri.-Sat.

COFFEE
BEEHIVE COFFEEHOUSE $

One of Pittsburgh's most iconoclastic locales in which to sip organic coffee while discussing Sartre and Nietzsche, the Beehive has been many different things to many different angst-ridden teens since its opening in 1991. The Beehive's interior decor vibe is strictly thrift store—think mismatched furniture and kitschy wall murals. It also offers pinball, wireless access, used paperbacks in the vending machine, and the best-pierced baristas in Pittsburgh. In other words, the spirit of the South Side under one roof.

MAP 4: 1327 E. Carson St., 412/488-4483, www.beehivebuzz.com; 8am-11pm Sun.-Mon., 8am-midnight Tues.-Wed., 8am-2am Fri.-Sat.

BIG DOG COFFEE ⑤

Looking for a quiet South Side café that's a sort of locals-only spot, and a bit off the beaten East Carson Street path? Owned by a Bulgarian violinist and his bassoonist wife, Big Dog sits in a restored, century-old former bakery, where it serves popular desserts and an unusual lunch menu that includes oatmeal, soups, sandwiches, cookies, and gelato. Coffee snobs take note: Big Dog serves Intelligentsia.

MAP 4: 2717 Sarah St., 412/586-7306; 6am-10pm Mon.-Fri., 7:30am-10pm Sat.-Sun.

Mount Washington

Map 4

CLASSIC AMERICAN
SHILOH GRILL ⑤⑤

Shiloh Grill is a Mount Washington mainstay, and it's a great place to go if you don't need the white linen tablecloths that are popular at some of the finer Grandview Avenue joints. You may not get that spectacular skyline view, but you can just as easily enjoy a summer evening on their casual patio. The menu is nothing fancy but offers the same fun and inventive twists on favorites, just like sister restaurant Harris Grill in Shadyside. You can't go wrong with the jerk chicken tacos or lobster mac-and-cheese.

MAP 4: 123 Shiloh St., 412/431-4000, www.theshilohgrill.com; 11:30am-11pm Mon.-Fri., 11:30am-1am Sat., 10am-11pm Sun.

ITALIAN
LA TAVOLA ⑤⑤⑤

If you've been to Italy, La Tavola is pretty successful at transporting you back. The Mount Washington restaurant approaches meals the same way Italians do: slowly. To someone with an hour lunch break or after-dinner plans, this may seem like a drawback. But if dining is the main event for your evening, La Tavola allows you to settle in, linger on a glass of wine, and share a meal with friends without feeling like you're being rushed. You'll find a menu of expertly and lovingly prepared Sicilian dishes, like veal piccata, chicken parmigiana, and house-made meatballs.

MAP 4: 1 Boggs Ave., 412/481-3336, www.latavolaitalianarestaurant.com; 5pm-10pm Tues.-Thurs., 5pm-11pm Fri.-Sat.

STEAK AND SEAFOOD
LEMONT RESTAURANT ⑤⑤⑤

The LeMont is a five-star locale offering traditional American cuisine, including seafood and old-school meat entrées. (The two house specialties, for instance, are steak Diane and chateaubriand.) And despite its hope-lessly out-of-date decor, LeMont also continues to be something of a hit for wedding receptions and business meetings. Dessert selections are appropriately filling and rich. For men, a coat and tie are required. This is a reservation-only venue.

MAP 4: 1114 Grandview Ave., 412/431-3100, www.lemontpittsburgh.com; 5pm-9pm Tues.-Thurs., 5pm-10pm Fri.-Sat., 4pm-8pm Sun.

MONTEREY BAY FISH GROTTO ❸❸❸

Inside a high-rise building at the far western end of Grandview Avenue, the Monterey Bay Fish Grotto offers an award-winning selection of fresh fish, flown in daily and served in a visually striking glass-enclosed dining room. The setting is truly remarkable; every table has a phenomenal view of The Point. The steaks and seafood will definitely set you back, but this is one of the few Mount Washington restaurants that have kept up with quality and service.

MAP 4: 1411 Grandview Ave., 412/481-4414, www.montereybayfishgrotto.com; 5pm-10pm Mon.-Thurs., 5pm-11pm Fri.-Sat., 5pm-9pm Sun.

GRANDVIEW SALOON & COAL HILL STEAKHOUSE ❸❸

It's easy to understand why the Grandview Saloon's two dining levels—as well as its two outdoor patios—are consistently packed with tourists and locals: The view afforded from either deck is just as stunning and romantic as any other you'll find along Restaurant Row, and yet the prices are a bit lower because the atmosphere is more casual. Sandwiches, wraps, chicken salads, burgers, and hoagies are all available, although USDA prime steaks are as well.

MAP 4: 1212 Grandview Ave., 412/431-1400, www.thegrandviewsaloon.com; 11:30am-10pm Sun.-Thurs., 11:30am-10pm Fri.-Sat.

Shadyside   Map 5

CLASSIC AMERICAN
HARRIS GRILL ❸❸

Something of a contemporary American lounge with a sense of humor, Harris Grill has a menu that is creative to say the least: Britney Spears (chicken tenders), Jamaican Tacos Tonight (pulled jerk chicken tacos), Sammiches (Pittsburghese for sandwiches), and Scooter's Mom's Black Bottom (a giant chocolate cupcake stuffed with chocolate cream cheese icing and topped with a raspberry drizzle) are highlights. Their most popular night is Bacon Night on Tuesdays, when you can order a basket of bacon for $1 or get it for free at the bar.

MAP 5: 5747 Ellsworth Ave., 412/362-5273, www.harrisgrill.com; 11:30am-2am Mon.-Fri., 11am-2am Sat., 10am-2am Sun.

NEW AMERICAN
CAFÉ ZINHO $$

Café Zinho resides in an actual garage in a residential neighborhood that's been transformed into something of a culinary hipster's haven. The decor at Café Zinho is strictly thrift-store chic, complete with mismatched furniture and ironically bad art. But entrées and even desserts are strictly first-class, and artfully built: Think gourmet dishes complete with lamb, mussels, and even wild game. The veggie rice bowls and remarkably constructed salads regularly earn approving clucks from discriminating foodies as well.

MAP 5: 238 Spahr St., 412/363-1500; 5pm-10pm Tues.-Thurs., 5pm-11pm Fri.-Sat.

ASIAN
SOBA $$$

For exquisitely crafted pan-Asian cuisine and a moderately formal ambience, look no further. Soba consists of two full floors, with a dining room and a well-tended bar on each. Starry-eyed lovers and local pseudo-celebrities can be seen digging into vegetable samosas and lemongrass strip steak. A relatively recent facelift modernized and brightened the place up quite a bit. Wander up to the third floor and you'll find Umi, a fantastic Japanese restaurant also affiliated with the Big Burrito Group.

MAP 5: 5847 Ellsworth Ave., 412/362-5656, www.sobapa.com; 5pm-10pm Mon.-Thurs., 5pm-11pm Fri.-Sat., 5pm-9pm Sun.

UMI $$$

On Soba's top floor but with its own separate entrance, Umi is probably Pittsburgh's most style-conscious Japanese eatery. The sushi and sashimi, prepared with high precision by a true *shokunin* (a master sushi chef), will set you back around $3 a piece. Not a terrible price to pay, considering that executive chef Mr. Shu is one of the city's top sushi celebrities. (Another is Chaya's Fumio Yasuzawa.) Fish-free dishes include teriyaki, miso soups, and even an octopus salad.

MAP 5: 5849 Ellsworth Ave., 412/362-6198, www.bigburrito.com/umi; 5pm-9pm Tues.-Thurs., 5pm-10pm Fri.-Sat.

ITALIAN
MERCURIO'S $$

This unassuming spot in Shadyside is known for two things: gelato and pizza. The casual family-owned joint started out as a gelato shop, serving up cups of the authentic Italian treat. Eventually, pizza was added to the menu—Neopolitan wood-fired pizza that tastes like it's straight out of Naples. Pizza purists should order the simple and perfect Marinara pizza, but you can also get more exotic with something like the Diavola, with tomato sauce, basil, salami, red pepper, and house-made mozzarella.

MAP 5: 5523 Walnut St., 412/621-6220, www.mercuriosgelatopizza.com; 1pm-9pm Sun.-Mon., 11am-10pm Tues.-Thurs., 11am-11pm Fri.-Sat.

MEDITERRANEAN
CASBAH $$$

Offering certainly one of the city's most satisfying culinary adventures, Casbah is tough to miss: It's the tan stucco block built to resemble a Moroccan mosque. Expect a wide spread of Mediterranean and North African cuisine that's simply unmatched elsewhere in Pittsburgh. A typical menu might offer Elysian Fields lamb with red wine jus, roasted duck broth soup, and Prince Edward Island mussels. The menu is seasonally based and features fresh food from area farms.

MAP 5: 229 S. Highland Ave., 412/661-5656, www.casbahpgh.com; 11:30am-2:30pm and 5pm-10pm Mon.-Thurs., 11:30am-2:30pm and 5pm-11pm Fri., 11am-2pm and 5pm-11pm Sat., 11am-2pm and 5pm-9pm Sun.

DESSERT
MILLIE'S HOMEMADE ICE CREAM $

Millie's is ice cream all grown up. The Shadyside ice cream shop hasn't been around for long, but Pittsburghers already know it by name and line up for scoops. They've applied the same popular "farm to table" philosophy to ice cream, using local all-natural milk and farm-fresh eggs from local suppliers. Though you can always get good old chocolate or vanilla, discerning palates will appreciate more mature flavors like Szechwan Peach and Pistachio Honey. The interior is fresh and spacious, with fun pink walls, exposed brick, and white subway tile. Grab a seat inside or at one of the picnic tables outside. There's a second location downtown (246 Forbes Ave., 412/709-6597).

MAP 5: 232 S. Highland Ave., 412/404-8853, www.millieshomemade.com; noon-10pm Sun.-Thurs., noon-11pm Fri.-Sat.

COFFEE
CRAZY MOCHA $

Another branch of the ever-growing Crazy Mocha chain, now with more than two dozen separate locations, this café retains a slightly rarified air and something of a neighborhood feel as well, due to its choice location on Ellsworth Avenue. Menu items are just what you'd expect: a full range of coffee and espresso drinks, with sandwiches and cheesecakes behind the counter. But even regular ol' coffee drinkers get their orders delivered straight to the table—a welcome concept in the too-often discourteous world of independent cafés.

MAP 5: 5830 Ellsworth Ave., 412/441-9344, www.crazymocha.com; 7am-9pm Mon.-Fri., 8am-9pm Sat.-Sun.

Squirrel Hill and Point Breeze

Map 6

DINERS
SQUARE CAFÉ 💲

One of the neighborhood's most popular early-morning eateries, the Square Café acts as a fairly standard neighborhood diner during its daily breakfast and lunch service. Breakfast fare includes tofu scrambles, breakfast quesadillas, French toast with challah bread, and granola, while lunch service is standard American fare (meat and pasta dishes mostly) with a light fusion twist. Soups, salads, sandwiches, and wraps are also served, as is a fairly standard kids' menu featuring PB&J, mac-and-cheese, and chicken fingers.

MAP 6: 1137 S. Braddock Ave., 412/244-8002, www.square-cafe.com; 7am-3pm Mon.-Sat., 8am-3pm Sun.

NEW AMERICAN
NU MODERN JEWISH BISTRO 💲💲

The neighborhood of Squirrel Hill houses nearly one-third of the entire Jewish population of Pittsburgh. So there's no better place to explore Jewish heritage and cuisine than at Nu Modern Jewish Bistro. The restaurant is an entirely creative concept: You pay one price to get in and then you choose your meal. There's a "nosh and nibble" table set up where you can taste little bits of Jewish specialties, like house-made bagels, noodle kugel, or latkes, making you feel like you're someone's dinner guest rather than a patron. The bistro is open only on the weekend.

MAP 6: 1711 Murray Ave., 412/422-0220, www.nujewishbistro.com; 10am-4pm Sat.-Sun.

ASIAN
★ CHENGDU GOURMET 💲💲

Of the countless Asian restaurants in Squirrel Hill, Chengdu stands out due to its authentic Sichuan dishes. The restaurant has two menus—one of standard Americanized Chinese fare and one with the real jewels, the traditionally prepared Sichuan dishes. Try the *mala,* a popular Sichuan dish of dried chilies, garlic, ginger and chili-bean paste, to get acquainted. Not sure where to start? The servers and chef Wei Zhu will be happy to point you in the right direction.

MAP 6: 5840 Forward Ave., 412/521-2088, www.chengdugourmetpittsburgh.com; 11am-10pm Mon.-Thurs., 11am-11pm Fri.-Sat., noon-10pm Sun.

CHAYA JAPANESE CUISINE 💲💲

As a general culinary rule of thumb, a Japanese restaurant filled with actual Japanese diners is usually a sign that you've found the real deal. Chaya, which boasts one of Pittsburgh's two best sushi chefs (Fumio Yasuzawa), operates under a similar assumption: Apparently, this is where the city's Japanese community congregates when they're feeling homesick. The

Clockwise from top left: unassuming Chengdu Gourmet, home to one of the top chefs in Pittsburgh; charcuterie at Cure; Apteka.

wasabi is made in-house, and what's more, fresh fish for sushi and sashimi is flown in chilled—not frozen—from Japan or New York.

MAP 6: 2032 Murray Ave., 412/422-2082, www.chayausa.com; 5pm-9:30pm Mon.-Thurs., 5pm-9:45pm Fri.-Sat.

CURRY ON MURRAY ⑤⑤

Pittsburgh's East End is relatively rich in Thai dining options, but in Squirrel Hill, Curry on Murray is generally a can't-miss choice. As its name suggests, curries are the go-to menu item, but the various noodle dishes are also popular. Fair warning to those who aren't accustomed to authentic Thai food: This stuff is *spicy*. If you can't handle the heat, be sure to let your server know.

MAP 6: 2121 Murray Ave, 412/422-3120; 11:30am-2:30pm and 4pm-9pm Mon.-Tues. and Thurs., 11:30am-2:30pm and 4pm-9:30pm Fri., noon-2:30pm and 4pm-9:30pm Sat., noon-2:30pm and 4pm-9pm Sun.

ITALIAN
MINEO'S ⑤

Claiming to be any city's best pizza joint can be a controversial undertaking, but the family-owned Mineo's has the awards to prove it—dozens of them, from nearly every Pittsburgh publication—lining the walls of their no-frills cafeteria-style shop. It's tough to put a finger on exactly why the pies and slices are so delectable. It could be the generous piling on of cheese, or maybe the always-fresh ingredients. Might be the sauces and toppings, both of which Mineo's steadfastly refuses to skimp on.

MAP 6: 2128 Murray Ave., 412/521-9864, www.mineospizza.com; 11am-1am Sun.-Thurs., 11am-2am Fri.-Sat.

CAFÉS AND LIGHT BITES
POINT BRUGGE CAFÉ ⑤⑤

Point Brugge Café was designed to feel and operate like a familiar neighborhood gathering spot. The atmosphere itself is a pleasant cross between traditional European sophistication and the laid-back vibe of the West Coast, while the dishes—Belgian-inspired cuisine with a twist—strike a balance between comfort food and modern decadence. As an added bonus, Belgian beers can often be found on tap. Reservations are recommended. Also worth a visit is the café's sister restaurant in Highland Park, the appropriately named **Park Bruges** (5801 Bryant St., 412/661-3334, www.park-bruges.com), which offers an upscale twist on poutine and serves the city's best Liège waffles and eggs Benedict during brunch.

MAP 6: 401 Hastings St., 412/441-3334, www.pointbrugge.com; 11am-10pm Tues.-Thurs., 11am-11pm Fri.-Sat., 11am-9pm Sun.

MAKE YOUR MARK ARTSPACE & COFFEEHOUSE ⑤

Just as popular for its vegetarian-friendly light lunches (panini, quesadillas, and soups) as for its artistically prepared selection of fair trade and organic La Prima coffees, Make Your Mark has done just that in the formerly unremarkable Point Breeze business district, which is slowly becoming something of a dining and leisure destination. As the café's name suggests, patrons can leave their own mark on a wall covered in stainless steel sheets and magnets.

MAP 6: 6736 Reynolds St., 412/365-2117; 7am-5pm Mon.-Fri., 8am-5pm Sat.

DESSERT
WAFFALONIA ❸

With two locations in Pittsburgh (the other is a food kiosk in Oakland's Schenley Plaza), Waffalonia is a fun little eatery that'll satisfy even the sweetest sweet tooth. The made-from-scratch and freshly ironed authentic Belgian waffles can be topped with the ice creams, spreads, fruits, and other confections of your choosing. The strawberry, banana, and Nutella waffle is a healthier alternative, but if you want to get the full Waffalonia experience, you'll want to pick a flavor of Dave and Andy's ice cream.

MAP 6: 1709 Murray Ave., 412/521-4902, www.waffalonia.com; 11am-10pm Mon.-Thurs., 11am-11pm Fri., 9am-11pm Sat., 9am-10pm Sun.

Bloomfield and East Liberty
Map 7

CLASSIC AMERICAN
WHITFIELD ❸❸❸

Whitfield is the restaurant for the new Ace Hotel in Pittsburgh's East Liberty neighborhood. The menu focuses on the hearty, traditional meals of the Western Pennsylvania region, while paying mind to seasonal ingredients. Meat-heavy meals like a 32-ounce rib eye or pork shank are served in the utilitarian-looking dining hall, which is housed in an old YMCA. Other than meat, there's a good variety of fish and vegetarian dishes. Make room for dessert: The head pastry chef doesn't skimp on decadence with the olive oil chocolate cake and butterscotch cheesecake.

MAP 7: 120 S. Whitfield St., 412/626-3090, www.whitfieldpgh.com; 7am-3pm and 5pm-10pm Sun.-Thurs., 7am-3pm and 5pm-midnight Fri.-Sat.

BRGR ❸❸

As its cheeky moniker suggests, BRGR is a gourmet burger joint, complete with handmade milkshakes and the ambience of a fairly upscale restaurant. And while the dry-aged prime beef patties are excellent, so too are the salmon, turkey, roasted corn, black bean, shrimp, and pork burgers. BRGR is very conscientious about dietary restrictions. BRGR also has a location downtown and several in the suburbs.

MAP 7: 5997 Centre Ave., 412/362-2333, http://brgrpgh.com; 11:30 am-11pm Mon.-Thurs., 11:30am-midnight Fri.-Sat., 11:30am-9pm Sun.

TESSARO'S ❸❸

Red meat fanatics should not miss out on a trip to one of the city's most mouthwatering eateries, Tessaro's, which looks and feels like a locals-only

Pittsburgh's Star Chefs

Pittsburgh may not be a huge city, but cutting-edge restaurants and superstar chefs are putting it on the foodie map. Pittsburgh is a great town for opening a restaurant, as the rent tends to be lower than in other big cities, so the risk to entry is much lower. For this reason, many amazing chefs have made Pittsburgh their home:

Justin Severino
Chef Justin Severino is no stranger to Pittsburgh—he graduated from the Pennsylvania Culinary Institute. After graduation, he spent some time working in California, in kitchens and a butcher shop. Now he's back in Pittsburgh and the city couldn't be happier. His two restaurants, **Cure** and **Morcilla,** are ever-present on lists of the city's best restaurants. In 2017 (and four other years), he was named as a semifinalist for the prestigious James Beard Award for Best Chef in the Mid-Atlantic Region.

Casey Renee
After a brief stint as a marketing professional in New York City, Casey Renee decided to make a big and risky life change, by quitting her job and enrolling in cooking school. Her schooling paid off and soon Renee landed a series of jobs at some of New York's most highly regarded and selective restaurants. But like many native Pittsburghers do, Renee decided to come back. She now brings her impressive résumé and rigorous training to her role as pastry chef at **Whitfield** in East Liberty. She was named a semifinalist for the James Beard Award in 2017 for Outstanding Pastry Chef.

Wei Zhu
Hailing from Chengdu, the capital of the Sichuan province of China, Wei Zhu's parents wanted him to go into the bakery business. But he preferred cooking to baking. After opening several restaurants in China, Zhu decided to move to New York to learn more about the restaurant business. He was disappointed in the quality of the Sichuan restaurants there and felt there wasn't much for him to learn. While visiting a friend in Pittsburgh before his planned return to China, Zhu was convinced to stay and open a restaurant with a couple of out-of-work PhD grads. The restaurant was extremely successful, but Zhu decided to leave the partnership for a while to open his own restaurant, **Chengdu Gourmet** in Squirrel Hill. His success at bringing authentic and spicy Sichuan dishes to Pittsburgh has paid off. He was also a semifinalist for the James Beard Award for Best Chef in the Mid-Atlantic region in 2017.

neighborhood eatery. It has been featured on many Food Network TV shows. Tessaro's regularly wins awards for the 'Burgh's best burgers. The secret, some say, is the bits of steak and filet mixed with the meat. If the idea of a gourmet burger isn't grabbing you, try a char-grilled steak or chop instead.

MAP 7: 4601 Liberty Ave., 412/682-6809, www.tessaros.com; 11am-11pm Mon.-Sat.

NEW AMERICAN
AVENUE B ⬤⬤⬤

Native Pittsburgh chef Chris Bonfili describes his culinary style at Avenue B as "sophisticated simplicity." This aesthetic is evident in the restaurant's short but impressive seasonally changing menu. The dishes rely on a farm-to-table philosophy, sourcing fresh ingredients locally and using what is in season. The chalkboard menu, prominently displayed in the dining room, features dishes that combine a lot of distinct flavors; for example, melon gazpacho with crab ceviche, crispy ham, smoked grapes, and almonds. Bonfili's style extends to the decor, which is casual and understated, with cool touches like hanging pendant lights and a huge chalkboard menu on the wall.

MAP 7: 5501 Centre Ave., 412/683-3663, www.avenueb-pgh.com; 5pm-10pm Tues.-Thurs., 5pm-11pm Fri.-Sat.

SPOON ⬤⬤⬤

Fawning food critics nationwide can't seem to say enough about Spoon, one of the East End's favorite avant-garde eateries, where seasonal and locally sourced ingredients are combined with unparalleled creativity. The brilliant menu is the result of executive chef Jamilka Borges's commitment to farm-to-table dining and an expertise in French, Italian, and Latin cuisine (in 2015 she was recognized by the James Beard Foundation as a rising star chef). Try the pork belly loin chop with rice polenta, wax bean salad, and pineapple barbecue sauce.

MAP 7: 134 S. Highland Ave., 412/362-6001, www.spoonpgh.com; 5pm-10pm Mon.-Thurs., 5pm-11pm Fri.-Sat., 11am-2pm and 5pm-9pm Sun.

DINETTE ⬤⬤

Dinette is a brilliantly designed minimalist bistro offering gourmet flatbread pizzas along with what is easily one of the city's most sophisticated wine lists. The name reflects the atmosphere here: a casual space offering a vibrant yet airy dining room with white walls, chrome tables, and bright red chairs. Aside from its daily-changing menu, Dinette has quite a lot to brag about: *Pittsburgh Magazine* has named it one of the city's 25 best restaurants several times, and chef-owner Sonja Finn has been a semifinalist for the prestigious James Beard Foundation award.

MAP 7: 5996 Centre Ave., 412/362-0202, www.dinette-pgh.com; 5pm-10pm Tues.-Thurs., 5pm-11pm Fri.-Sat.

ASIAN
PLUM PAN-ASIAN KITCHEN ⬤⬤

Long-time Pittsburgh-area diners might like to think of Plum as something of an upscale Spice Island Tea House, which is a pan-Asian eatery in Oakland appealing to the university set. And yet the Thai, Indonesian, Vietnamese, Malaysian, and Chinese offerings at Plum manage to be appropriately sophisticated while still maintaining a semblance of affordability. The space itself is gorgeous, and the sushi bar is among Pittsburgh's very best.

MAP 7: 5996 Penn Cir. S., 412/363-7586, www.plumpanasiankitchen.com; 11:30am-3pm and 5pm-10pm Mon.-Thurs., 11:30am-3pm and 5pm-11pm Fri.-Sat., 12:30pm-3pm and 4:30pm-9pm Sun.

THAI CUISINE ❸❺

The pad Thai at Thai Cuisine is some of the best in the city, the waiters are extremely good-natured and attentive, and the lunch menu is an absolute bargain. This is also a perfect choice for a first date. There are more than 100 items on the menu. Particularly popular is the *tom ka gai* (chicken coconut soup), which goes wonderfully with any entrée. Do save room for the black sticky rice with mango dessert if it's available.

MAP 7: 4627 Liberty Ave., 412/688-9661, www.thaicuisinerestaurant.net; 11am-2:30pm and 5pm-10pm Tues.-Fri., noon-10:30pm Sat.-Sun.

TRAM'S KITCHEN ❸❺

This is easily one of Pittsburgh's most popular Vietnamese restaurants, but even Tram's most loyal customers often feel compelled to describe the ambience with a qualifier, which I'll second: It's a hole-in-the-wall. But sit down with a steaming bowl of *pho* (Vietnamese soup) and order a round of spring rolls, and you likely won't care; the food at Tram's is always fresh and bursting with flavor.

MAP 7: 4050 Penn Ave., 412/682-2688; 10am-10pm Tues.-Sat., 11am-8:30pm Sun.

SMILING BANANA LEAF ❺

This restaurant specializes in authentic Thai dishes, with fresh herbs and other ingredients. The pad Thai is reliable, but try out some of the chef's specialties, like the mango tilapia, topped with a sweet and sour sauce. The decor is modern, but the dining area is rather small, so you may have to wait for a table. It's BYOB here.

MAP 7: 5901 Bryant St., 412/362-3200, www.smilingbananaleaf.com; 11am-3pm and 4pm-9pm Mon.-Thurs., 11am-3pm and 4pm-10pm Fri., 11am-10pm Sat., noon-9pm Sun.

ETHIOPIAN
TANA ETHIOPIAN CUISINE ❸❺

For those inexperienced with the cuisine, Ethiopian dishes are generally eaten with the hands, while using a soft yet sturdy type of flatbread called *injera* in place or a fork or spoon. To get a feel for the flavors, order a combination platter, which allows diners to sample up to five different meat and vegetable dishes. And yet just about anything found on the menu is likely to please the adventurous foodie.

MAP 7: 5929 Baum Blvd., 412/665-2770, www.tanaethiopiancuisine.com; 5pm-10pm Mon.-Thurs., 11:30am-2:30pm and 5pm-11pm Fri.-Sat.

FRENCH
PARIS 66 BISTRO 🟢🟢

As a self-described purveyor of "everyday French cuisine," this crepe hub prides itself on being the exact opposite of the stereotypical French restaurant in America: It's both affordable and non-exclusionary. At the same time, it manages to retain an entirely authentic vibe, thanks no doubt to the French-trained owner and head chef. Designed to look, smell, and feel like a Parisian sidewalk café, Paris 66 also serves up French pizza, Parisian pastries, and made-daily French desserts. Brunch is served on Sunday.

MAP 7: 6018 Penn Cir. S., 412/404-8166, www.paris66bistro.com; 11am-10pm Mon.-Thurs., 11am-11pm Fri.-Sat., 10am-3pm Sun.

INDIAN
TASTE OF INDIA 🟢

Don't be put off if you visit Taste of India around dinnertime and find the dining room nearly deserted—the crowd tends to thin after the midday all-you-can-eat buffet, a Pittsburgh trend that's repeated in nearly every area Indian restaurant. Nonetheless, the offerings at Taste of India unquestionably represent North Indian food at its finest, and the affordable portions are surprisingly generous to boot.

MAP 7: 4320 Penn Ave., 412/681-7700, www.tasteofindiapittsburgh.com; 11:30am-2:30pm and 5pm-10pm Mon.-Thurs., 11:30am-2:30pm and 5pm-10:30pm Fri.-Sat., 5pm-10pm Sun.

ITALIAN
THE LIVERMORE 🟢🟢

Opened in 2013 by the same team responsible for Bar Marco, the Livermore is a full-fledged Italian restaurant. The setting is cozy but casual (they occasionally host game nights), and the menu focuses on traditional recipes and simple ingredients. Bar Marco and The Livermore pay their employees a salary and vacation time, so tipping is not expected.

MAP 7: 124 S. Highland Ave., 412/361-0600, www.thelivermorepgh.com; 5pm-11pm Tues.-Sat.

SPAK BROTHERS PIZZA 🟢

Owned and operated by ambitious siblings who grew up in the city's suburbs, this Garfield-area pizzeria serves truly delectable versions of typical pizza shop fare. The Spaks, however, have also carved out a unique niche as purveyors of vegetarian and vegan offerings not available anywhere else in the region. Meat-free wings, tacos, cheese steaks, and even meatless sausage and pepperoni are all available. And what's more, the shop largely sources local and sustainable ingredients.

MAP 7: 5107 Penn Ave., 412/362-7725, www.spakbrothers.com; 11am-10pm Mon.-Thurs., 11am-11pm Fri., noon-11pm Sat., 3pm-10pm Sun.

POLISH
★ APTEKA $$

Vegan Polish food. It's kind of shocking that a cuisine that sounds so lack-luster won the title of Best New Restaurant in 2017, but that's a testament to how expertly the menu is executed. The owners of the Bloomfield eatery combine their Pittsburgh and Polish to serve up rich and complex dishes like *boczniaki z kapusta* (mushroom and cabbage in beer broth with butternut miso and rye crumbs) and, of course, pierogi (sauerkraut and mushroom or celeriac, apple, potato, and horseradish). The sparse decor of hanging bulb lights and whitewashed cinderblocks lets the menu shine.

MAP 7: 4606 Penn Ave., 412/251-0189, www.aptekapgh.com; 5pm-midnight Wed.-Sun. (21 and older after 10pm)

COFFEE
ZEKE'S COFFEE $

As the neighborhood's very own small-batch coffee roaster, Zeke's is a genuine first for East Liberty. And yet while the roaster itself does offer free Wi-Fi, it's not necessarily the sort of place you'd feel comfortable spending the entire day. (There's just one table.) Instead, pick up a pound to brew at home and enjoy a to-go cup of Zeke's rocket-fueled drip coffee while you wait. Fair warning: You'll never be able to purchase grinds at the grocery store again.

MAP 7: 6015 Penn Ave., 412/670-6231, www.zekescoffeepgh.com; 8am-7pm Mon.-Sat.

85

RESTAURANTS
LAWRENCEVILLE

Lawrenceville
Map 8

CLASSIC AMERICAN
FRANKTUARY $

Hot dogs have never been seen as fine dining, but Franktuary makes a successful attempt at changing this perception. Premium franks and sausages are topped with gourmet fixings like kimchi, apple compote, and grilled pineapple. Sides include garbanzo fries, miso kale salad, and chili. Pair your dog with a drink from the full bar, a glass of red wine, a mead cocktail, or a craft beer. Of course, this is no standard dog. You'll pay a premium for grass-fed and humanely raised meat and specialty sausages.

MAP 8: 3810 Butler St., 412/586-7224, www.franktuary.com; 11am-10:30pm Tues.-Thurs., 11am-11:30pm Fri.-Sat., 11am-8pm Sun.

NEW AMERICAN
CURE $$$

The food at this hugely popular and genuinely sustainable restaurant, where diners eat family-style around simple wood tables, is local, fresh, and tinged with something of a Mediterranean twist. Head chef Justin Severino takes ethical farming practices quite seriously and is deeply involved with his suppliers. As for the menu, it's tough to go wrong. Take full advantage of staff recommendations, as employees taste everything on offer and are well-versed on the ever-changing menu.

MAP 8: 5336 Butler St., 412/252-2595, www.curepittsburgh.com; 5pm-9:30pm Mon. and Wed.-Thurs., 5pm-10pm Fri., 5pm-9:30pm Sat.-Sun.

SMOKE 💲💲

The name of this Lawrenceville restaurant says it all: This casual but cool taqueria serves up all manner of smoked meats in freshly made flour tortillas. Dining in is an experience here, with a meat smoker as the centerpiece of the rustic and industrial charm (you'll probably carry that campfire smell out the door). The tacos are hefty and flavorful and the prices are surprisingly good. Burger Tuesday, when only burgers are offered, is a popular night.

MAP 8: 4115 Butler St., 412/224-2070, www.smokpgh.com; noon-9pm Mon., 3pm-10pm Tues., noon-10pm Wed.-Thurs., 11am-11pm Fri.-Sat., 11am-3pm Sun.

THE VANDAL 💲💲

At The Vandal, everything from the menu's font to the minimalist decor oozes hipster chic aesthetic. And that might make some dismiss the place as superficial, except for this: Executive chef Csilla Thackray absolutely nails everything. The Vandal calls itself a "hyper-seasonal café," so menu options change with the seasons. Despite this, the menu is actually pretty substantial, offering everything from lamb stew to smoked trout. The fried chicken sandwich with carrot slaw and chili honey (along with the house-made fries and addicting mustard aioli) should be on everyone's bucket list.

MAP 8: 4306 Butler St., 412/251-0465, www.thevandalpgh.com; 11am-3pm and 5pm-9pm Tues.-Thurs., 11am-3pm and 5:30pm-10pm Fri., 9am-2pm and 5:30pm-10pm Sat., 9am-2pm Sun.

ASIAN
PUSADEE'S GARDEN 💲💲

Pusadee's Garden easily serves up some of the best Thai in the city, but that's not really its biggest draw. What really sets Pusadee's apart is the garden itself, an outdoor sanctuary of lush plants and herbs that are picked by hand and used to flavor the restaurants delicious curries and noodle dishes. String lights and vining plants turn the back garden into one of the most romantic spots in the city. The garden seating is popular, so make reservations.

MAP 8: 5321 Butler St., 412/781-8724, www.pusadeesgarden.com; 4:30pm-10pm Mon.-Fri., noon-10pm Sat.-Sun.

UMAMI 💲💲

It's almost like Umami is a secret club. You'll be lucky to find the door, which is only indicated by a cryptic logo (it actually spells out the restaurant's name). The Japanese *izakaya*-themed casual restaurant is an experience in itself, especially if you're lucky enough to be seated in one of the private tatami rooms with low tables (your legs dangle into a hole built into the floor). The Umami dining experience focuses a lot on sharable small plates, like the *robatayaki*, which are grilled foods served on the skewer (try the chicken hearts or bacon-wrapped quail eggs). There's a large menu of sushi and cooked dishes that are inspired by Japanese street food. Umami also has a stocked bar with over-the-top cocktails, sake, and Japanese beers.

MAP 8: 202 38th St., 3rd floor, 412/224-2354, www.umamipgh.com; 4:30pm-midnight Tues.-Thurs., 4:30pm-2am Fri.-Sat.

BANH MI AND TI $

At this fun and fresh spot, two Vietnamese sisters are making a lot of Pittsburghers very happy by serving *banh mi. Banh mi* is a traditional Vietnamese sandwich filled with meat, cucumbers, cilantro, pickled carrots, chilies, mayonnaise, and cheese, on a French baguette, a nod to Vietnam's French colonial period. They offer several types of meat and a few twists on the classic *banh mi,* with ingredients like pâté and lemongrass. They also serve traditional and bubble teas, plus coffee from Café du Monde in New Orleans.

MAP 8: 4502 Butler St., 412/251-5030; 11am-8pm Tues.-Sat., noon-5pm Sun.

ITALIAN
PICCOLO FORNO $$

One long-standing restaurant that has survived and thrived in the barrage of new hip restaurants in Lawrenceville is Piccolo Forno. The warm and rustic Tuscan Italian restaurant has consistently relied on fresh ingredients and proven recipes since 2005. It's a great place to impress a date over dishes of fresh hand-made pasta or meet with a client for lunch.

MAP 8: 3801 Butler St., 412/622-0111, www.piccolo-forno.com; 11am-10pm Tues.-Thurs., 11am-11pm Fri.-Sat.

SENTI $$

Senti's service is impeccable, making its patrons feel like they are truly being served at their meal. This is not always a given, as some of the city's top restaurants rely on the reputation of their superstar chefs, while smug and aloof waiters are too cool to be hospitable. But not at Senti. With white linen tablecloths and attentive staff, they certainly earn their tips. The menu serves up authentic Italian dishes with modern touches. The portions are moderate but sufficient: Don't expect Olive Garden-sized heaps of pasta.

MAP 8: 3473 Butler St., 412/586-4347, www.sentirestaurant.com; 11:30am-2pm and 5pm-9pm Tues.-Thurs., 11:30am-2pm and 5pm-10pm Fri.-Sat., 4pm-8pm Sun.

SPANISH
MORCILLA $$$

Morcilla is another hit from Pittsburgh superstar chef Justin Severino (of neighboring Cure). The menu is Spanish cuisine, and charcuterie features heavily. Try a variety of *pinxtos* (skewered bite-sized food) and tapas or opt for an entrée-sized meal like the crispy suckling pork roast. The interior is almost as impressive as the food. With warm lighting, industrial-style chandeliers, and exposed brick walls, it's a great place to impress a date or gather with friends.

MAP 8: 3519 Butler St., 412/652-9924, www.morcillapittsburgh.com; 5pm-9pm Mon. and Wed.-Thurs., 5pm-10pm Fri., 4pm-10pm Sat., 4pm-9pm Sun.

CAFÉS AND LIGHT BITES

★ COCA CAFÉ ❸❸

Easily one of Pittsburgh's best coffeehouses in both food and drink quality as well as interior design, the arty Coca Café displays a regularly rotating selection of locally produced sculptures and multimedia work on the shelves and walls of its front room. The inventive menu shines just as bright as the coffee, with açai bowls, peach-and-mascarpone-stuffed French toast, and an amazing curry chicken salad. Sunday brunch (smoked salmon omelets, vanilla-orange yogurt with granola) is of the particularly pleasing and high-end variety.

MAP 8: 3811 Butler St., 412/621-3171, www.coca-cafe.net; 8am-3pm Tues.-Sat., 9am-2pm Sun.

BAKERIES

LA GOURMANDINE ❸

Owned and operated by a French couple who previously lived and worked in Paris, this traditional French bakery quickly became a darling of the Pittsburgh foodie community when it opened in the summer of 2010. And while the hand-crafted pastries and other French sweets are certainly big draws, La Gourmandine is probably best known for its breads, baguettes, and baguette sandwiches. Combination specials for breakfast or lunch, usually involving some grouping of croissant, sandwich, and made-from-scratch quiche, are offered daily.

MAP 8: 4605 Butler St., 412/682-2210, www.lagourmandinebakery.com; 7:30am-4:30pm Mon.-Fri., 9am-2:30pm Sat.-Sun.

COFFEE

ESPRESSO A MANO ❸

This Lawrenceville coffee shop is a hit with local creative types, and it can get especially packed in the summer months, which is also when the street-facing glass garage door is opened to the elements. The vibe is modern but warm, and the café is particularly popular for the artistic foam designs its baristas create when pouring lattes and cappuccinos. Craftsmanship, in other words, is a serious deal; coffee snobs won't go away disappointed.

MAP 8: 3623 Butler St., 412/918-1864, www.espressoamano.com; 7am-9pm Mon.-Fri., 8am-9pm Sat., 8am-6pm Sun.

Nightlife

Look for ★ to find
recommended nightlife.

Highlights

★ **Best View:** On warm summer nights, Pittsburghers gather at rooftop bar **Biergarten** to sip European beer under the stars (page 93).

★ **Best After-Hours Party:** Late-night partiers congregate at **Hot Mass,** a gay-friendly all-night club where anything goes (page 94).

★ **Best College Bar:** At **Hemingway's,** you'll find all the guilty pleasures of a good old-fashioned college bar: cheap drinks, greasy food, and hordes of undergrads ready to cut loose (page 96).

★ **Best Cocktail Bar:** Speakeasy-themed **Acacia** is known for its exquisitely crafted cocktails (page 97).

★ **Best Theme Bar:** If you want to feel like you're getting away from it all, visit **Hidden Harbor,** with its tiki decor and expertly mixed tropical cocktails (page 104).

★ **Best Bar for Beer Snobs:** Beer aficionados across the city flock to **Sharp Edge Beer Emporium,** where they can choose from obscure international draft and bottled brews (page 105).

★ **Best Bar for a First Date:** Chat over tacos and Coronas at the effortlessly hip **Round Corner Cantina** (page 106).

★ **Best Dive Bar:** Hipsters and locals alike adore the cheap swill at **Gooski's,** Pittsburgh's most legendary watering hole (page 110).

★ **Best Place to Try Something New:** Adventurous drinkers should sample from the selection of Italian grappa at **Grapparia** (page 111).

It can be easy to holler and moan about Pittsburgh's distinctive lack of serious nightlife options. This is a small town.

Although the city's nightlife scene certainly has a little something to offer almost everyone, chances are good that you may have to dig deep to truly find what you're looking for. For instance, where bigger urban areas may have dozens of gay clubs, or 10 different jazz bars, Pittsburgh may be home to only five or six. The major difference, however, lies in the sense of community that's ever-present. It's in the neighborhood bars and in the tiny East End art galleries that transform into cutting-edge live music venues on weekend nights.

Pittsburgh has its fair share of showy nightclubs, which you can primarily find around the Strip District and Station Square. But Pittsburghers tend to prefer proven neighborhood watering holes over bottle service and VIP areas. Pittsburgh is mostly a laid-back place that eschews pretention, and that mentality extends to nightlife. If you're visiting from New York or L.A. and ask about clubs with bottle service, you're likely to be met with an eye roll.

Making nice with locals and regulars is the key to learning about Pittsburgh's best bars and hidden nightlife secrets. So belly up to the bar, get to know your neighbor, and start exploring the Steel City like the locals do: with an open-mind and good friends in tow.

Previous: Salsa Friday at Cabaret Theater; Speakeasy at Omni William Penn Hotel.

Strip District

Map 1

LIVE MUSIC
MULLANY'S HARP AND FIDDLE

Mullany's Harp and Fiddle is one of the few authentic Irish pubs in Pittsburgh, serving Guinness and fish-and-chips to the Strip District crowds. Harp and Fiddle is especially popular on its live music nights, which happen quite often, and bring lively Irish folk music to stomping and clapping crowds. Not surprisingly, the place really comes alive on St. Patrick's Day, when throngs of parade-goers pack the place for a day of drinking and live music.

MAP 1: 2329 Penn Ave., 412/642-6622, www.harpandfiddle.com; 11:30am-1am Tues.-Thurs., 11:30am-2am Fri.-Sat.

BARS
THE BEERHIVE

With a name like The Beerhive, you might expect more than 16 beers on tap. They sort of make up for this in their selection of over 100 bottled beers. The knowledgeable bartenders really know their beer and will be happy to make suggestions. The food is typical bar fare with some surprises, like maple bacon wings and an out-of-this-world dill ranch dressing.

MAP 1: 2117 Penn Ave., 412/904-4502, www.thebeerhive.com; 11:30am-10pm Mon., 11:30am-midnight Tues.-Thurs., 11:30am-1am Fri., 10am-2am Sat., 11am-8pm Sun.; no cover

GAY AND LESBIAN
REAL LUCK CAFE

Lucky's has been around *forever,* and you may drive past it without even knowing: It's tucked back behind the green wooden shamrock sign where Penn Avenue meets the 16th Street Bridge. Aside from the super-friendly crowd, the nude male dancers are probably the biggest draw, although the pet-friendly deck doesn't hurt either. Lucky's is fairly popular with lesbians as well. Lucky's is also cash only.

MAP 1: 1519 Penn Ave., 412/471-7832, www.realluckcafe.com; 4pm-2am daily; no cover

Drinking Alfresco

Pittsburgh is not exactly known for its beautiful weather. The city gets some harsh winters and nightlife tends to slow down in the colder months, with few people brave enough to face the cold and ice. But in the summer months, watch out. Pittsburghers like to make up for lost time, soaking up as much vitamin D as possible during the day and enjoying warm breezes after the sun sets. If you want make like the locals and keep the party going outside, there are a few bars around the city where you can enjoy a cocktail under the stars.

- **Il Tetto** (page 93)

- **Local Bar + Kitchen** (page 98)

- **Round Corner Cantina** (page 106)

- **Arsenal Cider House** (page 110)

Downtown

Map 2

LIVE MUSIC
ANDY'S WINE BAR

Located in the Fairmont, Andy's Wine Bar is a contemporary wine bar, a live jazz club, and a restaurant, all in one. Inspired by the city's two most notable Andys—Warhol and Carnegie—Andy's Wine Bar is also home to a fantastic collection of artifacts that were discovered underground during the building's site excavation. The jazz shows (always free) are a history lesson unto themselves, regularly featuring some of the city's finest musical talent.

MAP 2: Fairmont Pittsburgh, 510 Market St., 412/773-8884, www.andyswinebar.com; 3pm-midnight Sun.-Thurs., 1pm-1am Fri.-Sat.; no cover

BEER GARDENS
★ BIERGARTEN

Open from spring through early fall, Hotel Monaco's rooftop German-inspired beer garden is a favorite spot for Pittsburgh's drinkers to mix and mingle. The relaxed vibe is enhanced with string lights, communal tables, and classic games like Jenga, cornhole, and a super-sized Connect Four.

MAP 2: 620 William Penn Pl., 412/471-1170, www.monaco-pittsburgh.com; 4pm-9pm Tues., 4pm-11pm Wed.-Thurs., 4pm-midnight Fri., noon-midnight Sat.

IL TETTO

On the rooftop of the restaurant Sienna Mercato resides Il Tetto, an open-air beer garden complete with stunning views of downtown. Lights are strung above the roof, making even cloudy nights seem starry. A retractable glass roof keeps the party going in the winter months. They also have wine, upscale cocktails, and more than 36 drafts, as well as a menu of bar snacks. Be prepared to wait at the bottom floor during busier hours, as bouncers only let a certain number of people up at a time.

MAP 2: 942 Penn Ave., 412/281-2810, www.siennamercato.com; 4pm-close daily

GAY AND LESBIAN
★ HOT MASS

Hot Mass isn't specifically labeled as a gay club, but its location under-neath a men's-only bathhouse strongly hints at its gay-friendly vibe. Every Saturday night, Hot Mass opens its doors to Pittsburgh's gay community, plus anyone else looking to dance the night away. The dance club, which plays house and techno music, hosts underground parties that are remi-niscent of something you'd see in Berlin or Amsterdam. Here's the catch: It's technically a members-only club, which allows it to stay open until the early morning, unlike the city's bars. But $15 at the door will get you a membership for the night.

MAP 2: 1139 Penn Ave., 412/471-6790, www.clubpittsburgh.com; midnight-7am Sat.; $15 nightly membership

TILDEN

Because it's technically a club (members apply and pay a $30 fee), Tilden can stay open past the time that the city's bars are required to close down. It's not specifically a gay bar, but it's a queer-friendly, welcoming environ-ment. Nights at Tilden are rumored to get pretty wild.

MAP 2: 941 Liberty Ave., 412/281-7100, www.tildenclub.com; 1am-3am Sun.-Thurs., 11pm-3am Fri.-Sat.; $30 membership

LOUNGES
SPEAKEASY

Tucked beneath the lobby of the historic Omni William Penn Hotel, this Prohibition-themed lounge feels like a secret club. Decorated with a 1920s aesthetic, including plush red seating and flocked wall coverings, the at-mosphere is dark and sensual, a welcome break from the city's many in-dustrial-themed bars. Sip on scotch or bourbon or a classic Pimm's cup or Tom Collins. The crowd tends to be more mature and quieter than at the trendier bars in the area.

MAP 2: Omni William Penn Hotel, 530 William Penn Pl., 412/281-7100, www.omnihotels. com; 5pm-11pm Tues.-Thurs., 5pm-12:30am Fri.-Sat.

Top: Biergarten. **Bottom:** Club Café.

BARS
★ HEMINGWAY'S

One of the University of Pittsburgh's most popular college bars is Hemingway's (or Hem's to the regulars). During the daytime, it's a great spot to get cheap and filling pub grub, and at night (especially on weekends) it's filled wall to wall with sweaty undergrads. The beer is cold, cheap, and plentiful and the shot pitchers get the job done. The bartenders, possibly hardened by years of dealing with drunk college students, are no-nonsense. With multiple happy hours per day and late-night half-off food specials, Hem's is hard to beat if you want the most bang for your buck.

MAP 3: 3911 Forbes Ave., 412/621-4100, www.hemingwayspgh.com; 11am-2am Mon.-Sat., no cover

PETER'S PUB

Only at Peter's Pub can one experience all the raucousness and debauchery of a Pitt frat party without actually having been invited. University athletes and undergrads who obsessively follow the NCAA playoffs are whom you can expect here; also count on ridiculously affordable daily beer specials, some as cheap as $1. On the second floor is a separate bar, as well as a dance floor that quickly grows sweaty and crowded on weekend nights.

MAP 3: 116 Oakland Ave., 412/681-7465, www.mypeterspub.com; 11am-2am daily; cover $1-5 Thurs.-Sat. after 9pm on DJ or live music nights

KARAOKE
KBOX KARAOKE HOUSE

Featuring authentic Asian-style private karaoke rooms, KBOX is definitely a first for the Steel City. In Asia, karaoke is a social and serious pastime that's often shared only with friends—thus, the private room. Roughly 100,000 songs are on tap at KBOX, including about 13,000 in English. Each room is kitted out with a 50-inch flat-screen TV, a video-on-demand system, and a pro-quality Shure microphone. A full bar, snacks, and Asian entrées are available.

MAP 3: 214 S. Craig St., 412/621-2860, www.kbktv.com; 7pm-midnight Mon.-Tues., 5pm-midnight Wed.-Thurs., 2pm-2am Fri.-Sat., 2pm-midnight Sun.; $30-60/room or $6-9/person

South Side

Map 4

LIVE MUSIC

CLUB CAFÉ

No other live music experience in Pittsburgh comes anywhere near to that at Club Café. The room is so small, and the seating so close to the stage, it's practically possible to reach out and touch the performers mid-song. Music is generally of the singer-songwriter variety; blues and indie-pop bands also show up with some regularity. Past artists include Nellie McKay, Ted Leo, and Clap Your Hands Say Yeah. The crowd generally consists of young professionals.

MAP 4: 56 S. 12th St., 412/431-4950, www.clubcafelive.com; bar until 2am daily; first show 7pm daily, door opens at 6pm; cover $10-25

REX THEATRE

Formerly a movie theater with a fantastic art deco facade, the Rex has since transformed itself into a midsize concert venue without actually transform-ing much. The reclining theater seats were never removed, for instance, so even during big-name punk shows, the energy level can feel rather lack-luster. The popcorn and candy counter in the front lobby is now a bar. The occasional alternative burlesque performance or independent film screen-ing also takes place.

MAP 4: 1602 E. Carson St., 412/381-6811, www.rextheatre.com; show times vary by performance; tickets $10-30

BARS

★ ACACIA

This Prohibition-themed cocktail bar demonstrates its authenticity with mixologists attired in period-appropriate costume, right down to the suit vest and the waxed handlebar mustache. And although you'll pay a princely sum for the artistically crafted cocktails, many of which call for incredibly complicated preparations, it's more than worth it just to soak in the detail-rich speakeasy atmosphere. Bourbon is a house specialty.

MAP 4: 2108 E. Carson St., 412/488-1800, www.acaciacocktails.com; 5pm-2am Mon.-Sat.

JEKYL AND HYDE

Halloween lovers rejoice: There is a place in Pittsburgh you can go to cel-ebrate the holiday any day of the year. Those who want to have fun with-out taking themselves too seriously will feel right at home at this haunted house/funhouse of a bar. How can you even attempt to look hip and cool with plastic vampire teeth and a bat ring on your finger? It gets crowded, and the service can be hit or miss, but that's to be expected at a South Side bar. Be forewarned; you'll leave smelling like smoke.

MAP 4: 140 S. 18th St., 412/488-0777, www.jekylandhydebar.com; 7pm-2am daily

LOCAL BAR + KITCHEN

Local is known for having the neighborhood's largest heated and enclosed rooftop deck. They use outdoor heaters for cooler nights, while giant paddle fans keep the breeze going in the summer. It also boasts a good kitchen (standard American pub grub, including pizza, wings, soups, and sandwiches) and a rustic pub atmosphere. Margaritas, martinis, and other cocktails are popular. This is a pretty popular destination on weekend nights, so get there early if you want to grab a table.

MAP 4: 1515 E. Carson St., 412/308-5183, www.localpgh.com; 11am-2am Mon.-Fri., 10am-2am Sat.-Sun.

OVER THE BAR BICYCLE CAFÉ

Pittsburgh has steadily grown into an enthusiastic bicycling city, and this bike-themed bar and café confirms that the cycling scene has become an important and lucrative business. Cyclists eat and drink here regularly, and even the delightfully toothsome pub-grub menu pays homage to the sport. You'll find bicycling tchotchkes and memorabilia hanging from—and nailed onto—nearly every available surface.

MAP 4: 2518 E. Carson St., 412/381-3698, www.otbbicyclecafe.com; 11am-2am daily

SMOKIN' JOE'S

The success of Smokin' Joe's is based on a relatively simple philosophy: Stock a larger variety of beer than the bar next door. *Way* larger. We're talking hundreds and hundreds, some on draft, some in the massive cooler just inside the front door. The interior is rather cramped and plain, and although budget wing nights are a draw for some, the pub grub really isn't much to write home about (try Fat Head's Saloon next door if you're really hungry). Don't pass Joe's by just because the bar is packed to overflowing; there's often ample seating on the second-floor balcony.

MAP 4: 2001 E. Carson St., 412/431-6757, www.smokinjoessaloon.com; noon-2am Mon.-Thurs., 10am-2am Fri.-Sat., 11am-2am Sun.

THE URBAN TAP

In terms of ambience and decor, not much sets The Urban Tap apart from the slew of other industrial decorated establishments of Pittsburgh, filled with exposed brick and beams. But if it's beer selection that you're after, you'll find over 140 different brews on tap. The windows, which are open to the street, provide an open-air atmosphere that's hard to find in the South Side, which is mostly crowded with cramped and dark bars. This feature also makes The Urban Tap a great place for people-watching, which never disappoints in the South Side.

MAP 4: 1209 E. Carson St., 412/586-7499, www.theurbantap.com; 11am-2am Mon.-Sat., 10am-2am Sun.

DANCE CLUBS

JIMMY D'S

If you want the complete South Side experience in all its sweaty, booze-soaked glory, head to Jimmy D's. Despite the sticky floor and abundance of

creepy dudes, the dance floor is always guaranteed to be bumping (literally;
it feels like the upstairs dance floor will cave in at any moment). The place
gets packed and the bouncers are notoriously aggressive, always maintaining a strict (sometimes described as discriminatory) dress code. Despite the
ticks against it Jimmy D's plays great music and has cheap drinks.
MAP 4: 1707 E. Carson St., 412/431-5095, www.jimmydspgh.com; 9pm-2am Thurs.,
7:30pm-2am Fri.-Sat.; occasional $5 cover for special events

DIVE BARS
DEE'S CAFÉ
Dee's is dirty, dank, and perpetually clouded in smoke; it's one of the few
bars in the city exempt from the smoking ban. Best of all, it's cheap and
probably the most fun you'll have in any of Pittsburgh's shot-and-a-beer
bars, especially if you hang around long enough to get to know the locals.
What does the crowd look like? Picture a Nine Inch Nails concert, circa
1994. The customers at the upstairs bar, where pint glasses are strictly ver-
boten, is a touch older and more upscale. Action around the billiards tables
on both levels is always in full effect.
MAP 4: 1314 E. Carson St., 412/431-1314, www.deescafe.com; 11am-2am Mon.-Sat.,
noon-2am Sun.

BAR 11
With an atmosphere that more closely resembles a house party than an
actual bar, it's perhaps surprising that the unmarked Bar 11 has stayed
such a well-kept secret for so long. Bar 11 is a tried-and-true dive; the even-
tempered waitstaff and the creative party-favor shtick keep things exciting.
The room is perpetually lit by black lights and covered in aluminum foil,
and patrons are encouraged to draw on each other with highlighter pens.
MAP 4: 1101 Bradish St., 412/381-0899; 8pm-2am Tues.-Sat.

JACK'S BAR
No one goes to Jack's for its beverage selection. Nor do they go for the atmosphere, the ambience, or the music. It says something about Pittsburgh
that its cheapest, smokiest, and sketchiest dive bar is consistently ranked
as the best in South Side. Expect raucous crowds, cheap booze, and plenty
of bar fights. In true Steel City style, Jack's is open early in the morning
until late at night.
MAP 4: 1117 E. Carson St., 412/431-3644, www.jacksbarpittsburgh.com; 7am-2am daily

THE SMILING MOOSE
The Moose is something of an unofficial headquarters for the city's tat-
tooed contingent, goth girls, old-school punk rockers, aging skinheads, and
Vespa-driving mods. Perhaps not surprisingly, fistfights aren't uncommon.
Obscure speed metal and punk bands play free shows in the back of the
bar most weekends; if the noise gets to be a bit too much, simply slip up to
the tiny second-floor bar, where conversation and a game of billiards can
be more easily accomplished.
MAP 4: 1306 E. Carson St., 412/431-4668, www.smiling-moose.com; 11am-2am daily

LOUNGES

DIESEL

Diesel is a glossy nightlife establishment. Comprising two levels and featuring dance floors and multiple bars, the weekend experience comes complete with big-name DJs, high-tech lighting, and overpriced VIP bottle service. There's even an all-white, mezzanine-level VIP lounge. *Très chic!* Headbangers should note, however, that rock, pop, and metal shows are also a big draw at Diesel, although discerning live music fans do frequently complain about the club's sound quality.

MAP 4: 1601 E. Carson St., 412/431-8800, www.dieselclublounge.com/pittsburgh; 9pm-2am Fri.-Sat. and during live events; cover $5-7, tickets $12-25

SKYBAR

Home to Pittsburgh's only rooftop pool and lounge, the year-round Skybar would almost certainly seem more at home in Miami's South Beach than it does on the gritty East Carson strip. Still, the city skyline somehow looks lovelier way up here in the air, where evening tables and even cabanas can be reserved. Outdoor fire pits and a retractable roof complete the atmosphere.

MAP 4: 1601 E. Carson St., 412/651-4713, www.skybarpgh.com; 1pm-8pm and 9pm-2am Sat., 1pm-8pm Sun.; cover $10

TIKI LOUNGE

Keep your eyes peeled for the massive Tiki god in the front window, as you'll have to pass through his massive mouth before gaining entry to the lounge. Inside, this Polynesian-themed bar is something of a South Pacific paradise, with wooden masks, bamboo stalks, and indoor waterfalls. The cocktail menu is equally exotic: Choose from such wonders as a Headhunter, a Fu Manchu, and a Coconut Kiss. DJs light up the relatively small dance floor with pop and house music on weekends.

MAP 4: 2003 E. Carson St., 412/381-8454, www.tikilounge.biz; 4pm-2am Mon.-Sat., 8pm-2am Sun.; no cover downstairs, $5-10 upstairs

PUBS

PIPER'S PUB

Piper's Pub has all the charm of an authentic English pub. At the bar, selections on draft include Strongbow, Old Speckled Hen, Smithwick's, and Boddingtons; the single-malt scotch menu is dozens of names long, and bottled beers are available from all across the British Isles and beyond. Try the Ploughman's platter (a cheese plate with apple slices and gherkins) or the Guinness stew. Traditional Irish bands perform most weekend nights, and live soccer matches are beamed in via satellite. Brunch is served Saturday and Sunday 8:30am-3pm.

MAP 4: 1828 E. Carson St., 412/381-3977, www.piperspub.com; 11am-midnight Mon.-Thurs., 11am-2pm Fri., 8:30am-2am Sat., 8:30am-midnight Sun.; cover $1-5 Thurs.-Sat. after 9pm on DJ or live music nights

BARS

BIGHAM TAVERN

Bigham Tavern is a welcome change from the expensive white-linen table-cloth restaurants that reside in Mount Washington. If you're into wings, beer, and sports (as are most Pittsburghers), you'll feel right at home at this neighborhood tavern. Wednesday's wing night is certainly Bigham's most popular draw, as the wings have consistently been ranked as some of the best in the 'Burgh. Fried up crispy with a huge selection of sauces, they meet all the requirements.

MAP 4: 321 Bigham St., 412/431-9313, www.bighamtavern.com; 11am-2am Mon.-Fri., 10am-2am Sat.-Sun.

REDBEARD'S

Both locals and Duquesne University students flock here for the many discount beer and wings nights. Redbeard's can accommodate quite a crowd on warm summer evenings, which is also when the umbrella-covered patio seating fills up especially fast. This spot is just steps from the lobby of the Monongahela Incline and the overlook decks of Grandview Avenue. There's a second location downtown, **Redbeard's on Sixth** (144 6th St., 412/261-2324, 11am-2am daily).

MAP 4: 201 Shiloh St., 412/431-3730, www.redbeardspgh.com; 11am-2am daily

THE SUMMIT

With skyline views, craft cocktails, and fun theme nights, this cozy bar has a relaxed but upscale vibe. Patrons take advantage of the bar's selection of board games while munching on elevated versions of bar foods, like goat cheese fritters and brown butter popcorn. The cocktail menu is what really shines, with house specialties like the Leora (strawberry vodka, pamplemousse liqueur, basil, blackberry, and Prosecco) and seasonal offerings like Uncle Bob's Hot Chocolate (whole milk, dark chocolate, cocoa powder, vodka, cognac, and turmeric whipped cream).

MAP 4: 200 Shiloh St., 412/918-1647, www.thesummitpgh.com; 5pm-2am daily

NIGHTLIFE
MOUNT WASHINGTON

Shadyside

Map 5

BARS
MARIO'S EAST SIDE SALOON

This location was for many moons home to the now-defunct Doc's Place, which always felt something like a pre-game frat party, but with manners. Thankfully, the old Doc's Place vibe still seems more or less in place. The upper-level outdoor patio (where smoking is allowed) is just as fun, and the burgers are just as burnt as they ever were. Not a bad choice if you're up for a low-key night with a relatively young crowd.

MAP 5: 5442 Walnut St., 412/681-3713, www.mariospgh.com/eastside; 11am-2am daily

DIVE BARS
LE MARDI GRAS

This dive bar stands out in the swanky Walnut Street neighborhood. Be forewarned (or excited): The drinks are notoriously strong. Decorated with random New Orleans trinkets, a few chandeliers, and a haze of smoke, this is a guilty pleasure hole-in-the-wall that will get your night kick-started or ended with a bang.

MAP 5: 731 Copeland St., 412/683-0912, www.lemardigras.com; 4pm-2am Mon.-Thurs., 2pm-2am Fri.-Sat., 3pm-2am Sun.

GAY AND LESBIAN
ELEMENT

Though it doesn't specifically market itself as a gay club, Shadyside's LGBT crowd does seem to have claimed Element as yet another boast-worthy attraction in what is probably Pittsburgh's most gay-friendly neighborhood. As for the interiors and the experience, both are very much what you'd expect from a place referring to itself as an ultra lounge: Patrons are generally stylish and upscale, as is the club itself. Dressing to impress is strongly encouraged.

MAP 5: 5744 Ellsworth Ave., 412/362-7746, www.elementpgh.com; 5pm-2am daily; cover from $5 Sat.-Sun. and special events

Top: upscale tiki bar Hidden Harbor. **Bottom:** Church Brew Works.

Squirrel Hill
and Point Breeze

Map 6

BARS
★ HIDDEN HARBOR

Hidden Harbor offers an upscale environment that's unusually well be-haved for a tiki bar. The sophisticated Polynesian-inspired craft cocktails and small plates are balanced out by the fun and relaxed tropical decor. Drinks can be pricey but are an experience, created with fresh ingredients and local liquors like Maggie's Farm Rum, and are served with over-the-top garnishes. Try one of the drinks meant to shared, like the Atlantis, a po-tent blend of two dozen ingredients intended only for the bravest drinkers.
MAP 6: 1708 Shady Ave., 412/422-5040, www.hiddenharborpgh.com; 5pm-midnight Tues.-Thurs., 5pm-1am Fri.-Sat.

SILKY'S SPORTS BAR & GRILL

Silky's is a sports bar with a friendly, welcoming vibe. Silky's can get a bit overrun with rowdy and overzealous fans when local sporting events are on television, but any other day of the week, it's a perfectly anonymous place to unwind with an Iron City beer, a burger, and a side of fries. Silky's two floors and upper balcony are quite roomy, making it a smart choice for large groups.
MAP 6: 1731 Murray Ave., 412/421-9222; 3pm-2am daily

SQUIRREL HILL CAFÉ

Known locally as "The Cage," this is a relatively unimposing room con-sisting of cafeteria-style booths, two TV sets tuned to sports or news, and a small balcony that opens only on busy nights. Even though rents have risen here, the vibe at The Cage remains. Grad students from CMU and Pitt have long populated the bar's booths; show up during the afternoon to spot English teachers grading term papers while sipping pints of Guinness or Penn Pilsner.
MAP 6: 5802 Forbes Ave., 412/521-3327; 4pm-2am Mon., 11am-2am Tues.-Fri., 5pm-2am Sat.

Bloomfield
and East Liberty

Map 7

LIVE MUSIC
BRILLOBOX
One of Pittsburgh's top see-and-be-seen spots, Brillobox is run by a husband-and-wife team who relocated here after establishing themselves in New York City's contemporary art world. (The name is a nod to the eponymous Warhol work.) The ground floor is strictly a drinking establishment where Cat Power and M.I.A. records serenade the hipster glitterati. Live music takes place on the second floor with local pop and indie-rock bands performing about as often as do national touring acts.

MAP 7: 4104 Penn Ave., 412/621-4900, www.brillobox.net; 5pm-2am Tues.-Sat.; 10am-3pm Sun.; no cover downstairs, $6-15 upstairs

MR. SMALL'S THEATRE
Cleverly located inside the nave of the former St. Ann's Catholic church in Millvale, Mr. Small's is a midsize venue with near-perfect acoustics. Performers run the gamut, although hip-hop, indie rock, and metal acts make up the vast majority of the club's schedule. What's more, a professional-grade recording studio is on-site, and the company also maintains its own low-key record label. For aspiring rock stars, Small's offers occasional workshops and music camps.

MAP 7: 400 Lincoln Ave., 412/821-4447, www.mrsmalls.com; show times vary by performer; tickets $10-50, VIP balcony seating available at additional cost

BARS
★ SHARP EDGE BEER EMPORIUM
Respected by beer snobs locally and countrywide, the Sharp Edge is perhaps best known for its extensive selection of obscure Belgian drafts. With more than 300 internationally crafted beers available, there's something for everyone, no matter which nation you'd like to explore in pint or bottle form. Burgers, sandwiches, pizzas, and assorted American finger foods are also a big draw. If you'd prefer your dinner party quiet, grab a table in the back room. There are several other locations, including one downtown.

MAP 7: 302 S. St. Clair St., 412/661-3537, www.sharpedgebeer.com; 11am-midnight Mon.-Thurs., 11am-1am Fri.-Sat., noon-9pm Sun.

KELLY'S BAR
Kelly's is practically synonymous with East End style and sophistication, but in a slightly retro and ironic sense. With its art deco design, Wurlitzer jukebox, and tiki-themed back deck, Kelly's has, unsurprisingly, played an important role in the revitalization of East Liberty. The bad news is the too-cool-for-school waitstaff, some of whom are infamous for their inattentiveness.

MAP 7: 6012 Centre Ave., 412/363-6012; 11:30am-2am daily

LOT 17

Less pretentious and more blue-collar than neighboring Lawrenceville, Bloomfield is a good place to go for a laid-back no-nonsense vibe. Lot 17 hits the mark with a tasty and affordable food menu, cold drinks, and a relaxed atmosphere. Their tagline is "where everyone is welcome," so it's no surprise that long-time Bloomfield locals mix with a younger crowd. There's a decent selection of craft and imported beers, but you also won't be judged for ordering a good old domestic light.

MAP 7: 4617 Liberty Ave., 412/687-8117, www.lot17pgh.com; 11am-2am Mon.-Fri., noon-2am Sat., noon-midnight Sun.

MIXTAPE

In a neighborhood that's just starting to transition, Mixtape is a clear indication that Garfield is up-and-coming. At this jack-of-all-trades hangout spot, you can grab a coffee and work on your laptop and then stay for a happy hour drink later in the day. Though they serve food, Mixtape allows patrons to bring in outside food, as long as you're buying some drinks. On the weekend evenings, Mixtape takes on more of a party vibe with DJs and occasional live music.

MAP 7: 4907 Penn Ave., 412/661-1727, www.mixtapepgh.com; 2pm-midnight Tues.-Thurs., 2pm-2am Fri., 7pm-2am Sat.

Lawrenceville   Map 8

BARS

★ ROUND CORNER CANTINA

Easily of one of Lawrenceville's hottest drinking and dining destinations, Round Corner Cantina is a gorgeously decorated Mexican-style bar and eatery catering to the young and artsy. Formerly a neighborhood dive, the cantina has been thoroughly refurbished with retro hand-painted signage and rickety wooden seating. The menu features a surprisingly authentic selection of Mexican beer and street food. Tucked away behind the restaurant, the outdoor patio feels like you're at a backyard barbecue with friends. There's ample seating and the area is surrounded by a high fence so you forget you're in the middle of an urban neighborhood. The vibe is laid-back, but it can still get crowded on summer evenings.

MAP 8: 3720 Butler St., 412/904-2279, www.roundcornercantina.com; 4pm-midnight Mon.-Thurs., 11am-2am Fri.-Sat., 11am-midnight Sun.

CHURCH BREW WORKS

Church Brew Works is located in a lovingly restored Catholic church where actual pews are used for seating and massive beer tanks sit atop the altar. The award-winning beers brewed here include a light and a dark lager, an English pale ale, a stout, and a specialty brew that changes on a monthly basis. Church Brew Works is probably just as well known for its gourmet

Clockwise from top left: Arsenal Cider House, Sharp Edge Beer Emporium; cocktail at Mixtape.

Brewed in the 'Burgh

What better way to support Pittsburgh than to buy locally brewed booze? The city has its fair share of independent breweries, and it seems like a new one pops up every week. But local producers aren't just about beer; there are several distillers, cider houses, and even a meadery in the region. Whatever your drink of choice is, you'll find plenty of options in Pittsburgh.

Apis Winery and Mead

The small town of Carnegie, just outside of Pittsburgh, is home to the region's first meadery. Mead is an alcoholic beverage, derived from fermenting honey, that may be the oldest alcoholic drink on earth. Vikings, Mayans, Egyptians, Greeks, and Romans all imbibed the ancient beverage. Now you can get a taste of mead at **Apis Mead & Winery** (212 E. Main St., Carnegie, 412/478-9172, www.apismead.com; 4pm-11pm Wed.-Thurs., 11am-midnight Fri.-Sat., noon-5pm Sun.) or at any of the restaurants and bars in town that stock the wine-like drink. Apis was started by David Cerminara, a former brewer at Penn Brewery in the North Side. Apis often has special events, like release parties where you can try out new flavors.

Wigle Whiskey

In the 1700s and 1800s, Western Pennsylvania was the center of American whiskey production. This whiskey distillery is actually named for Philip Wigle, a local distiller who protested a tax levied on whiskey producers. This act helped fuel the Whiskey Rebellion, and the rest is history. There are several ways to get your Wigle Whiskey fix. You can visit the **distillery and**

pub grub menu, featuring pasta, seafood, salads, sandwiches, and brick-oven pizza.

MAP 8: 3525 Liberty Ave., 412/688-8200, www.churchbrew.com; 11:30am-11pm Mon.-Thurs., 11:30am-midnight Fri.-Sat., 11:30am-9pm Sun.

HAMBONE'S

Hambones missed the memo that all Lawrenceville bars must be super-hipster and industrial-chic. Or maybe it just doesn't care. Nevertheless, Hambones is the ultimate Pittsburgh yinzer bar and has survived the revival of Lawrenceville, as is evidenced by the mix of older neighborhood regulars and younger cool kids lined up at the bar. It's a great place to grab a cheap drink if you want to escape the pretension at some of the neighborhood's newer establishments.

MAP 8: 4207 Butler St., 412/681-4318, www.hambonespittsburgh.com; 11am-2am daily

INDUSTRY PUBLIC HOUSE

Offering an even mixture of American comfort food, artisanal cocktails, and craft beer, Industry Public House hits a perfect balance between pre-Prohibition trendiness and gritty, industrial modernity. It's sometimes referred to as a gastropub, and it's certainly true that the carb-heavy menu is nearly as impressive as the ridiculously long list of microbrews on tap. The

tasting room (page 37) in the Strip District, check out the **tasting room and bottle shop** (530 William Penn Pl.) at the Omni William Penn Hotel downtown, or drop by the **Barrelhouse and Whiskey Garden** (1055 Spring Garden Ave.) for tastings, cocktails, and events in the North Side.

Arsenal Cider House

Arsenal Cider House (page 110) is a small-batch cider producer in Lawrenceville. Arsenal has been so successful that they have expanded beyond their home-based operation with two additional tap houses at Soergel Orchards and Trax Farms, two nearby farms. You can also taste their ciders at many fine Pittsburgh restaurants and bars.

Maggie's Farm Rum

Rum lovers are thrilled with the addition of Maggie's Farm Rum to the list of Pittsburgh distilleries. They are the first producers of rum in the state of Pennsylvania since Prohibition. The rum is produced in a Spanish-made copper still right behind the cocktail bar at their **Strip District location** (3212A Smallman St., 412/709-6480, http://maggiesfarmrum.com). Since its opening in 2013, Maggie's has racked up the awards, including Pennsylvania Distillery of the Year, Best-in-Class Rum, and Best-in-Show Spirit. Maggie's Farm Rum also offers distillery tours and tastings at their Strip District location.

NIGHTLIFE
LAWRENCEVILLE

wine and whiskey are also top-notch, and the creatively named cocktails are generous on the pour.

MAP 8: 4305 Butler St., 412/683-1100, www.industrypgh.com; 11am-2am Mon.-Sat.; 10am-2am Sun.

NEW AMSTERDAM

It's certainly no coincidence that one of Pittsburgh's favorite bastions of hipster cool, the bar and café known as New Amsterdam, is smack-dab in the heart of Lawrenceville's main drag. This bar is a squat brick square of a building with a garage door entrance opening onto the sidewalk, and it's quite unlike anything else in the area. The exterior is plastered with a gorgeous skull-motif mural by the local artist Matt Spahr.

MAP 8: 4421 Butler St., 412/904-2915, www.newamsterdam412.com; 4pm-2am Mon.-Fri., noon-2am Sat.-Sun.; cover $5-10 for special events

SPIRIT

It's difficult to describe exactly what Spirit is, as it combines a pizzeria, bar, and event hall to form a multifunctional nightlife destination. The uber-hipster venue, located in an old Moose Lodge, hosts events and live shows and serves up a mean selection of pizza by the slice. It could be said that Spirit tries a little too hard to look like it's not trying, with a style that could be described as "basement-chic." If you're feeling stifled by the crowds, head to the outdoor space, where you can drink on a dilapidated school bus.

MAP 8: 242 51st St., 412/586-4441, www.spiritpgh.com; 5pm-2am Tues.-Fri., 11am-2am Sat.-Sun.; cover $5-15 for special events

CIDERIES
ARSENAL CIDER HOUSE

Arsenal Cider House is a small-batch cider producer located near the Allegheny Arsenal, the inspiration for its name. It was founded by a married couple who decided to start making hard cider in the confines of their Lawrenceville home. They have transformed their house into a Civil War-themed tasting room and basement brewery, where you can sample varieties of their hard apple cider, with names like Fighting Elleck and Archibald's Aldo. They also have an outdoor Cider Garden in the lot behind the house. The fenced-in lawn has picnic table seating and lots of room to spread out blankets for picnic-style sipping and eating. They frequently have food trucks and live music, but when there is no food available, you're welcome to bring your own.

MAP 8: 300 39th St., 412/682-7699, www.arsenalciderhouse.com; 4pm-8pm Wed.-Thurs., 4pm-9pm Fri., noon-9pm Sat., noon-4pm Sun.

DANCE CLUBS
THE GOLDMARK

Opened in 2015, this spot made its mark quickly and has been called "the best new bar" and "the best place to dance" by several local publications. Owned and operated by a DJ, the focus of Goldmark is great music with different DJs spinning every night. The atmosphere is pure fun, and the eclectic mix of '90s R&B, pop, trap, reggae, and disco makes it difficult to keep from dancing. It's deceptively small and can get very crowded on weekend nights, but weeknights have a more relaxed vibe.

MAP 8: 4517 Butler St., 412/688-8820, www.thegoldmark.com; 8pm-2am Tues.-Thurs., 6pm-2am Fri.-Sat.; cover $5 after 10pm

DIVE BARS
★ GOOSKI'S

Call it a dive, call it a hipster hangout, or call it Pittsburgh's most legendary neighborhood watering hole—just make sure that before leaving town you spend at least one weekend night at Gooski's, preferably with a pitcher of cheap beer in front of you. It's long been known as one of the hardscrabble Steel City's most representative hangouts, but the true beauty of Gooski's lies in its diametrically opposed clientele: Saddle up to the bar, and you'll soon find yourself in conversation with an unemployed steel miner, or maybe a tough-talking motorcycle maven. Area hipsters—many who aren't from the area at all, but who've driven for miles just to make the scene—fill the bar's booths and the billiards room. On Saturday nights, local garage rock bands perform.

MAP 8: 3117 Brereton St., 412/681-1658; 3pm-2am daily; cover $4-7 for live music nights

BELVEDERE'S ULTRA-DIVE

A decidedly hip dive bar, Belvedere's also frequently doubles as a live music venue, hosting classic punk bands and newer hip-hop and indie acts. And while themed parties take place regularly, including a popular '80s night and karaoke and bingo nights, the real draw at Belvedere's is the truly unique energy and ambience of the place: gritty, honest, dirty, and downright fun.

MAP 8: 4016 Butler St., 412/687-2555, www.belvederesultradive.com; 11am-2am daily; cover $2-5

GAY AND LESBIAN
BLUE MOON

A seriously low-key neighborhood pub—basically a dive bar for Lawrenceville's LGBT crowd—the Blue Moon is not exactly the city's classiest queer joint. While a night out here can be rambunctious, it can also be a wildly good time, assuming you're willing to let loose and let go of your inhibitions. The frequently scheduled events (drag and fashion shows, for instance) are just as fun and equally goofy.

MAP 8: 5115 Butler St., 412/781-1119; 4pm-1am Mon., 5pm-2am Tues.-Sat., 5pm-1am Sun.

CATTIVO

A surprisingly massive gay bar and dance club tucked away in a somewhat sketchy area of Lawrenceville, Cattivo is especially popular with Pittsburgh's lesbian crowd. The crowd is exceptionally friendly and welcoming; Steelers games are shown on a big screen; and a pub-grub-style kitchen serving pizza, hoagies, and wings stays open until 1am. Every Friday and Saturday night, DJs get the crowd moving in Cattivo Sotto, the bar's lower-level dance floor.

MAP 8: 146 44th St., 412/687-2157, www.cattivopgh.com; 4pm-2am Wed.-Sat.; cover $5-10 during events

WINE BARS
★ GRAPPARIA

Grapparia serves up a curated selection of grappa and Italian wines. If you're unfamiliar with grappa, it's a super potent (70 to 120 proof) alcohol of Italian origin, derived from grapes. Grapparia is sister to Piccolo Forno, perhaps Pittsburgh's most lauded Italian restaurant. If you're not brave enough to try the grappa straight, they serve an innovative menu that includes grappa cocktails, like the LaVanda, which combines lavender-infused grappa, green pepper honey, and lemon juice.

MAP 8: 3801 Butler St., 412/904-3907, www.grappariapittsburgh.com; 4pm-midnight Tues.-Thurs., 4pm-2am Fri.-Sat.

ALLEGHENY WINE MIXER

For a city mainly focused on beer, this wine bar has been welcomed into Lawrenceville's hipster drinking scene with open arms. The selection of wines by the glass and bottle and even wine-inspired cocktails is impressive.

Check out the mix-and-match specials as well. They also serve a selection of cheese, meats, and small bites to accompany your glass.

MAP 8: 5326 Butler St., 412/252-2337, www.alleghenywinemixer.com; 5pm-midnight Tues.-Thurs., 5pm-1am Fri.-Sat.

Greater Pittsburgh Map 9

LIVE MUSIC
MOONDOG'S

Moondog's isn't particularly easy to get to without your own transportation—it sits north of the city in a blue-collar burgh along the Allegheny River—but if authentic local and national blues music is your bag, it's absolutely worth the trip. When live music isn't happening, Moondog's acts as a cozy neighborhood pub. But on most weekends, local blues acts and singer-songwriters like Norm Nardini take the stage. Sometimes true blues legends show up; Moondog's has hosted the likes of Keb' Mo', Koko Taylor, and Junior Wells.

MAP 9: 378 Freeport Rd., Blawnox, 412/828-2040, www.moondogs.us; 3pm-6pm Wed., 3pm-midnight Thurs., 3pm-2am Fri., 7pm-2am Sat.; tickets from $15

Arts and Culture

Highlights

★ **Widest Variety of Art:** Head to the Strip District's **Society for Contemporary Craft** to find works by Dale Chihuly and Frank Gehry. Temporary exhibitions might feature work from local high schoolers, artists from the Deep South, or Native American artisans (page 116).

★ **Best Place for Kids:** You won't find any "do not touch" signs at the **Children's Museum of Pittsburgh.** This hands-on museum is a great place for little ones to explore, learn and just be kids (page 116).

★ **Edgiest Art Gallery:** Check out **SPACE** for envelope-pushing work from local artists who might be exhibiting photography, visual art, or even installations (page 119).

★ **Best Place for Unexpected Art:** Unique **ToonSeum** is dedicated to the art of comics and cartoons. Don't miss the excellent gift shop (page 120).

★ **Funniest Night Out:** From improv nights to stand-up comedy acts, **Arcade Comedy Theater** is the best place for a laugh (page 122).

★ **Best Sports Museum:** An homage to Pittsburgh great Roberto Clemente, **The Clemente Museum** offers a wealth of memorabilia (page 130).

★ **Best Street Festival:** You don't need to have Italian ancestors to enjoy **Little Italy Days,** when Bloomfield comes alive with authentic eats, bocce tournaments, and live entertainment (page 134).

Pittsburgh is the new go-to town for creative types, artists, and makers. Up-and-coming neighborhoods and a supportive community make Pittsburgh an ideal home for artists.

It's also hard not to mention the city's general affordability, low cost of living, and proximity to schools and universities with great arts programs. This creative boom is evident in the number of galleries popping up all over the city, from the popular downtown Cultural District all the way to neighborhoods on the fringe, like Garfield and East Liberty. Because rent is more affordable in these farther-flung areas, the arts community is blossoming in places that previously didn't have much in the way of galleries, studios, or cultural centers.

The arts scene is more than stuffy museums or overpriced galleries. Many of the city's galleries also act as community centers, with classes for the public, open calls for submissions, and programs that give back to the community—especially the city's young residents. The August Wilson Center for African American Culture hosts a variety of performing arts productions while simultaneously housing exhibitions that document the African American experience in this region.

Offbeat and awe-inspiring museums like the ToonSeum and the Clemente Museum call Pittsburgh home and invite visitors and locals alike to see the depths of the Steel City. You can attend musical theater productions put on by the Pittsburgh Civic Lights Opera or a Pittsburgh Symphony Orchestra concert at historic Heinz Hall, or even witness acoustic perfection by going to a live performance at Carnegie Music Hall.

Previous: Heinz Hall; the Frick Art and Historical Center.

Strip District Map 1

GALLERIES
★ SOCIETY FOR CONTEMPORARY CRAFT

The Society for Contemporary Craft is basically a one-stop-shop for contemporary art, all packed into an industrial warehouse space. The society has been presenting exhibitions both conservative and eccentric since 1971. The permanent collection includes blown glass by Dale Chihuly and rare chairs by the likes of Frank Gehry and Mr. Imagination; clay, metal, and fiber crafts are also on display. Temporary exhibitions might feature anything from decoupage collages by high school kids to art from the Deep South and even Native American crafts. The gallery's gift shop, known simply as **The Store,** carries handmade purses, scarves, and stationery, as well as decorative items made of glass and wood. You'll also find a small selection of home furnishings, such as lamps, tables, and chairs.

MAP 1: 2100 Smallman St., 412/261-7003, www.contemporarycraft.org; 10am-5pm Mon.-Sat.; free

North Side Map 1

MUSEUMS
★ CHILDREN'S MUSEUM OF PITTSBURGH

With part of the building located in a disused U.S. Post Office and part in the former Buhl Planetarium, the Children's Museum of Pittsburgh holds 12 permanent exhibits, including puppets from the television show *Mister Rogers' Neighborhood;* the Makeshop, a DIY maker space where kids and families can explore woodworking, circuitry, and sewing; and the fantastic Waterplay exhibit, where children can pump, move, channel, and dam various flows of water. (Bring bathing suits for this one!) Kids love to explore The Attic and The Garage, where everyday activities and objects become learning experiences.

MAP 1: 10 Children's Way, Allegheny Square, 412/322-5058, www.pittsburghkids.org; 10am-5pm daily; $16 adults, $14 seniors and children, children under 2 free

CARNEGIE SCIENCE CENTER AND HIGHMARK SPORTSWORKS

Filled with kid-friendly and hands-on exhibits, the Carnegie Science Center features several floors of permanent and visiting exhibitions that intend to spark curiosity, allowing visitors to conduct experiments and figure out how things work—everything from the human body to giant robots. Admission includes entrance to the attached **Highmark SportsWorks,** a fun activity-based complex designed to let visitors explore the physics behind sports. There are nearly 30 different interactive experiences, where visitors, for instance, can race a virtual Olympic sprinter, climb a 25-foot rock wall, or attempt to pitch a fastball.

MAP 1: 1 Allegheny Ave., 412/237-3400, www.carnegiesciencecenter.org; 10am-5pm daily; $20 adults, $15 seniors, $12 children

MATTRESS FACTORY

The oddly named Mattress Factory is one of Pittsburgh's longest standing contemporary art museums—as well as one of the coolest and quirkiest. The museum supports emerging artists and features room-sized installation art that is unconventional and unexpected, almost always resulting in thought-provoking exhibitions. The museum has 17 permanent continuous installations. Some of the most stunning of these are James Turrell's odd and unsettling works of neon and light. Don't miss *Pleiades,* an entirely dark room where a presence of light may or may not appear. Another can't-miss is Yayoi Kusama's *Infinity Dots Mirrored Room;* entering it may just change your perspective on reality itself. On Tuesdays, admission is half price.

MAP 1: 500 Sampsonia Way, 412/231-3169, www.mattress.org; 10am-5pm Tues.-Sat., 1pm-5pm Sun.; $20 adults, $15 seniors and students, children under 6 free

PHOTO ANTIQUITIES MUSEUM OF PHOTOGRAPHIC HISTORY

A tucked-away space dedicated to the preservation of historical photography, the Photo Antiquities Museum is decorated with a quaint Victorian interior and boasts an archive of more than 100,000 negatives and prints. Beginning with the very earliest days of photography, the collection spans not only images, of which roughly 3,000 are always on display, but also cameras and other photographic accessories. The era of the earliest daguerreotype (roughly 1839) is documented, as is every important photographic era, including the digital cameras of the 21st century. The relatively small museum has hundreds of historical photographs on display, and at the onsite gift shop, visitors can purchase reproductions of any of the museum's images. Call ahead to ensure the museum will be open before visiting.

MAP 1: 531 E. Ohio St., 412/231-7881, www.photoantiquities.org; 10am-4pm Mon. and Wed.-Sat.; $10 adults, $8 seniors and students, children under 13 free

PERFORMING ARTS

NEW HAZLETT THEATER

The New Hazlett Theater considers itself an incubator for artists and is something of an anything-goes, all-purpose arts facility. Plays are staged on a regular basis, but so too are live music and spoken word performances, as well as various literary and artistic community gatherings. Performing arts organizations of all sorts pop up regularly at the New Hazlett, although new work by the decidedly quirky Barebones Productions theater company can be seen with some regularity.

MAP 1: 6 Allegheny Sq. E., 412/320-4610, http://newhazletttheater.org; show times and prices vary by performance

Clockwise from top left: Stage AE; exhibit at the Mattress Factory; the Children's Museum.

STAGE AE

Near the site of the old Three Rivers Stadium, this North Shore concert hall includes a large outdoor amphitheater as well as an indoor club area for concerts year-round. Featuring state-of-the-art acoustics and lighting, Stage AE is one of the most popular concert venues in the city, attracting national acts like Hall and Oates, Wiz Khalifa, and The Lumineers.

MAP 1: 400 North Shore Dr., 412/229-5483, http://promowestlive.com; show times and prices vary by performance

Downtown

Map 2

GALLERIES
★ SPACE

SPACE is arguably one of the city's hippest contemporary galleries. They're big on experimental work and explorations in new media. Special attention is paid to local artists whose work may be otherwise ignored or overlooked, especially those photographers, visual artists, or installation builders who consistently push the envelope. There are five shows a year exhibiting a wide variety of work, so the gallery appeals to a broad audience and does a great job of bringing art to the masses. Guest curators organize large and very popular group shows often.

MAP 2: 812 Liberty Ave., 412/325-7723, www.spacepittsburgh.org; 11am-6pm Wed.-Thurs., 11am-8pm Fri.-Sat., 11am-5pm Sun.; free

FUTURE TENANT

Consider this rough and ever-changing space a sort of laboratory setting for emerging artists to experiment and explore their creative expression via visual, written, and performance art. Exhibitions here might take the form of art installations, literary events, video art presentations, or anything else an artist might conceive of. Future Tenant partners with Carnegie Mellon University's Arts Management program, giving students the opportunity to plan, manage, budget, and market the gallery's programs throughout the year. Be sure to call or check online before visiting, as the gallery is periodically closed during exhibition installation or takedown.

MAP 2: 819 Penn Ave., 412/567-8861, www.futuretenant.org; 4pm-8pm Fri., 11am-8pm Sat., 11am-6pm Sun.; free

WOOD STREET GALLERIES

Wood Street Galleries is named for its location two floors above the Wood Street light rail station. The contemporary art gallery is known for its compelling and thought-provoking exhibitions, which often have a technological slant or feature other types of new media. Multidisciplinary artists both local and international have shown here; the curators seem to be especially fond of industrial-themed installation art and edgy video art. Wood Street Galleries is operated by the Pittsburgh Cultural Trust and is

Crawl the Cultural District's Galleries

One of the best ways to introduce yourself to the Pittsburgh arts scene is through the popular quarterly gallery crawls. For many people, stepping into a contemporary art gallery can be intimidating. You might feel like everyone there is cooler than you are, you're not sure if the crumpled-up piece of paper on the floor is trash or modern art, or you start to feel ashamed of the IKEA "art" hanging in your living room.

Gallery Crawl (http://crawl.trustarts.org; free), which is put on four times a year by the Pittsburgh Cultural Trust, is a great introduction to art and a fun way to explore the Cultural District. Gallery Crawl is free, and many of the stops include complimentary wine or beer, so the event takes on a fun party atmosphere.

The stops on the crawl include the Cultural District's many galleries, but you'll also find live music, dance and theater performances, free film showings, public art, and even culinary arts (the Culinary Arts program at the Art Institute of Pittsburgh often gets involved). It's a fun night out with friends, even if you've always thought contemporary art wasn't really your thing.

The crawl occurs quarterly, usually on a Friday. Check the website for specific dates.

the sister gallery to **SPACE** (812 Liberty Ave., 412/325-7723, www.space-pittsburgh.org).

MAP 2: 601 Wood St., 412/471-5605, www.woodstreetgalleries.org; 11am-6pm Wed.-Thurs., 11am-8pm Fri.-Sat., 11am-5pm Sun.; free

MUSEUMS
★ TOONSEUM

ToonSeum is one of just a few museums in the country that are dedicated exclusively to cartoon art. The museum's space is very small, but they manage to pack in over 100 pieces of art at a time and rotate exhibits every couple of months. Examples of past exhibits include *Draw Me: The Art of Cartooning Schools and "How to Cartoon" Culture in America* and *From MLK to March: Civil Rights in Comics and Cartoons.* Because the museum's mission involves promoting a deeper understanding of cartoon artists and their work, original programs and educational workshops occur on a regular basis. The gift shop is worth a visit for its wonderful selection of comics, graphic novels, and cartoon-related ephemera.

MAP 2: 945 Liberty Ave., 412/232-0199, http://toonseum.org; 11am-5pm Wed.-Sun., $8 adults and children 13 and over, $7 seniors and students, $4 children 6-12, children 5 and under free

FORT PITT MUSEUM

This museum, located next to Point State Park and just below the Fort Pitt Bridge, is actually part of the **Heinz History Center** (1212 Smallman St., 412/454-6000), whose main building is in the Strip District. The two-story, 12,000-square-foot museum focuses on the events that shaped the birth of

Clockwise from top left: cutting-edge gallery SPACE; ToonSeum; Wood Street Galleries.

Pittsburgh and the impact the city had on America's history. Check out art, artifacts, and life-size dioramas that bring important historical eras to life. **MAP 2:** Point State Park, 101 Commonwealth Pl., 412/281-9285, www. heinzhistorycenter.org; 10am-5pm daily; $8 adults, $7 seniors, $4.50 children ages 6-17, children 5 and under free

SENATOR JOHN HEINZ HISTORY CENTER

The Heinz History Center is Pennsylvania's largest history museum and a Smithsonian Institution Affiliate. The museum does a great job of bringing Pittsburgh and Western Pennsylvania history to life and bringing it into a context that's relevant and engaging for its visitors. Because so many exhibitions are interactive and creatively curated, the museum is also enjoyable for children. On the museum's third floor is Discovery Place, a hands-on historical exhibit specifically designed for younger guests. Kids also love sitting in the driver's seat of the restored 1949 streetcar trolley, which is in the ground floor's Great Hall, where you'll find Kidsburgh, a small play area built above Reymer's Old-Fashioned Deli. Admission to the center includes entrance to the **Western Pennsylvania Sports Museum** (on the 2nd and 3rd floors), a must-see for any black-and-gold sports buff. **MAP 2:** 1212 Smallman St., 412/454-6000, www.heinzhistorycenter.org; 10am-5pm daily; $16 adults, $14 seniors, $6.50 students and children 6-17, children 5 and under free

PERFORMING ARTS
★ ARCADE COMEDY THEATER

Named the "Best Place to See Live Comedy" multiple times by *Pittsburgh Magazine*, downtown's 75-seat comedy club features stand-up, improv acts, sketch comedy, and more to get you rolling in the aisles. The atmosphere is as fun as the performances, complete with a pinball machine in the lobby. The nonprofit theater also offers workshops, classes, internships, and improv pop-up nights if you want to dip your toes into the world of comedy. **MAP 2:** 943 Liberty Ave., 412/339-0608, http://arcadecomedytheater.com; show times vary based on performance; tickets $7-20

AUGUST WILSON CENTER FOR AFRICAN AMERICAN CULTURE

Pittsburgh is the birthplace of American playwright and two-time Pulitzer Prize winner August Wilson. The city pays homage to him in the form of this cultural center, which offers a wide range of programming, events, and exhibitions. The 492-seat theater hosts live music, dance, and theater performances. The center is also home to an impressive collection of ongoing and changing exhibits that document and celebrate the African American experience throughout Western Pennsylvania and beyond. **MAP 2:** 980 Liberty Ave., 412/471-6070, www.trustarts.org; hours and prices vary by performance and exhibition

BENEDUM CENTER FOR THE PERFORMING ARTS

The Benedum Center is one of downtown's most significant buildings, thanks to its opulent 2,800-seat theater and its offering of some of the

The Legacy of August Wilson

It's not possible to talk about arts in Pittsburgh without talking about Pulitzer Prize-winning playwright August Wilson (1945-2005). Wilson was born and raised in the Hill District neighborhood; this became the backdrop and inspiration for many of his plays, including *Fences,* which earned Wilson a Pulitzer Prize and was made into an Academy Award-nominated movie in 2016.

Wilson was born in 1945 and lived with his five siblings, his mother, and a mostly absent father. Wilson dropped out of high school at the age of 16 and began working menial jobs. This did not mean the end of his education, however. He spent much of his time at the Carnegie Library studying black writers and reading voraciously. The library eventually awarded him an honorary high school diploma, the only one they've ever handed out.

Wilson pursued his passion, spending time writing on napkins and bits of paper at cafés and bars, finding inspiration in the people and situations around him. He was also inspired by Malcolm X and the teachings of both Islam and the Black Power movement. He converted to Islam when he married Brenda Burton, a Muslim.

Wilson co-founded a theater in the Hill District in 1968, where his first play, *Recycling,* was performed. Wilson eventually moved to Minnesota, then Seattle, where he produced more plays and earned many accolades.

Wilson's legacy is his contribution to the advancement of black theater and to arts in the black community. The impact of his work is still felt and celebrated in Pittsburgh, particularly in the establishment of the **August Wilson Center for African American Culture,** a theater and arts center that promotes the accomplishments of African American artists and writers.

best Broadway shows in America. Built in 1928, the theater was originally named the Stanley Theater and saw acts such as Frank Zappa and The Grateful Dead. It's where Bob Marley played his last show and where Prince kicked off his 1981 *Controversy* tour. Today the Benedum is home to the Pittsburgh Opera, Pittsburgh Ballet Theater, and Pittsburgh Civic Light Opera.

MAP 2: 237 7th St., 412/456-6666, www.trustarts.org; show times and prices vary by performance

BYHAM THEATER

A landmark building in Pittsburgh's Cultural District, this 1904 theater was originally a vaudeville house before it was renovated and reopened as the Byham Theater, complete with old-fashioned lit marquee, in 1990. Today the Byham offers a classic music hall experience, with red velvet seating, elegant Renaissance-style paintings on the ceiling above the stage, and world-class musical, theater, and dance acts. The fully restored, 1,500-seat interior houses the opulent Cherub Lobby, a full balcony, and friendly ushers who escort latecomers to their seats with a flashlight.

MAP 2: 101 6th St., 412/456-6666, www.trustarts.org; show times and prices vary by performance

Clockwise from top left: Arcade Comedy Theater; August Wilson Center for African American Culture; Senator John Heinz History Center.

Heinz Hall has been a cultural destination since the 1800s, even before it carried its current name. Once used as a hotel for actors, it was eventually purchased by the Howard Heinz Endowment in 1971 and became the new home of the Pittsburgh Symphony Orchestra. The PSO has consistently been recognized as one of the country's greatest orchestras. The theater maintains the feel of its original era thanks to its plush red velvet curtains and crystal chandeliers. Each year more than a half million patrons fill the 2,675 seats and attend events ranging from symphony orchestra performances to Broadway shows and children's performances.

MAP 2: 600 Penn Ave., 412/392-4900, www.pittsburghsymphony.org; box office 9am-8pm Mon.-Fri., noon-4pm Sat., show times vary by performance; tickets from $20

PITTSBURGH CIVIC LIGHTS OPERA

The Pittsburgh CLO has been producing musical theater in the city since 1946. The organization prides itself on bringing Hollywood and Broadway stars to the Pittsburgh stage and launching the careers of local performers as well. In 2014, for the first time ever, Pittsburgh CLO developed a new musical for Broadway, a stage adaptation of *An American in Paris*. The production garnered 12 Tony Award nominations. Pittsburgh CLO performs at the **Byham Theater** (101 6th St., 412/456-6666, www.trustarts. org), the **Benedum Center for the Performing Arts** (237 7th St., 412/456-6666, www.trustarts.org), and the **CLO Cabaret Theater** (655 Penn Ave., 412/456-6666).

MAP 2: 412/456-6666, www.pittsburghclo.org; show times vary by performance; tickets $20-90

PITTSBURGH PUBLIC THEATER

Pittsburgh Public Theater sprang up in the mid-1970s, when the theater scene in the city was lacking. PPT's inaugural season was met with great success and rave reviews. The company moved into its current home, the O'Reilly Theater (built by superstar architect Michael Graves), in 1999. The 650-seat auditorium was built with acoustics in mind and features a "thrust" stage, a shape that allows the audience to surround it on three sides. The Public Theater shows artistically diverse performances, new works, and even world premieres.

MAP 2: O'Reilly Theater, 621 Penn Ave., 412/316-1600, www.ppt.org; show times vary by performance; tickets $25-60

CONCERT VENUES
A. J. PALUMBO CENTER

Although technically the home of the Duquesne University Dukes and Lady Dukes basketball teams, the A. J. Palumbo Center frequently transforms into a pop and rock concert hall after dark. Only the biggest artists at the top of their game perform here; years past have seen Public Enemy, Green Day, and Kings of Leon take the stage. Other entertainment and sporting events happen occasionally, such as wrestling and boxing. Insider tip: To avoid being crushed on the floor during a rock show, arrive early and grab a seat in the general admission bleachers nearest the stage.

MAP 2: 600 Forbes Ave., 412/396-5140, www.duq.edu; show times and prices vary by performance

PPG PAINTS ARENA

PPG Paints Arena is not just the home of the Pittsburgh Penguins, it's also a destination venue for some of the biggest performances that come to Pittsburgh. The capacity for concerts is almost 20,000 guests, so this is where you go to see major stars like Lady Gaga, Katy Perry, and Ed Sheeran, just to name a few.

MAP 2: 1001 5th Ave., 412/642-1800, www.ppgpaintsarena.com/events; show times and prices vary by performance

Oakland   Map 3

PERFORMING ARTS
CARNEGIE MUSIC HALL

Built in 1895 and described as "acoustically perfect," Carnegie Music Hall is nestled into the same complex as the Carnegie Museums of Art and Natural History. Entering the opulent and ornately decorated hall feels like stepping back in time. The theater seats 1,950 and has welcomed famous musicians, actors, and writers to its stage. The hall is also home to the world-class **Chamber Music Pittsburgh** (www.chambermusicpittsburgh. org; tickets $39-46).

MAP 3: 4400 Forbes Ave., 412/622-3131, www.carnegiemuseums.org; show times and prices vary by performance

PITTSBURGH PLAYHOUSE

Pittsburgh Playhouse is home to several theater companies, including Point Park University's professional company, The REP, and its three student companies, including a children's theater and a dance company. There's always a lot going on here. In fall of 2018, the playhouse moves to its new location in downtown Pittsburgh.

MAP 3: 222 Craft Ave., 412/392-8000, www.pittsburghplayhouse.com; show times and prices vary by performance

South Side Map 4

PERFORMING ARTS
CITY THEATRE
If you want to see a show that's never been seen before, innovative City Theatre is the place to do it. It's the largest theater in Pittsburgh that puts out only new work, so it's a great place to see edgy contemporary performances. The facility houses the Mainstage Theater, which holds 254 seats. The smaller Hamburg Studio Theater seats 110 for a more intimate experience.

MAP 4: 1300 Bingham St., 412/431-2489, www.citytheatrecompany.org; show times vary by performances; tickets $40-65

Shadyside Map 5

GALLERIES
GALLERIE CHIZ
Gallerie Chiz is an eclectic gallery that specializes in paintings, sculptures, handmade books, jewelry, furniture, and other handcrafted items. All art pieces are selected by owner Ellen Chisdes Neuberg. The quirky and interesting finds are the work of local, regional, and international artists. Come to browse and be inspired by the art or look for something new for your home.

MAP 5: 5831 Ellsworth Ave., 412/441-6005, www.galleriechiz.com; 11am-5:30pm Tues.-Fri., 11am-5pm Sat., or by appointment; free

MENDELSON GALLERY
Since 1980, the Mendelson Gallery has been home to an extensive collection of modern art, including works by famous artists such as Mapplethorpe, Keiffer, Beuys, Man Ray, and Rauschenburg, mixed with a selection of work from local artists, as well as owner Steve Mendelson's own eclectic artwork. The building was once a 19th-century bordello and was eventually purchased at an IRS auction.

MAP 5: 5874 Ellsworth Ave., 412/361-8664, www.mendelsongallery.net; noon-5pm Wed.-Sat.; free

PITTSBURGH CENTER FOR THE ARTS
Housed in a cheerful yellow Tudor Revival mansion that was a gift from Pittsburgh industrialist Richard Mellon to his daughter Sarah Scaife, the Pittsburgh Center for the Arts is a piece of Pittsburgh history and a hub for an active arts community. The work displayed in the gallery of this non-profit arts campus is produced largely by Southwestern Pennsylvanians

with various skill levels. You'll find works by well-established artists displayed alongside pieces by newcomers.

MAP 5: 6300 5th Ave., 412/361-0873, www.pittsburgharts.org; 10am-5pm Tues.-Sat., noon-4pm Sun.; adults $5, seniors $4, students $3, children 12 and under free

Squirrel Hill and Point Breeze
Map 6

GALLERIES
FRICK ART AND HISTORICAL CENTER

Visiting the Frick is like stepping back in time to the Victorian age. Set on the estate grounds and mansion of the late industrialist, Henry Clay Frick, the house has been transformed into a museum to display the Frick family's impressive art collection. Collections include Renaissance art, Baroque sculptures, decorative arts, Chinese porcelain, photographs, costumes, and more. Don't forget to visit the Car and Carriage Museum on the grounds as well.

MAP 6: 7227 Reynolds St., 412/371-0600, www.thefrickpittsburgh.org; 10am-5pm Tues.-Thurs. and Sat.-Sun., 10am-9pm Fri., free

PERFORMING ARTS
THE SPACE UPSTAIRS

The Space Upstairs, in its industrial loft space above the building-materials supply warehouse Construction Junction, is one of Pittsburgh's most unique venues for art performances. The space hosts experimental drama and dance performances, and the audience is encouraged to lounge around on couches, cushions, even the floor, so that the separation between audience and artists is casual and intimate. Improvisational post-jazz performances feature heavily here, where experimentation and the unexpected are embraced.

MAP 6: 214 N. Lexington St., 412/225-9269, www.thespaceupstairs.org; show times and prices vary by performance

Bloomfield and East Liberty
Map 7

GALLERIES
BOXHEART GALLERY

Artist-run BoxHeart Gallery exhibits artwork from local, regional, and international artists, both established and emerging. If you're thinking about purchasing your first piece of original art, this is the gallery you want to visit. BoxHeart exhibits everything from photography and digital media to paintings, sculpture, and even wearable pieces.

MAP 7: 4523 Liberty Ave., 412/687-8858, www.boxheartgallery.com; 11am-6pm Tues., 10am-6pm Wed.-Sat., 1pm-5pm Sun.; free

THE IRMA FREEMAN CENTER FOR IMAGINATION

The Irma Freeman Center for Imagination is part community center and part art gallery, housed within a unique building that reflects the importance of sustainable building practices and renewable energy. Irma Freeman was a German-born immigrant who eventually settled in Pittsburgh and dedicated herself to creating art. Freeman's life is the inspiration for IFCI, and the center provides arts education and outreach for the community. The center also showcases visual arts exhibits, including a rotating selection of paintings by the late Irma Freeman herself—an incredibly prolific Pittsburgh artist. The gallery space is open only when there's an exhibition running, so call ahead to confirm hours before visiting.

MAP 7: 5006 Penn Ave., 412/924-0634, www.irmafreeman.org; 2pm-5pm Sat. and by appointment during exhibitions; free

PITTSBURGH GLASS CENTER

The Pittsburgh Glass Center is not just a gem of the Pittsburgh arts scene; it's also considered one of the top glass centers in the world. Pittsburgh is well known for its past steel production, but did you know the region was also a main producer of glass as well? PGC is honoring that history by keeping the art of glass-making alive with its diverse offering of contemporary glass art exhibitions from around the world. A visit to the glass center includes a self-guided tour, where you'll see the current exhibition and observe artists at work in their studios on-site.

MAP 7: 5472 Penn Ave., 412/365-2145, www.pittsburghglasscenter.org; 10am-7pm Mon.-Thurs., 10am-4pm Fri.-Sun.

SILVER EYE CENTER FOR PHOTOGRAPHY

Though Pittsburgh is a hub for art galleries, it's hard to find very many exhibits dedicated solely to contemporary fine art photography. That's why Silver Eye Center for Photography is such a vital asset to the city's art scene. The gallery offers 3-5 exhibitions per year with work from local, regional, and international fine art photographers, and also holds a juried exhibition each year.

MAP 7: 4808 Penn Ave., 412/431-1810, www.silvereye.org; noon-6pm Tues.-Sat.; free, donations accepted

MUSEUMS
THE CENTER FOR POSTNATURAL HISTORY

There's history, and then there's postnatural history. If you have an appreciation for the weird and freaky, this is a must-visit. Postnatural history is the study of the origins, habitats, and evolution of organisms that have been intentionally altered by humans. Meaning: Humans have messed with nature, and the results are fascinating. Past exhibits have included a collection of photos of lab rats, a genetically modified mosquito, and a BioSteel goat (I dare you to find out what that is).

MAP 7: 4913 Penn Ave., Garfield, 412/223-7698, www.postnatural.org; noon-4pm Sun. or by appointment; free, donations accepted

PERFORMING ARTS
KELLY STRAYHORN THEATER

Kelly Strayhorn Theater is named for two incredible talents of Pittsburgh's past: Gene Kelly and Billy Strayhorn. Kelly was a Highland Park native who made it to the Broadway stage in New York and then Hollywood, dancing alongside icons like Judy Garland and directing films such as *Hello Dolly*. Strayhorn was a prolific composer, often overshadowed by his collaborator, Duke Ellington. Today the theater is a destination for contemporary and innovative performances.

MAP 7: 5941 Penn Ave., 412/363-3000, www.kelly-strayhorn.org; show times and prices vary by performance

Lawrenceville   Map 8

MUSEUMS
★ THE CLEMENTE MUSEUM

Although visiting this loving monument to professional baseball legend Roberto Clemente can only be done by a pre-arranged tour, the experience is nevertheless worth the trouble—especially for anyone with a serious interest in Major League Baseball or the immigrant experience in America. Clemente, also known as The Great One, was a Puerto Rican athlete who spent all 18 of his pro baseball seasons, from 1955 until his untimely death in a plane crash in 1972, with the Pittsburgh Pirates. Not only is he still considered one of the finest to ever play the game, he was also well known for devoting much of his time off the field to humanitarian work.

At the two-story Clemente Museum, which is inside the historical Engine House 25, visitors will find thousands of pieces of Clemente memorabilia, including photographs and family snapshots, all manner of gear, letters, telegraphs, and other personal curios, a large collection of bats, and even a set of actual seats from Oakland's Forbes Field.

MAP 8: 3339 Penn Ave., 412/621-1268, www.clementemuseum.com; tours given by appointment only; $20 adults, $10 students and children

Greater Pittsburgh   Map 9

MUSEUMS
PENNSYLVANIA TROLLEY MUSEUM

Just about a half an hour south of Pittsburgh in Washington County is the Pennsylvania Trolley Museum, a quirky gem of a museum for anyone interested in the nostalgia of railway travel. Streetcars played a major role in 20th-century transportation and in the growth of American cities. But as they were phased out, groups of passionate trolley aficionados worked together to preserve their history for generations to come. One of these groups was the Pittsburgh Electric Railway Club, whose three-car collection eventually grew into the Pennsylvania Trolley Museum. Today you can see nearly 50 street and electric railway cars, some of which still operate on the museum's four-mile tracks. Each year, children impatiently wait for the PA Trolley Museum's Santa Trolley, when Santa visits the Trolley Museum and children can board the operational train for a magical holiday ride and festivities.

MAP 9: 1 Museum Rd., Washington, 724/228-9675, http://pa-trolley.org; 10am-4pm Sat.-Sun. Apr.-May and Sept.-mid-Dec., 10am-4pm Tues.-Sun. June-Aug.; $10 adults, $9 children ages 3-15, children 2 and under free

Festivals and Events

WINTER
LIGHT UP NIGHT

Light Up Night is a fun November tradition that officially marks the start of the holiday season and gets Pittsburghers geared up for the (often long) winter ahead. On the third Friday of November, thousands of people pack into the downtown area for a night of entertainment, delicious food, and ice skating, which culminates in the lighting of multiple Christmas trees, as well as a fireworks display. Many of the downtown businesses get involved with holiday decorations and lights, turning the area into a winter wonderland.

Downtown: www.downtownpittsburghholidays.com; third Fri. in Nov.; free

HIGHMARK FIRST NIGHT PITTSBURGH

The Pittsburgh Cultural Trust's New Year's Eve celebration is one of the biggest events in the city, when thousands of people pack into the Cultural District for a night of food, fun, and entertainment leading up to the countdown at midnight and an epic fireworks display. The event is an arts-focused celebration, so you'll see a lot of musical and dance performances. This event is family friendly and booze free, so if you're looking for a little libation to warm you up, you'll have to stop in one of the many open bars around the area.

Downtown: Cultural District, 412/456-6666, http://firstnightpgh.trustarts.org; 6pm-midnight Dec. 31; $10

SPRING
ST. PATRICK'S DAY PARADE

Get this: Pittsburghers are so nuts about St. Paddy's Day that, depending on which day the holiday actually falls on, it's sometimes celebrated *twice*. It works like this: The St. Patrick's Day Parade always takes place on a Saturday in March, so if St. Paddy's Day falls on a weekday, the parade will happen the Saturday before the actual holiday. The parade, which begins as early as 10am and snakes through downtown, is arguably Pittsburgh's biggest annual party, replete with floats and marching bands. And no, you don't have to be Irish to join in. The parade itself is family friendly, but be

Clockwise from top left: Pittsburgh Marathon; Highmark First Night Pittsburgh; Pittsburgh Glass Center.

forewarned that as the day continues on and the green beer is flowing, **133**
much of the celebration becomes more adult-oriented.

Downtown: Begins at Liberty Ave. and 11th St., www.pittsburghirish.org/parade; Sat.
preceding Mar. 17; free

PITTSBURGH MARATHON

Despite unpredictable weather and long winters, Pittsburgh is a very athletic and active city. Runners spend months training for the Pittsburgh
Marathon, in early May. Pittsburgh's notoriously hilly terrain makes for
a challenging course, which meanders through city neighborhoods such
as North Shore, South Side, Oakland, Shadyside, and Bloomfield. Register
early to secure your spot.

Citywide: Starts downtown, 412/586-7785, www.thepittsburghmarathon.com; early
May; $95-155

SUMMER
PITTSBURGH PRIDE

Pittsburgh Pride is a 10-day-long celebration of the city's proud and active
gay community put on by the Delta Foundation of Pittsburgh. The celebration features several popular events. **PrideFest** (Liberty Ave. between 6th
St. and 10th St.) is a free two-day celebration featuring vendors, family-
friendly entertainment, and a dance party. **Pride in the Street** (Liberty
Ave.) features a concert by a different performer each year (past musicians
include Kesha, Nick Jonas, and Jennifer Hudson). The **Equality March**
(starts at PPG Paints Arena, follows Grant St. to Liberty Ave.) is a lively
parade featuring floats, entertainment, and performers.

Downtown: 412/332-2800, www.pittsburghpride.org; early June; prices vary based
on event

THREE RIVERS ARTS FESTIVAL

Usually held in June, the Three Rivers Arts Festival marks the unofficial
start to summer. The 10-day event is a celebration of arts and culture in
Pittsburgh's downtown area. The celebration consists of musical and theatrical performances, gallery shows, a popular artists market, children's
events, and, of course, food. The festival has a reputation for being rained
on each year, as June is Pittsburgh's rainiest month. But that never stops the
crowds from coming downtown to check out the attractions.

Downtown: Point State Park and other locations, 412/456-6666, www.3riversartsfest.
org; early June; free

FOURTH OF JULY FIREWORKS

Each year on Independence Day, the city launches an impressive fireworks
display from a barge on the river. Thousands gather near Point State Park
to see the show. If you're going to brave the traffic and crowds, get there
early and bring blankets and lawn chairs. If you're not keen on crowds,
locals may give you tips on some out-of-the-way spots that allow for great
views without the traffic.

Downtown: Point State Park; July 4; free

EQT THREE RIVERS REGATTA

One of the city's favorite ways to celebrate its many waterways is with the EQT Three Rivers Regatta, which takes place in early August in Point State Park. It's a four-day-long celebration featuring boat races, watercraft shows, fishing competitions, and boating demonstrations. The event also features on-land attractions like hot-air-balloon rides, a canine Frisbee show, and live music.

Downtown: Point State Park, 412/875-4841, www.yougottaregatta.org; early Aug.; free

★ LITTLE ITALY DAYS

Bloomfield was settled by Italian immigrants from the Abruzzi region of Italy and is still home to many working-class Italian Americans. The best time of year to visit Bloomfield is during Little Italy Days in mid-August. The streets are closed to vehicle traffic, and vendors sell everything from beer and spicy Italian sausages to overstuffed cannoli and homemade meatballs. Don't miss the crowning of Miss Little Italy, the Italian Idol competition, or an intense round of bocce.

Bloomfield and Lawrenceville: Liberty Ave. from Ella St. to Gross St., http:// littleitalydays.com; mid-Aug.; free

FALL
A FAIR IN THE PARK

A contemporary arts and crafts festival that has been organized by the Craftsmen's Guild of Pittsburgh since 1970, the three-day A Fair in the Park, held in early September, has long been one of the Pittsburgh art community's most anticipated annual celebrations. More than 20,000 craft obsessives from Pittsburgh and beyond arrive each year to shop for handmade works of jewelry, glass, metal, clay, and much more. A packed schedule of activities and entertainment is also a big part of the fun: Glassblowers, metalsmiths, and sculptors can be observed in the act of creation, and a wide variety of musicians and performing artists set up shop as well.

Shadyside: Mellon Park, 412/370-0695, www.afairinthepark.org; early Sept.; free

Sports and Activities

Highlights

★ **Best Spectating:** You don't have to be a baseball fanatic to enjoy the nostalgic atmosphere of a **Pittsburgh Pirates** game. Just sit back and enjoy the sparkling lights of the city skyline and some serious ballpark food (page 139).

★ **Most Iconic Pittsburgh Experience:** To truly understand this city, you must tailgate at a **Pittsburgh Steelers** game (page 139).

★ **Best Scenic City Hike:** Check out views of Pittsburgh's bridges, landmarks, and skyline vistas as you navigate the riverside **Eliza Furnace Trail** (page 141).

★ **Best Place to Escape in Nature:** The city's largest park, **Frick Park** is home to an extensive trail system and more than 100 species of birds (page 146).

★ **Best Bowling Night:** You're guaranteed to have a great time at funky, old-school **Arsenal Bowling Lanes** (page 148).

Pittsburgh takes its sports seriously. "The City of Champions" lives for its winning sports teams— and locals cheer just as hard for the less successful ones.

But there's more to do here than just spectating. The city's most popular leafy escapes, Schenley Park and Frick Park, provide recreation and respite. Entering their gates feels like entering an entirely different world, right in the center of town. Joggers and walkers can enjoy miles of trails inside Schenley Park, and the mountain-biking paths that run through Frick Park are said to be some of the best in the country. And unlike in some bigger towns, locals are generally amenable to welcoming out-of-towners into Ultimate Frisbee or pickup basketball games.

During winter, you'll find families ice skating in Schenley Park and at PPG Place. Skiing and snowboarding excursions aren't more than an hour away in the Laurel Highlands. No matter what the season, you won't need to dig deep during your time in Pittsburgh to discover just about any sort of outdoor fun.

Previous: skyline from Mt. Washington; Steelers fans at Heinz Field.

PARKS
NORTH SHORE RIVERFRONT PARK

This park along the Allegheny and Ohio Rivers is directly across from downtown and offers stunning views of the city. It's part of the city's Three Rivers Park, an effort to provide continuous greenspace linking existing and future riverfront destinations. The park features walking and biking trails, large grassy spaces, an esplanade and pier, and three war memorials. Kids especially will love the interactive Water Steps: part art piece and part water park.

MAP 1: Roberto Clemente Bridge to the Carnegie Science Center, 412/393-0200, www. pgh-sea.com

GUIDED AND WALKING TOURS
PNC PARK TOURS

With its classic style and modern amenities, PNC Park is considered by many to be one of the finest ballparks in the country. Which is why no baseball fan should forgo the opportunity to tour the facility and get a behind-the-scenes look at the home of the Pittsburgh Pirates. The 90-minute walking tour leaves ample time to see parts of the park that you won't see on game day, like the dugout, batting cages, and press box.

MAP 1: PNC Park, 115 Federal St., 412/325-4700, http://pirates.mlb.com; 10am, noon, and 2pm Mon.-Fri. and one Sat. per month Mar.-Sept.; adults $10, seniors and children over 5 $8

HIKING AND BIKING TRAILS
THREE RIVERS HERITAGE TRAIL

Stretching for 24 miles along both sides of the Allegheny, Monongahela, and Ohio Rivers, the well-maintained Three Rivers Heritage Trail begins as a concrete path on the North Shore, where it runs alongside the Allegheny River. The trail is well-traveled by cyclists, joggers, and walkers and promises unforgettable views and access to many of the city's best attractions and neighborhoods. The North Side section of the trail is home to the **Vietnam Veterans Monument,** the **Korean Veterans Memorial,** and the striking **Mister Rogers statue.** The dirt trail turns to rock and begins to peter out around the 40th Street Bridge. The trail connects to other popular trails, like the Great Allegheny Passage, the Erie-to-Pittsburgh Trail, and many others.

MAP 1: Heinz Field to the 40th St. Bridge, alongside the Allegheny River, http:// friendsoftheriverfront.org; 24 hours daily

ROWING AND KAYAKING
KAYAK PITTSBURGH

Kayak Pittsburgh offers what may very well be the most enjoyable and affordable way to explore Pittsburgh's waterways. The company rents flat-water kayaks that even the completely inexperienced can easily navigate and has been consistently ranked as one of the city's top places for rentals and guided trips. They also offer rowboat, canoe, stand-up paddleboard, and pedal boat rentals.

MAP 1: North side of Roberto Clemente Bridge, 412/337-1519, www.ventureoutdoors. org; 11am-8pm Mon.-Fri., 10am-8pm Sat.-Sun.; rentals $16-24.50/hour

SPECTATOR SPORTS
Baseball
★ PITTSBURGH PIRATES

Despite the Pirates' infamously dismal record, catching a game is still the city's best spectator sports experience. A good baseball game is all about the ambience: the gorgeous ballpark, a spectacular skyline view, fireworks for every home run, and racing pierogi mascots. **PNC Park** is considered a classic-style ballpark, with its rhythmic archways and steel truss work, though it also features plenty of modern amenities, like upscale restaurants. The park offers an intimate viewing experience, with the highest seat only 88 feet from the field.

MAP 1: PNC Park, 115 Federal St., 800/289-2827, http://pirates.mlb.com; Apr.-Sept.; tickets from $19

Football
★ PITTSBURGH STEELERS

In Pittsburgh, the Steelers are not a football team. They are a conversation starter, a way of life, and, to some, a religion. The Steelers are the fifth oldest team in the NFL, and the team's history is rife with championships, the reason why Pittsburgh is dubbed "The City of Champions." The ultimate way to experience a game is by tailgating beforehand. **Heinz Field** opens five hours before kickoff, but fans also set up in other parking lots nearby. Pack in some beer and gear for grilling, then get ready to make a lot of new friends. Game tickets are pricey and hard to come by, but they're worth it.

MAP 1: Heinz Field, 100 Art Rooney Ave., 412/323-1200, www.steelers.com; Sept.-Jan.; tickets from $50

PITT PANTHERS FOOTBALL

For fans of college football, a University of Pittsburgh Panthers game is an unforgettable experience. You get the fun college football atmosphere with the luxury of a pro football stadium (the Pitt Panthers play at **Heinz Field,** home of the Pittsburgh Steelers). I recommend braving the freezing cold weather and nabbing tickets (before they sell out!) to the Backyard Brawl, the notorious showdown between Pitt and their rival, the West Virginia University Mountaineers. Or try for seats to Pitt versus Penn State. The schools' mutual disdain for each other makes for a fun tailgate. The Pitt football program has a fruitful history and has churned out quite a few football greats over the years, including icons like Dan Marino, Tony Dorsett, Mike Ditka, and Pop Warner, not to mention dozens of other NFL athletes.

MAP 1: 100 Art Rooney Ave., Heinz Field, 412/648-7488 or 800/643-7488 (tickets), www. pittsburghpanthers.com; late Aug.-Dec.; tickets $50-285

Top: the Eliza Furnace Trail. **Bottom:** PNC Park, home of the Pittsburgh Pirates.

Downtown

Map 2

HIKING AND BIKING TRAILS

★ ELIZA FURNACE TRAIL

The Eliza Furnace Trail, a part of the larger Three Rivers Heritage Trail, is an urban pathway for joggers, walkers, and bikers to get around the city. The 3.5-mile paved trail winds through downtown, along the Monongahela River, and into Oakland. A large part of the trail runs alongside a major highway, so don't expect a peaceful escape into nature. It does, however, offer great views of the city's bridges and skyline. You may also hear locals refer to the Eliza Furnace Trail as the "Jail Trail" due to its proximity to the county jail.

MAP 2: Trailhead starts in downtown and ends in Oakland, north of Schenley Park; 24 hours daily

ICE SKATING

ICE RINK AT PPG PLACE

The MassMutual Pittsburgh Ice Rink at PPG Place is Pittsburgh's answer to Rockefeller Center. And would you believe, Pittsburgh's version is actually 2,000 square feet larger? Located in the shadow of the dramatic PPG Place building, the rink opens for the holiday season on Light Up Night (usually mid-November) and closes toward the end of February. The skating rink has been around since 2001 and has quickly become a Pittsburgh tradition, whether for a family outing or a sweet date night.

MAP 2: PPG Place, 3rd. Ave. at Market St., 412/394-3641, www.ppgplace.com/rink; 11am-10pm Mon.-Thurs., 11am-midnight Fri.-Sat., noon-8pm Sun. mid-Nov.-late Feb.; adults $8, seniors and children $7; skate rental $4

SPECTATOR SPORTS

Hockey

PITTSBURGH PENGUINS

Starting in October each year, Pittsburgh becomes a hockey town. The Pittsburgh Penguins are the city's champion professional ice hockey team. The team, which plays its games at **PPG Paints Arena** (www.ppgpaintsar-ena.com), has qualified for six Stanley Cup finals and has won four times, including back-to-back seasons in 2016 and 2017. The Pens have featured hockey greats such as Mario Lemieux and Jaromir Jagr, as well as current superstar players like Evgeni Malkin, Sidney Crosby, and Kris Letang.

MAP 2: PPG Paints Arena, 1001 5th Ave., 412/642-1800, http://penguins.nhl.com; Oct.-Apr.; tickets $45-215

Oakland Map 3

PARKS
SCHENLEY PARK

Located near the University of Pittsburgh and Carnegie Mellon University, 456-acre Schenley Park is a great nature retreat for university students and urban dwellers alike. The park was donated by Mary Schenley in 1889 and is on the National Register of Historic Places. The park is an outdoors-lover's oasis, with miles of hiking trails, 13 tennis courts (free), an ice-skating rink, a public swimming pool (adults $5, children $3), and even an 18-hole disc golf course. Schenley Park attracts crowds for the many events held throughout the year; the one that draws the most fans is the annual **Pittsburgh Vintage Grand Prix** (www.pvgp.org). Each July, a quarter million spectators gather in the park to watch vintage sports cars race around the winding roads of the tree-lined park.

MAP 3: Bounded by Schenley Dr., Murdoch St., I-376, and Boundary St., 412/687-1800, www.pittsburghparks.org; 6am-sunset daily, visitors center 10am-4pm daily; free

ICE SKATING
SCHENLEY PARK SKATING RINK

Schenley Park features an ice skating rink that operates daily throughout the winter. Because of its location near the University of Pittsburgh and Carnegie Mellon University, the rink is especially popular with college students, but special deals such as family nights and adults-only nights bring in a variety of crowds. The facility hosts three events in particular that are very popular: "Skate with Santa" in December, "Mascot Skate" in January, and "Valentines on Ice" in February.

MAP 3: 1 Overlook Dr., 412/422-6523, www.pittsburghpa.gov; hours vary Nov.-Mar.; adults $5, seniors $4, children 17 and under $3; skate rental $3

SPECTATOR SPORTS
Basketball
PITT PANTHERS BASKETBALL

Pittsburgh doesn't have a professional basketball team, but the Pitt Panthers are a great substitute. The Panthers are the NCAA Division I men's basketball team for the University of Pittsburgh. They boast 15 First Team All-American Selections, have appeared in 25 NCAA and eight National Invitation Tournaments, and have reached one Final Four tournament. Catch a game on campus at the impressive **Petersen Events Center.** You'll likely get a view of the "Oakland Zoo," Pitt's notoriously lively cheering section, primarily made up of enthusiastic undergrads.

MAP 3: Petersen Events Center, 3719 Terrace St., 800/643-7488 (tickets), www.pittsburghpanthers.com; Nov.-Feb., tickets from $45

Top: The Pittsburgh Steelers play at Heinz Field, which looks out to the beautiful city skyline. **Bottom:** one of the amphibious vehicles from Just Ducky Tours.

South Side

Map 4

GUIDED AND WALKING TOURS

JUST DUCKY TOURS

Whether you're a local or a visitor, you must indulge in the city's most touristy experience with Just Ducky Tours. These vintage World War II amphibious vehicles, able to traverse both land and water, will take you around town and through the rivers, bombarding you with essential Pittsburgh trivia and history. Be sure to wave at the pedestrians who are surely shaking their heads at you. It's all in good fun!

MAP 4: 125 W. Station Square Dr., 412/402-3825, www.justduckytours.com; Apr.-Nov.; adults $25, children 3-12 $15, children 2 and under $5

PITTSBURGH HISTORY AND LANDMARKS FOUNDATION TOURS

In an effort to save some of Pittsburgh's historical landmarks and buildings from demolition, the Pittsburgh History and Landmarks Foundation was formed in 1964. The group offers an impressive variety of tours to educate the public on the history of Pittsburgh. These guided walking tours are typically an hour long and include well-researched information and trivia. The tours, offered on Fridays from May through October, are free but donations are encouraged. Popular tours include the Old Allegheny County Jail, Market Square, and Fourth Avenue Historic District.

MAP 4: 100 W. Station Square Dr., Ste. 450, 412/471-5808, www.phlf.org; Fri. May-Oct.; free, donations encouraged

THE PITTSBURGH TOUR COMPANY DOUBLE DECKER TOURS

This is Pittsburgh's only hop-on, hop-off bus tour, with double-decker buses making 21 stops on the route through the city. The lively tour guides give a fun and entertaining explanation of Pittsburgh during your ride. This is one of the most convenient and thrilling ways to explore the city. The bus travels from the SouthSide Works plaza to Station Square before heading to venues like the Heinz History Center and Wholey's Fish Market in the Strip District, and then to downtown before returning again to the SouthSide Works.

MAP 4: SouthSide Works, 445 S. 27th St., 412/381-8687, www.pghtours.com; all-day passes adults $30, children $20

SEGWAY PITTSBURGH

Pittsburgh has its own Segway tour, Segway Pittsburgh, where even newbies to the two-wheeled contraptions will be navigating the streets of Pittsburgh in no time. Besides being a fun, futuristic ride, the tour also highlights interesting and historic sights and landmarks around the city. Don't be intimidated by the machinery involved: This tour is for all ages and abilities. Options include a tour of downtown, a sunset tour, and the nighttime City

MAP 4: 125 W. Station Square Dr., 412/337-3941, http://segwaypittsburgh.com; $39-69

SPECTATOR SPORTS
Soccer
PITTSBURGH RIVERHOUNDS

The Pittsburgh Riverhounds are the only pro soccer team in the immediate area, and they're headquartered right on Pittsburgh's South Side. The club plays in the Eastern Conference of the United Soccer League. They play their matches at the 3,500-seat **Highmark Stadium** (http://highmarkstadium.com) at the Station Square complex. The team has its own fan league, the Steel Army, who meet at Piper's Pub in the South Side. If you get tickets to a game, check out the Steel Army at their post at the South Gate end of the stadium: It's quite a sight!

MAP 4: Highmark Stadium, 510 W. Station Square Dr., 412/224-4900, www.riverhounds. com; Apr.-Sept.; season tickets $192-288, check website for individual ticket prices

SWIMMING
OLIVER BATH HOUSE

This indoor swimming facility, designed by Daniel Burnham in the Tudor style, is also a cool piece of Pittsburgh history. The Oliver Bath House was built in 1910 at the base of the South 10th Street Bridge and then donated to the city when Henry Oliver gave the city $100,000 to build a public bath for mill workers or anyone without indoor plumbing to use. The phrase "the great unwashed" was used to describe anyone who needed to use these facilities. Eventually, a new housing code made indoor plumbing mandatory, so public bath houses were no longer necessary. Now, Oliver Bath House is Pittsburgh's oldest swimming pool and is still used by the public.

MAP 4: 38 S. 10th St., 412/488-8380, www.pittsburghpa.gov; daily fall-spring; adults $5, children 3-15 $3

Mount Washington   Map 4

PARKS
EMERALD VIEW PARK

Emerald View Park is actually three different parks (Grandview, Olympia, and Mount Washington) that are linked together, surrounding Duquesne Heights and Mount Washington and running along scenic Grandview Avenue. The land, once the site of heavy mining and illegal dumping, has been totally revitalized, with trails, playgrounds, playing fields, and scenic overlooks.

MAP 4: Mount Washington, 412/481-3220, http://mwcdc.org; 6am-11pm daily

Shadyside

Map 5

PARKS
MELLON PARK

Just beyond the Pittsburgh Center for the Arts lies the small but worth-while Mellon Park. The former grand estate of Pittsburgh mogul Richard Mellon, the grounds contain the Walled Garden, which was designed by landscape architects Vitale and Geiffert. The gardens are maintained to this day by volunteers. Park-goers love to escape in this hidden gem and play among the beautifully tended plants and fountains. On the opposite side of bustling 5th Avenue you'll find Mellon Park's **Tennis Bubble** (reservations $20-30), a set of courts with a bubble-like covering that protects players from the biting cold throughout the winter and early spring, and is air-conditioned in the summer.

MAP 5: Bounded by 5th Ave., Shady Ave., Mellon Park Rd., and Beechwood Blvd., 412/682-7575, www.pittsburghpa.gov; 6am-sunset daily

Squirrel Hill and Point Breeze

Map 6

PARKS
★ FRICK PARK

The heavily wooded, 644-acre Frick Park is a bird-watcher's paradise, where over 100 species have been recorded. A well-marked and extensive trail system meanders throughout the park. The trails are also very popular with mountain bikers, with some challenging routes. Even if you've never been to Pittsburgh, you may have heard of Frick Park's playground. Pittsburgh rapper Mac Miller gave Blue Slide Park its 15 minutes of fame when he named his debut album after the playground. The park also features a popular off-leash dog park.

MAP 6: Bordered by Forbes Ave., S. Braddock Ave., I-376, and Beechwood Blvd., no phone, www.pittsburghparks.org; 6am-11pm daily

ROCK CLIMBING
THE CLIMBING WALL

Looking for a way to break outside your normal workout routine? Build your physical strength, push your mental stamina, and learn new skills at The Climbing Wall in Point Breeze. This state-of-the-art gym features over 14,000 square feet of climbing, top roping, and bouldering. Not sure what any of this means? Don't worry, all skill levels are welcome!

MAP 6: 7501 Penn Ave., 412/247-7334, www.theclimbingwall.net; introductory class (includes equipment rental) $30; day pass $12

Top: Frick Park. Bottom: Arsenal Bowling Lanes is a retro-style bowling alley with a full bar.

Bloomfield
and East Liberty Map 7

PARKS
HIGHLAND PARK

Located in an East End neighborhood of the same name, Highland Park sits on an overlook atop the Allegheny River, close to the Pittsburgh Zoo. Because of its enviable vista, the park is especially popular with joggers but also with walkers who enjoy circling the 0.75-mile path around the reservoir, a historical city site officially known as Reservoir No. 1. The sand volleyball courts are a popular destination in the summer, as is the swimming pool, which is the only long-course pool in Pittsburgh.

Highland Park was originally created as a reservoir for drinking water, but people were drawn to the spot because of its natural beauty, and residents began congregating around the reservoir for picnics and recreation. It was eventually made into an official park and today contains beautiful gardens, a reflecting pool, bike tracks, and jogging trails. The sand volleyball courts are popular in the summer.

MAP 7: Highland Ave., 412/682-7575, www.pittsburghpa.gov; 6am-sunset daily

Lawrenceville Map 8

PARKS
ARSENAL PARK

Rarely do you find such a fun and carefree place with such a destructive history. Arsenal Park is a playground and park on the former site of the Allegheny Arsenal, which produced cartridges for the U.S. Army, peaking during the Civil War. The arsenal employed over 1,100 workers during the Civil War, most of them women. On a September afternoon in 1862, three explosions occurred at the arsenal. Tragically, 78 workers, almost all women, were killed—the worst civilian disaster in the Civil War. The exact site of the explosion is now buried beneath a ballfield in the 20-acre park, which also features basketball courts, tennis courts, a playground, and tree-lined walking paths.

MAP 8: Bounded by 39th St., 40th St., Butler St., and Penn Ave., www.arsenalpark.org; dawn-dusk daily

BOWLING
★ ARSENAL BOWLING LANES

At this funky old-school bowling alley with a full bar and restaurant and a hip nightclub vibe, you'll find everything you need for an unforgettable night out. The bowling alley has been around for seemingly forever—and that's reflected in the decor: low lights, polished hardwood floors, fabric-covered walls, and old-school scoring machines. Special events include live bands, '80s- and '90s-themed nights, karaoke, and more. College students are especially fond of Arsenal, thanks to its affordable food and drink specials and deals on bowling. It's popular on weekend nights, so call ahead and reserve a lane for the busy 9pm-midnight unlimited bowling slot. They sell out pretty quickly!

MAP 8: 4310 Butler St., 412/683-5992, www.arsenalbowl.com; noon-midnight Mon. and Wed.-Thurs., 10am-midnight Tues., noon-2am Fri., 11am-2am Sat., 11am-midnight Sun.; open-6pm $3.75/game/person, 6pm-close $4.35/game/person

Greater Pittsburgh   Map 9

ADVENTURE SPORTS
GO APE ZIPLINE PARK

Think you need to go on a tropical vacation to zipline through the forest canopy and swing through the trees like Tarzan? Not true! This treetop obstacle course is just north of Pittsburgh in Allegheny County's gorgeous North Park. It's set atop the park's 63-acre lake and features ziplines, Tarzan swings, suspension bridges, and amazing views of the park below. Don't worry if you're a bit faint of heart, though, as there are bypass routes throughout the course. The minimum age is 10.

MAP 9: North Park, 991 Tennis Court Rd., Allison Park, 800/971-8271, http://.goape.com; daily Jun.-Aug., weekends and select weekdays Mar.-May and Sept.-late Nov.; online reservations recommended; adult $58, child 10-15 $38

PITTSBURGH INTERNATIONAL RACE COMPLEX

The Pittsburgh International Race Complex is the area's top destination for auto racing. The complex features a 2.8-mile full circuit track with 19 corners, a six-acre vehicle dynamics area for performance and evasive driving training, and a 0.8-mile Wilson Circuit kart track, which is one of the fastest kart tracks in Pennsylvania. They rent out 9.5-horsepower go-karts ($22.50 per 10-minute session). Pitt Race also offers specialty driving courses.

MAP 9: 201 Penndale Rd., Wampum, 724/535-1000, www.pittrace.com; hours and prices vary based on activity

GUIDED AND WALKING TOURS
RIVERS OF STEEL HERITAGE TOURS

Comprising 3,000 square miles throughout seven counties of Southwestern Pennsylvania, the Rivers of Steel Heritage Area was created by U.S. Congress in 1996. The purpose was to honor the industry of Big Steel—an industry that no longer exists in this region. In Pittsburgh's Homestead neighborhood, however, it's now possible to tour the areas where steel production took place. Tours and their themes occasionally change, so it's best to call or check the organization's website before planning a trip. Past tours, however, have explored the infamous site of the Homestead Steel Strike of 1892 and the remains of the Carrie Furnace. Visitors can also take narrated, self-guided tours of the immediate area by renting audio devices with headphones.

MAP 9: 623 E. 8th Ave., Homestead, 412/464-4020, www.riversofsteel.com; tour times vary, May-Oct.; adults $21-25, seniors and students $17-20, children $14-17

ROLLER DERBY
STEEL CITY ROLLER DERBY

If you're interested in seeing female athletes kick some serious butt in a vintage sport that's made a major comeback, head to a Steel City Roller Derby bout. Pittsburgh's all-women roller derby league plays competitive teams from other cities and within the league. Their bouts, which are two 30-minutes periods, are played at the **Pittsburgh Indoor Sports Arena** (www.pisausa.com) in Cheswick, about 30 minutes northeast of the city. The at-home games generally run September through March. Check the website for specific bout dates.

MAP 9: Pittsburgh Indoor Sports Arena, 22 Rich Hill, Cheswick, www.steelcityrollerderby.org; Sept.-Mar.; tickets $10-15

SKATEBOARDING
AE RIDE SKATEPARK

Located behind the Cranberry Municipal Center, this BMX bike and skate park is open year-round during daylight hours. The park was built on a 120- by 80-foot pad of concrete and features ramps, steps, rails, benches, and platforms. All materials were provided by a grant from the American Eagle Outfitters Foundation and national organization KaBoom!

MAP 9: Cranberry Township Municipal Center, 2525 Rochester Rd., Cranberry, 724/779-4386, www.cranberrytownship.org; daily dawn-dusk, weather permitting; free

IMPERIAL SKATEPARK

This skate park just south of the airport has a reputation as being one of the more challenging and exciting skate parks in the area. Local skaters flock to the concrete park for its assortment of ramps, rails, and half-pipe. Skateboarders, inline-skaters, and BMX riders will be thrilled by the kidney-shaped pool and the concrete snake run. This park is open late and is well lit year-round.

MAP 9: Leopold Lake Park, 810 Rte. 30, Imperial, 724/695-0500, www.findlaytwp.org; 8am-11pm daily May-mid-Nov., 8am-9pm daily mid-Nov.-Apr., weather permitting; free

SKI RESORTS
HIDDEN VALLEY FOUR SEASONS RESORT

Laurel Highlands, about 60 miles east of the city, is a popular weekend getaway destination for Pittsburghers, and this ski resort is one of the most popular spots there. The resort features 26 slopes and trails, two terrain parks, and nine lifts for skiers and snowboarders. For warmer weather visits, the resort also features a gorgeous 18-hole golf course and a full spa.

MAP 9: 1 Craighead Dr., Hidden Valley, 814/443-8000, www.hiddenvalleyresort.com; 9am-9pm daily; adult lift tickets $42-67 Mon.-Fri., $45-123 Sat.-Sun.

If you want a five-star luxury experience that's within a two-hour drive of Pittsburgh, Nemacolin Woodlands Resort will not disappoint. Nestled in the picturesque Laurel Highlands, this extravagant resort features every experience you could want to pack into a weekend getaway, including animal safaris, ziplines, fine dining, spa treatments, and unspoiled nature. Want to try your hand in dog sledding? Dance in a ballroom? Participate in a clay shoot? The sky's the limit at Nemacolin. However, all this finery is going to cost you. The resort is the priciest in the area.

MAP 9: 1001 Lafayette Dr., Farmington, 866-344-6957, www.nemacolin.com; adult day pass $43, cross-country skiing or snowshoeing $20

SEVEN SPRINGS MOUNTAIN RESORT

Seven Springs Mountain Resort is probably the most popular skiing destination in the area. Set in the Laurel Highlands, this resort features 33 slopes and trails, seven terrain parks, and 10 lifts. The mountain's elevation reaches nearly 3,000 feet, with a 750-foot vertical drop, and there are about 285 acres of skiable terrain. The resort is known for its winter activities but also boasts year-round activities like golf, clay-shooting, fly-fishing, and a spa, making Seven Springs a great place to visit any time of year.

MAP 9: 777 Waterwheel Dr., Champion, 814/352-7777, www.7springs.com; adult lift tickets $59-159

SPECTATOR SPORTS
Horse Racing
THE MEADOWS

The Meadows is a giant entertainment complex just a half hour south of Pittsburgh. It boasts a casino, hotel, and racetrack. The unique racetrack conducts harness races year-round, with live racing over 200 days of the year. Races are usually held on Monday and Tuesday afternoons. Make a day of it by visiting the adjacent casino and restaurants. Check out the website for racing schedules and wagering information.

MAP 9: 210 Racetrack Rd., Washington, 877/824-5050, www.meadowsgaming.com; races usually Mon.-Tues.; free admission

WATER PARKS
SANDCASTLE

On a hot summer day, Pittsburghers cool off at Sandcastle. One of the city's few amusement parks, and the closest one to downtown, this water park features 14 water slides of various thrill levels, a lazy river, a giant wave pool, hot tubs, and a children's area. When you're ready to take a break from the water, the park offers an array of tempting amusement park grub.

MAP 9: 1000 Sandcastle Dr., Homestead, 412/462-6666, www.sandcastlewaterpark.com; from 11am daily early June-late Aug.; from $36, children 3 and under free

Shops

Pittsburgh has never really been known as a fashion mecca. But thanks to an influx of boutiques and their fashion-forward owners, cutting-edge fashion is becoming more and more accessible in the city.

Explore the urban areas of Pittsburgh and you'll find a growing variety of specialty shops, fashion boutiques, gift stores, and booksellers who carry items you would never find at a big box store. Shoppers can expect to find one-of-a-kind, handcrafted goods by local designers and artisans in stores throughout the city.

A growing concern for responsible consumerism has led to an increased demand for environmentally friendly production practices, fair labor environments, and locally made goods. It's easier than ever to find ethical and sustainable fashion, cosmetics, gifts, and other products. You'll find small-batch waxed canvas bags at Moop Shop, ethically created fashions at Mid-Atlantic Mercantile, and eco-friendly underwear at Calligramme.

The shopping havens of Shadyside, South Side, and Lawrenceville hold a plethora of establishments to please even the pickiest of shoppers. If your budget is endless and you demand the best labels and high-end fashion, a shopping trip to Shadyside will supply you with numerous options. The budget-minded thrift shopper will love getting lost in the racks of the numerous vintage clothing shops of the South Side. Lawrenceville is a favorite hot spot for hipster threads and trendy boutiques.

Previous: shops in Shadyside; some of the South Side's many storefronts.

Highlights

★ **Best Yinzer Gear:** Find luxuriously soft, Pittsburgh-designed cotton tees at **Steel City** (page 156).

★ **Best Place to Get Lost in a Book:** You could search through the shelves of used books at **Caliban Bookshop** for hours on end (page 157).

★ **Best Bike Gear:** Pay a visit to the friendly folks at **Thick Bikes,** a fantastic neighborhood spot with all manner of biking paraphernalia (page 161).

★ **Most Wearable Vintage Clothes:** East Carson Street's **Highway Robbery** carefully selects vintage pieces that can be seamlessly integrated into modern wardrobes (page 163).

★ **Best Way to Feel Like a Kid Again:** Get lost in the whimsy and imagination of **S.W. Randall Toyes and Giftes,** Pittsburgh's oldest and largest specialty toy store (page 163).

★ **Best Designer Shoes: Emy Mack Collective** offers luxury shoes that are made in Italy (page 166).

★ **Best Potential for a Wardrobe Overhaul:** Women's boutique **Pavement** carries on-trend labels that can't be found anywhere else in the 'Burgh (page 173).

★ **Best Retail Smorgasbord:** Offering everything from handmade T-shirts and housewares to uber-creative greeting cards and jewelry, **Wildcard** is ground zero for the city's crafting scene (page 175).

SHOPPING DISTRICTS AND CENTERS
STRIP DISTRICT

Although the Strip District is often referred to as Pittsburgh's only 24-hour neighborhood, the hardiest shoppers will want to arrive during the daylight hours on Friday, Saturday, or Sunday, when the widest variety of curbside vendors and street performers set up shop along Penn Avenue. The Strip is also something of a public market, and with a bit of poking around it's possible to procure everything from gourmet coffee and cheeses to imported Italian meats and high-end kitchen gadgets. The best fun, however, can usually be had by simply wandering the streets and exploring at length. And don't forget to check out Smallman Street, which runs parallel to Penn Avenue and is home to a few unusual shopping surprises of its own.

MAP 1: Penn Ave. and Smallman St. between 16th St. and 24th St., www. neighborsinthestrip.com

ARTS AND CRAFTS
LOOM EXQUISITE TEXTILES

It's no wonder sewing and fabric fiends rave about Loom—it has the most impressive selection of cloth in the city. This awesome little boutique is jam-packed with high-quality and hard-to-find fabrics, tassels, trims, patterns, buttons, buckles, bling, how-to books, and even vintage couture clothing and jewelry. It also stocks rugs, fine textiles, and various home decor items. Sewing classes and private instruction are also available, as are interior consultations, custom upholstery, and window treatments.

MAP 1: 2124 Penn Ave., 412/586-4346, www.loomshowroom.com; 10am-4pm Mon.-Sat., also by appointment

CLOTHING AND ACCESSORIES
LUCY'S HANDMADE CLOTHING

Lucy's is an unexpected little gem right in the heart of Pittsburgh's Strip District—a corner of the city that's much better known for its gourmet food offerings. Once you work your way past the fun finds displayed out on the sidewalk, you'll find the main floor packed with pashmina scarves, jewelry, handbags, and other unique accessories, while the second floor contains an impressive array of beautiful, handmade clothing—all at surprisingly affordable prices.

MAP 1: 2021 Penn Ave., 412/281-1081, www.lucyspgh.com; 9am-5pm daily

HOME DECOR AND FURNISHINGS
HOT HAUTE HOT

Specializing in eclectic and truly one-of-a-kind furniture pieces, the artists at Hot Haute Hot select used, vintage, or antique furniture items and customize each with a unique touch of creativity and top-notch craftsmanship. In other words, this is the perfect showroom for anyone on the hunt for a singular gem. The shop also creates custom items on commission for interested shoppers and for commercial spaces. To put it plainly, Hot Haute Hot is the polar opposite of your run-of-the-mill, standard contemporary furniture shop.

MAP 1: 2124 Penn Ave., 412/338-2323, www.hothautehot.net; 10am-5pm Mon.-Fri., 9am-5pm Sat., 11am-3pm Sun.

Downtown Map 2

BOOKS AND MUSIC
AMAZING BOOKS AND RECORDS

Amazing Books and Records is downtown's only used bookstore. Alongside the standards—literary fiction, counter-cultural authors, psychology, and philosophy, to name just a few—the store also has a decent selection of works by local authors and poets, and an impressive collection of first editions. The space is made up of rows of wooden bookshelves and offers plenty of room to move around and browse.

MAP 2: 929 Liberty Ave., 412/471-1899, www.amazingbooksandrecords.com; noon-6pm Mon.-Thurs., 11:30am-sunset Fri., noon-4pm Sun.

CLOTHING AND ACCESSORIES
★ STEEL CITY

Steel City is the best place to go for fashionable Pittsburgh-themed gear. Started by a married Pittsburgh couple, Steel City sells luxuriously soft cotton T-shirts with vintage-looking graphics and clever text. Big retailers like Nordstrom, Dick's Sporting Goods, and Urban Outfitters carry the company's designs, but it's worth the experience of visiting their cool storefront.

MAP 2: 625 Smithfield St., 412/338-2333, www.shopsteelcity.com; 10am-8pm Mon.-Sat., 10am-6pm Sun.

LARRIMORS

This boutique is known for its upscale selection of designer men's and women's fashions. You'll find designer labels here that are hard to find elsewhere in the city. Though many items are on the expensive side, the prices are fair compared to other retailers. They also have impeccable customer service, with employees who know the merchandise and are happy to help.

MAP 2: 249 5th Ave., 412/471-5732, www.larrimors.com; 9am-6pm Mon.-Wed. and Fri.-Sat., 9am-8pm Thurs.

MOOP SHOP

This studio and storefront on 1st Avenue sells handcrafted small-batch bags. The waxed canvas bags are stylish, durable, and made right in front of your eyes in the store. The brand was started by a Pittsburgh woman, Wendy Downs, on Etsy and built up so much popularity that she opened this brick-and-mortar location. Downs is committed to creating her bags as responsibly as possible, using recycled materials and local vendors. This shop is only open weekdays.

MAP 2: 429 1st Ave., www.moopshop.com; 9am-6pm Mon.-Fri.

SOCIAL STATUS

Social Status is an urban boutique that sells a mix of designer clothing and premium sneakers. This is the go-to spot for high-end street wear and limited-release sneakers. You'll find brands like Just Don, Human Made, A Bathing Ape, and Publish Brand. The downtown location has a hip minimalist vibe and frequently displays work from local artists.

MAP 2: 717 Liberty Ave., 412/456-2355, www.socialstatuspgh.com; 11am-7pm Mon.-Thurs., 11am-8pm Fri.-Sat.

Oakland Map 3

ARTS AND CRAFTS
IRISH DESIGN CENTER

The real gems at the Irish Design Center, an Irish import shop offering all the standard tchotchkes (rings, books, etc.), are the authentic sweaters and other cozy knits and linens. All are hand-knit, and all are absolutely the real deal (not mass-produced, in other words). What's more, the knits—blankets, throws, pullovers, and shawls—are all uniquely styled. A crowd favorite is Inis perfume, which has been described by more than one devotee as "Ireland in a Bottle."

MAP 3: 303 S. Craig St., 412/682-6125, www.irishdesigncenter.com; 10am-5:30pm Mon.-Fri., 10am-5pm Sat., extended holiday season hours

BOOKS AND MUSIC
★ CALIBAN BOOKSHOP

Specializing in rare first editions, leather-bound books, and fine arts and philosophy tomes, Caliban Bookshop carries the sort of printed curiosities you simply aren't going to stumble across at the neighborhood Barnes & Noble. Treasures seem to show up almost daily, and if you're looking to sell something rare and counterculture-esque, Caliban may be looking to buy. Just about every last item from the *McSweeney's* catalog is stocked, and a tiny music store, Desolation Row, can be found in the back corner.

MAP 3: 410 S. Craig St., 412/681-9111, www.calibanbooks.com; 10am-5:30pm Mon.-Sat., noon-5:30pm Sun., open most Thurs. till 8pm

PHANTOM OF THE ATTIC COMICS

With a roomy location right above Top Notch Art Center (look for the giant pencil), Phantom of the Attic has long been a Pittsburgh comic book institution. Regulars tend to show up in droves every Wednesday, when upwards of 100 new issues are added to the shelves. The inventory, in other words,

Clockwise from top left: Caliban Bookshop; Steel City; Social Status.

The best way to support Pittsburgh fashion designers is to shop locally. Pittsburgh has a surprising number of accomplished fashion designers, some of whom are listed here.

Emy Mack
Emy Mack's beautiful shoe designs are produced in Italy, then sold in her Shadyside store, **Emy Mack Collective** (page 166).

Diana Misetic
Diana Misetic moved to the United States in 1994 to pursue a fashion career in the United States and escape war-torn Bosnia. She is now the owner of the eponymous **Diana Misetic** (page 164).

Kiya Tomlin
Kiya Tomlin took the comfortable fabric of sweats and transformed it into dresses, rompers, accessories, and more at **Uptown Sweats** (page 171).

Wendy Downs
Wendy Downs got her start by listing a bag she had designed and sewn on Etsy. So many bags sold that she opened the brick-and-mortar **Moop Shop** (page 156), where the bags are designed, sewn, and sold.

is serious. And because Phantom's well-lit space is so sprawling and large, you're nearly guaranteed to find what you need.
MAP 3: 411 S. Craig St., 412/621-1210, www.pota-oakland.com; 10am-7pm Mon.-Tues. and Thurs.-Sat., 10am-8pm Wed., 10am-5pm Sun.

THE UNIVERSITY STORE ON FIFTH
Not content to exist solely as a locale for new Pitt students to purchase textbooks and school supplies, this massive bookstore has a well-stocked selection of fiction and nonfiction titles, as well as gifts and accessories. Non-students are always welcome.
MAP 3: 4000 5th Ave., 412/648-1455, www.pittuniversitystore.com; 8:30am-6pm Mon.-Tues. and Thurs., 8:30am-8pm Wed., 8:30am-5pm Fri., 10am-5pm Sat., noon-4pm Sun.

GIFT AND SPECIALTY
SNOWLION IMPORTS
Snowlion Imports is Pittsburgh's first and only location for Tibetan and Himalayan arts, artifacts, religious items, and handicrafts, the vast majority of which were acquired by the owners during trips to Nepal, India, and Tibet. The shop's South Craig Street location carries items such as silver and turquoise jewelry, books and CDs, statues, Tibetan religious items, trinkets and carpets.
MAP 3: 203 S. Craig St., 412/687-5680, http://snowlionimport.com; 11am-5pm Mon.-Fri., 11am-4pm Sat.

SKATEBOARDING AND CYCLING

IRON CITY BIKES

Located in the heart of South Oakland, the somewhat rough-around-the-edges Iron City Bikes carries a wide variety of high-quality bicycles, accessories, apparel, and merchandise from manufacturers including Norco, Surly, Velocity, ToPeak, and Haro. Iron City also provides bicycle maintenance services, and it boasts an amazing collection of used bikes starting at just $20. Be forewarned that while staffers are extremely knowledgeable, they can seem a bit intimidating to cycling newbies.

MAP 3: 331 S. Bouquet St., 412/681-1310, www.ironcitybikes.com; 11am-7pm Mon.-Fri., 11am-5pm Sat., noon-4pm Sun.

South Side

Map 4

SHOPPING DISTRICTS AND CENTERS

SOUTHSIDE WORKS

An outdoor shopping center complete with exclusive boutiques, big-box chain stores, cafés and restaurants, a movie theater, and even high-end apartment buildings, SouthSide Works has earned a reputation as one of the city's most successful retail projects. Clothiers include Urban Outfitters, Forever 21, and H&M. You'll also find a slew of restaurants like Hofbräuhaus Pittsburgh and Claddagh Irish Pub. Parking is affordable, and a Hyatt House hotel is on-site. Don't miss the human-size chess board, directly behind REI.

MAP 4: Bounded by E. Carson St., S. 28th St., Tunnel Blvd., and S. 26th St., 412/481-8800, www.southsideworks.com; hours vary by merchant

ARTS AND CRAFTS

FIREBORN STUDIOS

Every piece of functional pottery sold in this South Side studio and shop is created on the premises by Fireborn's founders, the master potters Dan Vito and Donna Hetrick. Heavily inspired by the 19th-century Arts and Crafts movement, the gallery is as warm, accessible, and inviting as the work found inside it, and Fireborn's "fat" mugs are the best thing to happen to coffee since the home grinder. Fireborn also provides classes for aspiring potters of all skill levels.

MAP 4: 2338 Sarah St., 412/488-6835, www.fireborn.com; noon-4pm Tues.-Sat.

CLOTHING AND ACCESSORIES

DECADE

If you're looking for a perfectly hip and comfortable T-shirt, look no farther than Decade. This boutique has an excellent selection of tees from local producers like Steel City Cotton Works as well as accessories for men and

women. The storefront has a hip urban vibe to it that makes it a pleasure
to sort through the merchandise.

MAP 4: 1407 E. Carson St., 412/720-1677, www.shopdecade.com; 11am-7pm Mon.-Sat.,
11am-5pm Sun.

GIFT AND SPECIALTY
CULTURE SHOP

A wonderfully unique import shop offering clothing, accessories, and gifts
from (mostly) India and the Far East, the Culture Shop feels something like
a cross between a Haight-Ashbury head shop and a magic store straight out
of a Harry Potter novel. Bohemian accoutrements abound: incense, peasant
dresses, silver rings, and statues bearing the likeness of Ganesha. But many
come specifically for the striking jewelry, as should you, assuming you're
looking for something expressly unique without the requisite high price tag.

MAP 4: 1602 E. Carson St., 412/481-8284; noon-9pm Mon.-Thurs., noon-10pm Fri.,
11am-10pm Sat., noon-5pm Sun.

HOME DECOR AND FURNISHINGS
PERLORA

Offering trendy contemporary furniture, Perlora is located in a retrofitted
building that is now a loft-style showroom. Perlora also staffs a few interior
designers who can help with projects of all sizes, which makes sense given
the ultra-modern and traditional designs for sale, not to mention the er-
gonomic chairs and mattresses available. And while it's true that Perlora's
furniture can be pricey, the originals are quite striking and not easily available elsewhere in the city.

MAP 4: 2220 E. Carson St., 412/431-2220 or 800/611-8590, www.perlora.com; 10am-6pm
Mon.-Sat., noon-5pm Sun.

SKATEBOARDING AND CYCLING
★ THICK BIKES

Originally located in Brooklyn, Thick Bikes is a full-service repair shop
that has been fabricating chromoly bicycle frames and other custom parts
since 1996. And while the small showroom is packed tight with some of the
best bikes and cycling products on the market, including a wide selection of
used cycles and messenger gear, Thick Bikes is probably best known among
locals for its honesty and its concern for safety. For those ready to make a
serious investment, the shop also deals in made-to-order bicycles—some
so stylish they'll even have drivers drooling.

MAP 4: 62 S. 15th St., 412/390-3590, http://thickbikes.com; 11am-8pm Mon.-Fri.,
9am-5pm Sat. summer, 11am-7pm Tues.-Fri., 9am-5pm Sat. winter

ONE UP SKATE

Something of a cross between an upscale boutique and an old-school skate
shop, One Up quickly became a South Side institution after opening its
doors in 2003. The store boasts an impressive collection of skate shoes and
apparel, with labels like Vans, Adidas, and Dickies all well represented.
Check out the dizzying array of beautifully shiny skate decks—neatly

Clockwise from top left: modern and classic toys on display at S.W. Randall Toyes and Giftes; Thick Bikes; SouthSide Works.

stacked floor to ceiling on brackets. The quite knowledgeable and surprisingly friendly staff offer private skate lessons by appointment at Mr. Smalls Funhouse in Millvale.

MAP 4: 1923 E. Carson St., 412/432-7007, www.oneuppgh.com; noon-8pm Mon.-Sat., noon-5pm Sun.

VINTAGE AND ANTIQUES
★ **HIGHWAY ROBBERY**

To describe Highway Robbery owner Kate Colussy as a vintage clothing savant would probably be an understatement; she has an eye for what she calls "vintage casual" style, and it's one you don't often find outside of the most pricey and pretentious big city retro boutiques. Highway Robbery has a carefully curated selection of clothing that represents roughly the last six or seven decades of fashion, with each and every piece being hand-selected to blend effortlessly into modern wardrobes—reasonable price tags and all. Colussy is obsessed with customer service, and the store has a wonderfully bright and airy ambience.

MAP 4: 1411 E. Carson St., 412/251-0818, www.highwayrobberyvintage.com; noon-8pm Mon.-Sat., noon-5pm Sun.

Shadyside

Map 5

CHILDREN'S CLOTHING AND TOYS
★ **S.W. RANDALL TOYES AND GIFTES**

With the ambience of an old-fashioned toy store and a huge collection of dolls, unique toys, and gifts that you simply won't find at a department or discount store, S.W. Randall has been one of Shadyside's most treasured gems for years. Just off of Walnut Street, this truly magical shop is a rare treat for children and grown-ups alike. Staffers are wonderfully talented at recommending uncommon, age-appropriate gifts, and can place special orders for most items, including collectible dolls. Fans of yo-yos will be delighted to learn new skills and tricks at the shop's Saturday Yo-Yo Club, led by resident pro Ky Zizan. S.W. Randall also has locations in Squirrel Hill (5856 Forbes Ave., 412/422-7009) and downtown (630 Smithfield St., 412/562-9252).

MAP 5: 806 Ivy St., 412/687-2666, www.swrandalltoys.com; 10am-6pm Mon.-Tues. and Thurs.-Sat., 10am-8pm Wed., 11am-4pm Sun.

THE PICKET FENCE

Budding fashionistas will be right at home in this charming Shadyside children's boutique. The Picket Fence carries lines like Freshly Picked and Appaman in addition to clothing for both new moms and babies, specialty toys, household decor, candles, and gifts. Fashion-forward moms flock to the store often to get their hands on up-and-coming labels that aren't readily available in other area shops, or even online.

MAP 5: 5425 Walnut St., 412/246-0350, www.picketfenceshadyside.com; 10am-5pm Mon.-Tues., 10am-6pm Wed.-Sat., 11am-3pm Sun.

CLOTHING AND ACCESSORIES
DIANA MISETIC

Designer and former Bosnian refugee Diana Misetic has been a local fashion institution since she opened her first boutique, Little Black Dress, years ago. Misetic releases two ready-to-wear collections each year out of her eponymous shop, in addition to providing custom designs. Misetic's custom designs don't come cheap: Expect to pay anywhere from $300 to thousands for a dress.

MAP 5: 809 Ivy St., 412/363-6442, www.dianamisetic.com; by appointment only

E.B. PEPPER

This shop is an absolute must for stylish women. The lower level at E.B. Pepper consists mainly of career and formal attire, while the top floor is not to be missed for its endlessly chic casual wear. You'll find suiting by the ever popular Milly and casual clothing by Alice and Olivia, as well as all the standards in premium denim, such as J Brand and Strom.

MAP 5: 5411 Walnut St., 412/683-3815, www.ebpepper.com; 10am-5:30pm Mon.-Tues. and Thurs.-Sat., 10am-7pm Wed., noon-5pm Sun.

MAXALTO

Simply visiting MaxAlto, a super funky and fun little boutique where customers sit on plush velvet couches while deciding what to purchase, is an experience in and of itself. The shop carries lines by Rundholz, High, Lilith, and others of similar ilk. The decor is unique and spunky: antique hatboxes used as shoe displays, fitting rooms with long velvet curtains. The owner is particularly nice, and wonderful sale items can always be found in the back of the shop.

MAP 5: 5426 ½ Walnut St., 412/683-0508, www.maxaltofashion.com; 10am-5pm Mon.-Sat.

MODA

Carrying designer collections and "it" labels from Alexander Wang and Rag & Bone to Ted Baker, Vivian Westwood, and Theory, Moda is one of the Pittsburgh area's most fashion-forward clothing stores for men, complete with a decent shoe collection and a somewhat snooty staff. While the store does carry a small but fantastic selection of suiting, its primary focus is more casual, ready-to-wear merchandise, like designer denim, casual button-downs, graphic tees, and trendy accessories and watches.

MAP 5: 5401 Walnut St., 2nd Fl., 412/681-8640, www.modapittsburgh.com; 11am-7pm Mon.-Fri., 11am-6pm Sat., noon-5pm Sun.

PURSUITS

A bit more bohemian and New Age-y than your average women's clothing store in Shadyside, Pursuits is a wonderfully eclectic boutique that carries way too many brands to mention. Don't expect big-name designer gear, but rather relaxed fashions, dresses, and more affordable indie labels. If you're going for a more effortless, bohemian-chic vibe, you'll find everything you need (and then some) at Pursuits, without breaking the bank. Candles and other accessories are also available.

MAP 5: 740 Filbert St., 412/688-8822, www.pursuitspittsburgh.com; 10:30am-5:30pm Mon.-Sat., noon-4pm Sun.

GIFT AND SPECIALTY
KARDS UNLIMITED

Hardly your average card store, this Shadyside favorite is more of a well-edited novelty shop that also carries an impressive stock of books, comics, graphic novels, posters, candles, T-shirts, wrapping papers, and unusual jewelry items, such as jewel-encrusted cigarette cases and lighters. Anyone looking for witty gifts from Knock Knock, stylish Blue Q products (for home and body), or yummy-smelling Yankee candles would do well to take a look, as Kards Unlimited's selection is the largest in town.

MAP 5: 5522 Walnut St., 412/622-0500, http://kardsunlimited.com; 9:30am-9pm Mon.-Sat., noon-5pm Sun.

KAWAII GIFTS

Shadyside's fantastic Kawaii Gifts (the store's name is Japanese for "cute") stocks the region's largest (and arguably only) selection of Japanese imports, including collectible vinyl toys, plushies, housewares, stationery, miniatures, and more. Stuffed floor to ceiling with toys and baubles in every color of the rainbow, Kawaii is a must-visit for fans of brands like San-X, Iwako, Momiji, and Ugly Dolls. The store can be easy to miss, as it's tucked away at the bottom of a small staircase off Walnut Street.

MAP 5: 5413-B Walnut St., 412/687-2480, www.shopkawaii.com; 11am-7pm Mon.-Sat., 11am-5pm Sun.

SCRIBE

Self-described as Pittsburgh's premiere paper boutique, Scribe is the perhaps the city's finest destination for all things communication related. It offers the most distinctive letterpress, stationery, and print design work from the likes of Gilah, Rifle Paper Company, Ink + Wit, Retro 1951, and others. Scribe's calligraphy and gift-wrapping services are extraordinary, and the boutique stocks a lovingly curated collection of journals, notebooks, greeting cards, and fine wrapping papers and ribbons. Unlike similar neighborhood stationery shops, Scribe's customer service is welcoming and unpretentious.

MAP 5: 731 1/2 Filbert St., 412/682-1644, www.scribepgh.com; noon-6pm Tues., 11am-7pm Wed., 11am-6pm Thurs.-Sat., Sun. seasonal

TOADFLAX

This gorgeous floral shop and gift boutique offers a true feast for the senses, thanks in large part to the bouquets of fine freshly cut flowers dotting the otherwise minimalist decor. Whether you're selecting a single lily or rose stem, or asking the shop to arrange a bouquet for that special someone, Toadflax does an exquisite job. The shop also stocks gift items, including fine candies and chocolates, richly scented premium candles, coffee-table books, and modern ceramic and blown-glass vases.

MAP 5: 5500 Walnut St., 412/621-2500, www.toadflax.com; 10am-5pm Mon.-Sat.

HOME DECOR AND FURNISHINGS
WEISS HOUSE

Carrying high-end furniture lines like B&B Italia, Cassini, and Ligne Roset, Weiss House employs a highly educated crew of interior designers who specialize in custom work, contemporary kitchen design, and residential renovations. The store has a large selection of carpeting, as well as exotic wood flooring materials. Recently added items include Asian antiques—all of them hand-selected and one of a kind. Weiss House also has home decor items and gifts, such as coffee-table books and candles.

MAP 5: 324 S. Highland Ave., 412/441-8888, www.weisshouse.com; 10am-6pm Mon.-Fri., 10am-5pm Sat.

SHOES
★ EMY MACK COLLECTIVE

Designer shoe addicts don't have to go to New York City to find luxury heels and boots, with the Emy Mack Collective located right on Filbert Street. Designer Emy Mack Jamison started the brand of luxury leather heels, flats, and boots in 2011, and the brand has taken off, appearing in Mercedes-Benz Fashion Week in NYC and on the feet of celebrities like Kerry Washington. Though prices are what you would expect for designer shoes, she also has a sale room with serious markdowns.

MAP 5: 723 Filbert St., 412/687-2666, www.emymack.com; 11am-5pm Tues.-Sat.

FOOTLOOSE

Footloose is a relatively small boutique specializing almost entirely in high-end women's designer lines from Italy, Spain, and France. You'll find a very well-chosen collection of pumps, platform stilettos, sandals, and boots, and prices accurately reflect their quality. Ladies with a fascination for sky-high heels, chunky platform wedges, and adorable ballet flats will likely find themselves in metaphorical footwear heaven. Footloose has been in Shadyside since 1987 and has built a very loyal following for good reason. Most shoes are priced $150-500.

MAP 5: 5411 Walnut St., 412/687-3663, www.footlooseshadyside.com; 10am-5:30pm Mon.-Tues. and Thurs.-Sat., 10am-7pm Wed., noon-5pm Sun.

TEN TOES

If you're looking for affordable shoes in Shadyside, Ten Toes has a trendy selection of women's shoes that you can't find in the major department

Clockwise from top left: Eons Fashion Antique; Emy Mack Collective; Highway Robbery.

stores. You might discover a great new pair of heels or fall boots for under $100—and the sales are great, too. The staff is friendly and knowledgeable.

MAP 5: 5502 Walnut St., 412/683-2082, 10am-7pm Mon.-Tues. and Thurs.-Sat., 10am-8pm Wed., 11:30am-5pm Sun.

VINTAGE AND ANTIQUES
EONS FASHION ANTIQUE

A great spot for men's and women's fashions from the "1880s through the 1980s," as the store's tagline suggests, Eons is possibly best known for its sidewalk mannequin, which is dressed daily by the store's owner, Richard Parsakian. The best finds are definitely dresses, costume jewelry, and hats, although there are also loads of very feminine pieces and some wonderful pants and shirts for guys.

MAP 5: 5850 Walnut St., 412/361-3368; noon-5pm Sun.-Fri., 11am-5pm Sat.

Squirrel Hill and Point Breeze

Map 6

ARTS AND CRAFTS
KNIT ONE

Simply put, Knit One is every knitter's paradise. A large and well-lit store decorated with woven area rugs, Knit One also offers the largest amount and widest variety of both yarns and knitting classes in the city. Even the inventory itself is artistic, displayed as it is in modular shelving that is cleverly attached to the shop's walls. Knit One's owner offers private lessons to help even the most impatient and distracted of aspiring crafters complete their own yarn-spun creations.

MAP 6: 2721 Murray Ave., 412/421-6666, www.knitone.biz; noon-8pm Tues.-Thurs., noon-5pm Fri. and Sun., 10am-5pm Sat.

BOOKS AND MUSIC
JERRY'S RECORDS

Vinyl enthusiasts have been known to travel from as far away as Japan to dig through the crates holding more than one million records at this Squirrel Hill institution, named by no less an authority than *Rolling Stone* magazine as one of the best record shops in the country. Turntables and accessories are also sold, and prices on all but the rarest of finds are surprisingly affordable.

MAP 6: 2136 Murray Ave., 412/421-4533, www.jerrysrecords.com; 10am-6pm Mon.-Sat., noon-5pm Sun.

CLOTHING AND ACCESSORIES
CAPRICCIO BOUTIQUE

One of the few boutiques in Squirrel Hill, Capriccio is an upscale women's boutique featuring designer duds and the price tags to match. Labels include names like Katherine Barclay, Joseph Ribkoff, and Samuel Dong. If

you follow their Facebook page, you'll be alerted to their generous sales, **169**
which they have quite often.

MAP 6: 5867 Forbes Ave., 412/422-4225, www.capriccioboutique.com; 10am-5:30pm
Mon., Wed., and Fri.-Sat., 10am-7pm Tues. and Thurs., noon-4pm Sun.

SHOES
LITTLE'S SHOES

While Pittsburgh today has more to offer the modern, stylish man than
ever before, there was a time when Little's was one of the city's few independently owned shops offering a large collection of well-chosen, casual
men's shoes. The shop is quite large, and on the many racks and shelves
you'll find everything from sneakers to formal styles. In the women's section, which is significantly larger than the men's section and offers much
trendier choices, you'll also find handbags and accessories.

MAP 6: 5850 Forbes Ave., 412/521-3530, www.littlesshoes.com; 9:30am-9pm Mon.-Sat.,
noon-5pm Sun.

SKATEBOARDING AND CYCLING
BIKETEK

In the heart of Squirrel Hill, Biketek is perhaps the city's most mainstream
cycling shop. With a vibe and interior design not unlike that of REI, Biketek
offers a wide range of expensive rides, along with a professional staff. Bike
repair and bike-fitting services are also available, along with cycling apparel and accessories.

MAP 6: 5842 Forbes Ave., 412/521-6448, www.biketek.com; 11am-7:30pm Mon.-Thurs.,
11am-5pm Fri.-Sat., noon-3pm Sun.

FREE RIDE

Staffed by the sort of cycling enthusiasts you'd expect to find leading a
Critical Mass rally, Free Ride is a recycle-a-bike shop where old and dis-
carded rides are given a new lease on life. The program works like this:
Bikes are donated to Free Ride in a generally sorry state of disrepair.
Volunteers spend hours in the shop bringing the bikes up to code. The
resulting mountain bikes, road bikes, and BMX bikes are then sold at affordable rates.

MAP 6: 214 N. Lexington St., 412/731-2474, www.freeridepgh.org; 1pm-5pm Sat.,
6pm-10pm Sun.

VINTAGE AND ANTIQUES
CONSTRUCTION JUNCTION

Though not technically a vintage or antiques shop per se, Construction
Junction is actually Pittsburgh's used building-materials supply warehouse,
an excellent place to find anything and everything for that home-improve-
ment project you're working on—everything, that is, from decorative doors
and windows to old toilets, filing cabinets, and plywood for a fraction of
the original retail price.

MAP 6: 214 N. Lexington St., 412/243-5025, www.constructionjunction.org; 9am-6pm
Mon.-Fri., 9am-5pm Sat., 10am-5pm Sun.

Bloomfield and East Liberty

Map 7

SHOPPING DISTRICTS AND CENTERS

BAKERY SQUARE

Located on a stretch of Penn Avenue in East Liberty that was once home to a bustling Nabisco plant, Bakery Square is a self-described "lifestyle center" and one of Pittsburgh's "it" places to work, shop, dine, and play. The facility is home to retail shops like West Elm, Coffee Tree Roasters, and Free People. Budding makers can find inspiration and assistance at TechShop, a popular community workshop space and prototyping studio.

MAP 7: 6425 Penn Ave., 412/683-3810, www.bakery-square.com; hours vary by merchant

EASTSIDE

Although it calls itself "a retail development connecting Shadyside and East Liberty," Eastside really isn't a cohesive shopping center in the traditional sense. It's an ever-expanding and constantly morphing collection of smaller retail shops and trendy restaurants that is quickly becoming a very pleasant place to shop and dine. Anchored by a Whole Foods Market (5880 Centre Ave.) on its southwest end and an enormous Target (6231 Penn Ave.) on its northeast end, Eastside also has a covered walkway attached to the upper level of the parking garage, making it possible to stroll over to Shadyside's Ellsworth Avenue business district, where art galleries and more bars and restaurants are located.

MAP 7: 5966 Penn Cir. S., 412/391-7171; hours vary by merchant

BOOKS AND MUSIC

THE BIG IDEA INFOSHOP

A volunteer-run bookshop specializing in leftist politics, queer issues, and other radical and alternative cultures, the Big Idea originally existed only as a small corner of a small room in the original Mr. Roboto Project in Wilkinsburg. Along with the standard collection of neo-anarchist lit, the shop also stocks a good selection of zines and other independent publications. Volunteers are always needed, and the store hosts numerous discussion groups. A small café sells coffee, tea, and vegan snacks.

MAP 7: 4812 Liberty Ave., 412/687-4323, www.thebigideapgh.org; 11am-9pm Mon. and Wed.-Fri., 11am-5pm Tues., 11am-7pm Sat.-Sun.

EAST END BOOK EXCHANGE

The East End Book Exchange (EEBX) started out as a pop-up shop. It's since grown into a fully respectable general interest store on Bloomfield's main drag, where it sells a great selection of mostly used titles—everything from fiction and history to travel and cooking—with some rare volumes thrown in for good measure. The EEBX buys books, but don't expect to unload your old romance novels; the shop is clearly curated by someone who knows their stuff.

MAP 7: 4754 Liberty Ave., 412/224-2847, www.eastendbookexchange.com; 11am-7pm Tues.-Sat., noon-4pm Sun.

CLOTHING AND ACCESSORIES
TRIM PITTSBURGH

Men who have been considering upgrading from department store boxers will find everything they need and more at TRIM Pittsburgh, an underwear and swimwear retailer just for men. The store features a wide selection of styles and brands from all over the world. This includes underwear, socks, swimwear, and shirts from emerging and established designers. Owner Thomas West brings brands like Parke & Ronen, Happy Socks, and Kevin Love to his Pittsburgh store.

MAP 7: 5968 Baum Blvd., 412/512-9251, www.trimpittsburgh.com; 11am-8pm Mon.-Fri., 11am-6pm Sat., noon-5pm Sun.

UPTOWN SWEATS

Owned by fashion designer Kiya Tomlin (if her name sounds familiar it's because she's married to Steelers football coach Mike Tomlin), Uptown Sweats is making a name for itself in the fashion world and in the closets of the women of Pittsburgh. She has taken the comfortable fabric of sweats and transformed it into flattering and stylish designs that you can wear at home, work, or out at a party. Tomlin's designs are sold at her East Liberty storefront, and she even offers free alterations.

MAP 7: 5983 Broad St., 412/361-2100, www.uptownsweats.com; 10am-5pm Tues.-Fri., 11am-4pm Sat.

SHOES
BEST-MADE SHOES

Aside from brands like Dansko and Alegria, you won't find the most fashion-forward shoes at Bloomfield's Best-Made. You will, however, find the city's best selection of comfort footwear, custom shoes, and orthotics, all being sold by board-certified pedorthists and master shoemakers. In addition to offering custom shoes and custom molded orthotic inserts, the family-owned Best-Made also provides the largest selection of Birkenstock shoes and orthotics in the area and stocks extra-large and wide width sizes.

MAP 7: 5143 Liberty Ave., 412/621-9363, www.bestmadeshoes.com; 10am-4pm Tues.-Sat.

SHOPPING DISTRICTS AND CENTERS
16:62 DESIGN ZONE

Officially starting in Pittsburgh's Strip District before reaching the Lawrenceville neighborhood, the 16:62 Design Zone is essentially Pittsburgh's arts, crafts, and interior design district. As such, it's overflowing with galleries, boutiques, and open studios. And as Lawrenceville has found itself home to some of the best independently owned and operated shops in the city (Wildcard, Pavement, and Who New? all come to mind), shopping in the 16:62 Design Zone has become a great way to support local artists. Numerous events are organized throughout the year, including the annual **Joy of Cookies Cookie Tour** (www.lvpgh.com/cookietour) and the hugely popular **Art All Night party** (www.artallnight.com), where guests enjoy a full 24 hours of art and music. Most area studios offer open houses, and tours are held throughout the year. Exhibit openings are generally timed with first Friday gallery crawls, during which local galleries and shops stay open late and offer complimentary snacks and drinks along with a bevy of special events and programming.

MAP 8: Between Penn Ave. and Butler St. from 16th St. to 62nd St., www.1662designzone. com; hours vary by merchant

ARTS AND CRAFTS
GALLERY ON 43RD STREET

Lifelong weaver Mary Coleman's shop is just off of the hustle and bustle of Lawrenceville's Butler Street. It features one-of-a-kind arts and crafts from throughout Western Pennsylvania. Coleman's impressive rugs, runners, and placemats can be seen throughout the gallery shop, and while you won't find the latest cutting-edge or controversial exhibit, you can always expect to find beautifully crafted and tasteful work in more traditional mediums, such as ceramics, pottery, and porcelain.

MAP 8: 187 43rd St., 412/683-6488, www.galleryon43rdstreet.com; 11am-6pm Thurs.-Sat.

BOOKS AND MUSIC
THE COPACETIC COMICS COMPANY

Much more than just a run-of-the-mill comic book shop, Copacetic is also home to one of the city's better collections of independent and self-published comics, books, and zines. It also stocks a huge library of classic lit (everything from Homer to Whitman), classic and obscure DVDs, and jazz and indie CDs. Regardless of its eclectic and well-edited inventory, though, the truth is that many of Copacetic's best customers stop by just for a chance to shoot the bull with owner Bill Boichel—a veritable encyclopedia of American pop culture and perhaps Pittsburgh's chattiest boutique owner.

MAP 8: 3138 Dobson St., 3rd Fl., 412/251-5451, www.copaceticcomics.com; 11am-5pm Mon.-Fri., 11am-7pm Sat., noon-5pm Sun.

Nine Stories is a small but well-curated bookstore featuring a selection of new and used reads. If you need a recommendation or just want to chat about all things literary, the owner is friendly and knowledgeable. The store frequently hosts events like book signings, releases, readings, and club meet-ups. There's also a Sunday morning story time for children. While you're there, make sure to browse their collection of unique gifts, like locally made candles, pins, and more.

MAP 8: 5400 Butler St., 412/347-8635, www.ninestoriespgh.com; 11am-7pm Tues.-Sat., 10am-5pm Sun.

CHILDREN'S CLOTHING AND TOYS
BRAMBLER BOUTIQUE

Brambler Boutique is not only the best place in Pittsburgh to go to for trendy, design-forward fashion for kids and babies, it's also a great resource for mothers, fathers, and parents-to-be. It has a great selection of baby supplies like innovative feeding tools, unique board books, and organic bath products. Plus, they know what it's like to shop with kids, so they provide snacks by request, coffee for the grownups, and a comfortable area to feed your baby.

MAP 8: 3609 Butler St., 412/682-1327, http://bramblerboutique.com; 11am-6pm Tues.-Fri., 10am-5pm Sat., 10am-3pm Sun.

CLOTHING AND ACCESSORIES
★ PAVEMENT

Pavement was a desperately needed and instantly adored addition to the city's shoe scene when it opened back in 2006, and even today this shop boasts a carefully and creatively curated assortment of designer shoes, as well as a complementary selection of clothing and hand-made accessories, jewelry, and gifts from designers and labels such as Ella Moss, Free People, Prairie Underground, and Alternative Apparel. Perhaps not surprisingly, the owners and staff are exceedingly knowledgeable and stylish.

MAP 8: 3629 Butler St., 412/621-6400, www.pavementpittsburgh.com; 11am-6pm Tues.-Sat., 11am-4pm Sun.

CALLIGRAMME

Women who hold their lingerie to a higher standard will love Calligramme's eco-friendly and U.S.-made offering of intimates and loungewear. Founder Marissa Vogel combines her love of responsible consumerism and romanticism by sourcing lingerie in a wide range of styles and sizes from mostly women-owned manufacturers. You can shop the racks at the Butler Street location or find an even wider selection on their website, which boasts the largest selection of U.S.-made lingerie anywhere.

MAP 8: 5417 Butler St., 412/621-3256, www.calligramme.com; 11am-7pm Wed.-Sat., 11am-4pm Sun.

GLITTER AND GRIT

The idea for Glitter and Grit was born when owner Erin Szymanski decided she wanted to give brides the opportunity to break with tradition and wear a wedding gown that reflects their personal style. Brides who don't want the cookie-cutter white dress and are looking for something more original will be delighted by Glitter and Grit's carefully curated selection of wedding gowns. This bridal boutique offers unique designs and individual attention that you won't find at the chain stores.

MAP 8: 5300 Butler St., 412/781-2375, www.glitterandgritpgh.com; by appointment only

KINSMAN

This boutique is exclusively a men's shop, featuring a carefully curated collection of high quality and rugged yet stylish clothing. The prices aren't exactly cheap, but you're paying for a wardrobe that's both on trend and durable. The store is located in an old barber shop that has been redesigned with a minimalist vibe.

MAP 8: 3818 Butler St., 412/204-7316, www.kinsmanshop.com; noon-6pm Wed.-Fri., noon-5pm Sat.-Sun.

MID-ATLANTIC MERCANTILE

This shop stocks sustainable and ethically created styles for both men and women and is hands-down the best source for raw Japanese denim in Pittsburgh. All the labels carried—Rogue Territory, Tellason, and Naked & Famous, to name just a few—are manufactured in small batches with the utmost attention paid to durability and detail. Owner Emily Slagel is nearly always on-site to offer a wealth of information about the shop's goods, and the spacious and naturally lighted fitting rooms ensure you won't wind up with buyer's remorse.

MAP 8: 4415 Butler St., 412/965-4095, www.midatlanticmercantile.com; 11am-6pm Tues.-Sat., noon-4pm Sun.

NO. 14

No. 14 was started by a mother-daughter duo with a love of fashion in 2014. They stock their boutique with on-trend fashions at reasonable prices and have frequent sales. Look for brands like Jack, BB Dakota, BCBGeneration, and Moon River.

MAP 8: 4601 Butler St., 412/260-6088, www.no14boutique.com; 11am-6pm Tues.-Sat., noon-4pm Sun.

VESTIS

Men looking for well-made basics like T-shirts, button-downs, and denim will appreciate the selection and brands offered at Vestis. The store focuses on ethically produced clothing that is made in America. Of course, you're going to pay more for higher quality goods, but Vestis focuses on durable clothing that is made to last decades rather than a season. You'll also find a nice selection of luggage, grooming supplies, and belts.

MAP 8: 5124 Butler St., 412/784-1112, www.vestispgh.com; 11am-7pm Tues.-Sat., noon-4pm Sun.

★ WILDCARD

With eye-popping colors and impressive inventory that includes greeting cards, stationery, wallets, jewelry, T-shirts, and tons more (much of it made by Pittsburgh crafters), Wildcard is part gift shop and part art gallery, all wrapped up in one handsomely designed little package. It's been a neighborhood staple since 2009, when it was opened by Rebecca Morris, a Pittsburgh native.

MAP 8: 4029 Butler St., 412/224-2651, www.wildcardpgh.com; 11am-7pm Mon.-Wed. and Sat., 11am-8pm Thurs.-Fri., 11am-5pm Sun.

CITY GROWS

If you're bummed out about a lack of yard space at home, City Grows has you covered. The Lawrenceville business considers itself an urban organic garden shop, where their plants and gardening supplies fit the specific needs and limited space of the urban dweller. You'll find organic plants, decorative succulents and air plants, and gardening containers that are just the right size for a windowsill or porch stoop. City Grows also holds occasional classes and events to help get your green thumb up to snuff.

MAP 8: 5208 Butler St., 412/781-2082, www.citygrowspgh.com; 11am-6pm Tues.-Wed. and Fri., 11am-8pm Thurs., 10am-6pm Sat., 11am-5pm Sun.

THE GILDED GIRL BEAUTY EMPORIUM

Beauty junkies will go wild for the incredible selection of luxury and indie beauty brands at the Gilded Girl. The products are hard to find anywhere else, especially in Pittsburgh. This is the place to go for small-batch and handcrafted goods as well as organic and vegan products. The store also offers bridal makeup services and makeup classes so you can put your favorite beauty finds to work.

MAP 8: 5104 Butler St., 412/450-0578, www.thegildedgirl.com; by appointment Mon., 1pm-6pm Wed.-Fri., 11am-6pm Sat., noon-5pm Sun.

HOME DECOR AND FURNISHINGS
ASIAN INFLUENCES

Each and every item in this Butler Street homage to the Far East has been personally selected by shop owner and interior designer Susan Fischer. Many of her antique and one-of-a-kind pieces were acquired during years of shopping and auction-going, both in the United States and abroad. Unique lamps and lighting fixtures are sold at Asian Influences, which is also something of a paradise for those who love containers like baskets, boxes, and tins.

MAP 8: 3513 Butler St., 412/621-3530, www.asianinfluences.com; 11am-6pm Wed.-Fri., 11am-5pm Sat.

VON WALTER AND FUNK

Store owners and partners Jamie McAdams and Shawn Aversa drew upon their international travels and family influences to bring unique luxury gifts and goods to their Pittsburgh storefront, which they named for their

respective maternal grandmothers. This is the kind of place you go to to find a gift for the person who has everything. You'll find things like luxury Japanese towels, Muhle shaving kits, designer wallpaper, and metal jewelry.
MAP 8: 5210 Butler St., 412/784-0800, www.vonwalterandfunk.com; noon-6pm Tues.-Fri., 10am-6pm Sat., 10am-4pm Sun.

VINTAGE AND ANTIQUES
THRIFTIQUE
Thriftique comes from the National Council of Jewish Women in Pittsburgh. You can shop the store's selection of clothing, furniture, housewares, and home decor while knowing that your purchase will be helping to support area women, children, and families. Donations are graciously accepted, and the store is always looking for volunteers.
MAP 8: 125 51st St., 412/742-4951, http://www.ncjwthriftique.com; 10am-6pm Mon.-Wed. and Fri., 10am-8pm Thurs., 9am-6pm Sat.

TOLL GATE REVIVAL
Self-described as "Rust Belt vagabonds," the people at Toll Gate Revival specialize in finding American vintage decor, repurposed furniture, and reclaimed materials for your home. They hunt down their treasures in abandoned steel mills, barns, and warehouses. Their Lawrenceville showroom is jam packed with vintage trunks, metal signs, well-loved leather furniture, and much more.
MAP 8: 3711 Butler St., 724/288-6618, www.kinsmanshop.com; 1pm-7pm Wed.-Fri., 11am-5pm Sat., 11am-3pm Sun.

WHO NEW?
Easily the best place in Pittsburgh for midcentury decor, Who New? is owned and operated by two men who could best be described as 20th-century design encyclopedias. The shop carries a wide-ranging selection of retro home furnishings, the vast majority from the 1950s through the '70s, including an incredible selection of vintage barware and kitchen items.
MAP 8: 5156 Butler St., 412/781-0588; noon-6pm Wed.-Sat., also by appointment

Greater Pittsburgh Map 9

SHOPPING DISTRICTS AND CENTERS
THE GALLERIA OF MT. LEBANON

An upscale if slightly small indoor shopping mall deep in the South Hills, the Galleria is home to treasured retailers, many of which have no other locations in the city. To name just a few, you'll find Anthropologie, Pottery Barn Kids, Janie and Jack, Godiva Chocolatier, and Restoration Hardware, as well as a movie theater and a decent food court. As far as malls go, the Galleria is almost never terribly noisy or crowded, with the exception of the holiday shopping season, of course.

MAP 9: 1500 Washington Rd., Pittsburgh, 412/561-4000, www.galleriapgh.com; 10am-9pm Mon.-Sat., noon-5pm Sun.

THE WATERFRONT

Perched along the Monongahela River in between Squirrel Hill and Munhall, The Waterfront is an enormous outdoor shopping center on the former site of U.S. Steel's Homestead Steel Works plant. Roughly a dozen of the mill's smoke stacks were preserved; they can be seen and even touched at the complex's southwest corner, next to a LongHorn Steakhouse restaurant on 5th Avenue. You'll find just about everything you'd expect in a traditional suburban shopping center, including multiple specialty stores, dozens of eateries, a grocery store, and chains like Macys, Barnes & Noble, Target, and Starbucks. Travelers can stay overnight at The Waterfront, as three different hotel chains have locations here.

MAP 9: 149 W. Bridge St., Homestead, 412/476-9157, www.waterfrontpgh.com; 10am-9pm Mon.-Sat., 11am-6pm Sun.

BOOKS AND MUSIC
ARKHAM GIFT SHOPPE

The owner of Arkham had two decades of retail comic store experience before branching out on his own to open this store. This is a true comic-lover's dream store, where offerings include everything from action figures and T-shirts to graphic novels and both new and old comic titles. Naturally, a comic subscription service is available for hard-core collectors. And Arkham is a wonderful place to simply hang out and chew the fat with the shopkeepers. A few miles west of Hartwood Acres Park, Arkham is a bit of a hike from downtown, but it's definitely worth the drive.

MAP 9: 3973 Rte. 8 (Wm. Flynn Hwy.), Allison Park, 412/486-3140, www. arkhamgiftshoppe.com; noon-8pm Wed., 1pm-8pm Thurs.-Fri., noon-7pm Sat., noon-5pm Sun.

MYSTERY LOVERS BOOKSHOP

This Raven Award-winning shop just a few miles east of the city has been an Oakmont community staple since first opening its doors in 1990, and it has welcomed numerous touring mystery writers over the years. One of the largest specialty mystery book shops in the country, Mystery Lovers is also known for hosting several book clubs and for regularly offering intimate catered dinners with popular authors. Various readings, lectures, and workshops take place throughout the year.

MAP 9: 514 Allegheny River Blvd., Oakmont, 412/828-4877, www.mysterylovers.com; 10am-5pm Mon.-Sat., 11am-2pm Sun.

CLOTHING AND ACCESSORIES
RAGGED ROW

Owned by a pair of Pittsburgh sisters, Ragged Row stocks contemporary designer brands and also specializes in activewear fashion lines like Alo Yoga, P.E. Nation, and Varley. You'll also find go-to favorites like Citizens of Humanity, Rag & Bone, and Velvet. Their boutique is located in the village-like well-to-do Sewickley, just a few miles northwest of the city. They also have a second location at Bakery Square in East Liberty.

MAP 9: 439 Beaver St., Sewickley, 412/441-1730, www.pavementpittsburgh.com; 10am-5pm Tues.-Fri., 10am-4pm Sat.

HOME DECOR AND FURNISHINGS
FRESH HEIRLOOMS

Fresh Heirlooms offers handmade items created from reclaimed and repurposed materials. Most products are designed and made in-house by the shop's owner and her family, all of whom are skilled craftspeople committed to making high-quality products that will stand the test of time. While it's located outside the city in New Kensington, the shop and the classes and workshops they host are well worth the trip.

MAP 9: 887 5th Ave., New Kensington, 412/512-5098, www.freshheirlooms.com; 10am-2pm Thurs.-Sun.

Hotels

Highlights

★ **Best Urban Bed-and-Breakfast:** In a unique section of the North Side, **The Inn on the Mexican War Streets** is a beautifully restored inn with a gay-friendly vibe (page 182).

★ **Most Historic Boutique Hotel:** Originally a Benedictine monastery, **The Priory** is full of historical details and modern luxuries (page 182).

★ **Best Luxury Hotel:** The **Fairmont Pittsburgh** is the opulent choice—and the place to spot celebrities and sports figures visiting the city (page 184).

★ **Best Design:** If you prefer bold design rather than the neutral palette typical of most hotel chains, the **Kimpton Hotel Monaco Pittsburgh** will delight you with its quirky details and pops of color (page 184).

★ **Best View:** To see the spectacular skyline right from your room, stay across the river at the **Sheraton Hotel Station Square** and take in the sparkling city lights from a giant picture window (page 189).

★ **Best Renovation:** The lavish **Mansions on Fifth** is the historical home of Henry Clay Frick's attorney. It's listed on the National Register of Historic Places and features both an art gallery and a wine cellar (page 191).

★ **Hippest Hotel:** Built inside an old YMCA, the **Ace Hotel Pittsburgh** features midcentury finishes and a trendy restaurant—all near the active arts scene of the eastern side of town (page 192).

PRICE KEY

💲 Less than $100 per night

💲💲 $100–200 per night

💲💲💲 More than $200 per night

Y ou'll almost never have a difficult time finding a place to stay in Pittsburgh. In fact, recent years have brought on a lodging boom, with developers adding new, hip hotels at a furious pace.

As some of the city's grittier areas like East Liberty are gentrifying, new hotels are cropping up in neighborhoods that visitors might not have previously thought to stay in. However, the developers may have been a little overzealous. The hotel boom has left Pittsburgh with more rooms than it can fill and the market has been oversaturated. This is not great news for hotel owners, but it is does mean lower room rates for travelers. It's possible to stay in a luxury hotel here for less than it would cost to stay at a budget motel in a big city.

CHOOSING A HOTEL

Some travelers prefer the large corporate **chain hotels** due to their predictability and consistency, and there's nothing wrong with that. Pittsburgh certainly has a huge variety of these, whether you prefer Marriott, Wyndham, or Hyatt. If you prefer something more unique, several **boutique hotels** will fit that bill. Kimpton Hotel Monaco Pittsburgh features trendy colorful and quirky modern decor that you won't find in most hotel chains. Hotel Indigo in East Liberty seems like an independently owned boutique hotel but is owned by the same group as Hampton Inn. And then there's the popular Ace Hotel with its hip design, located inside a historical YMCA building.

Pittsburgh also has its share of privately owned **bed-and-breakfasts** and **inns,** ranging in price and quality. The city's rich history means the area is rich with historical homes and buildings that have since been

Previous: Renaissance Pittsburgh Hotel; Mansions on Fifth.

restored. It's possible to spend a night in the home of an old bank at Drury Plaza Hotel or a former Benedictine monastery at The Priory.

Of course, many visitors pick where they're going to stay depending on neighborhood. There are plenty of places to stay **downtown,** whether you want all-out luxury at the Fairmont Pittsburgh or more of a budget stay (but comfortable) at the Pittsburgh Marriott City Center.

For more information on hotels and other accommodations, check out **Visit PA** (http://visitpa.com), Pennsylvania's official tourism site, or **VisitPittsburgh** (www.visitpittsburgh.com), the official tourism agency for Allegheny County. Another option, to truly feel like a local, is to check out the Pittsburgh homes available on **Airbnb** (www.airbnb.com). You'll find options ranging from cool downtown lofts to budget apartment accommodations.

All the rates in this guide are based on the average cost of a double occupancy king room in the summer, Pittsburgh's high season.

North Side   Map 1

★ THE INN ON THE MEXICAN WAR STREETS ❸❸

Of the few bed-and-breakfasts in Pittsburgh, The Inn on the Mexican War Streets is arguably the best. The Mexican War Streets section of the North Side is a few streets of beautifully restored historical homes and the inn is no exception. The inn is the renovated former home of a department store owner, Russell H. Boggs. There are eight rooms to choose from, each with elegant decor and different amenities. The inn also has a private restaurant for guests only as well as a library bar. This bed-and-breakfast is gay-owned (though currently up for sale, as the owners are retiring) and very gay-friendly, but of course everyone is welcome!

MAP 1: 604 W. North Ave., 412/231-6544, www.innonthemexicanwarstreets.com

★ THE PRIORY ❸❸

The Priory is a gorgeously restored historical boutique hotel located in the Deutschtown area of the North Side. Once a Benedictine monastery, the hotel retains a lot of the historical charm while adding modern amenities you might expect from a luxury hotel. Relax with a drink at the Monk's Bar or settle into one of the 40-some guest rooms, filled with antiques, vintage reproductions, and exquisite woodwork. The Priory, with its Grand Hall, is also a popular place for events, especially weddings. Guests can relax in the beautiful courtyard. Amenities include a fitness center and a business center.

MAP 1: 614 Pressley St., 412/231-3338, www.thepriory.com

HYATT PLACE PITTSBURGH NORTH SHORE ❸❸

If you're in town for a ball game, the seven-floor, 178-room Hyatt Place Pittsburgh North Shore is conveniently located right next to PNC Park and within walking distance of Heinz Field. The lobby and rooms have a

Top: The Inn on the Mexican War Streets. **Bottom:** The Priory.

sleek and modern yet comfortable design. The rooms also feature sitting areas with either a sofa or sofa-bed and separated sleeping quarters. The free breakfast goes beyond the typical hotel breakfast buffet—think cage-free eggs, tomato bruschetta, and roasted parmesan potatoes. You can also order meals from the 24/7 gourmet room service menu.

MAP 1: 260 North Shore Dr., 412/321-3000, http://pittsburghnorthshore.place.hyatt.com

THE PARADOR $$

A lovely bed-and-breakfast in the North Side, The Parador has a distinctly tropical vibe, inspired by the owners' love of Florida. The house was built in 1870 and was known as the Rhodes Mansion. The nine rooms' decor and furniture stay true to the historical appeal of the inn, but Caribbean decor and lush colors set it apart from other B&Bs. Each room features a full private bath, gas fireplace, central air, cable television, and other standard hotel amenities. A full breakfast is served each morning, and there are plenty of communal areas and lounges to make friends with other guests. There's also a beautiful garden filled with tropical plants.

MAP 1: 939 Western Ave., 412/231-4800 or 888/540-1443, www.theparadorinn.com

RESIDENCE INN NORTH SHORE $$

The Residence Inn on the North Shore is convenient whether you're staying for one night or an extended trip. It's close to all the popular North Shore destinations, like Heinz Field, PNC Park, and Stage AE. Downtown is just a quick ride or walk across the Roberto Clemente Bridge. The 180 suites feature full kitchens, living rooms, and dining areas. The comfortable and spacious rooms have a modern decor, making you feel at home no matter how long your stay. On-site parking is an additional $25 per day.

MAP 1: 574 W. General Robinson St., 412/321-2099 or 800/228-9290, www.marriott.com/pitrn

Downtown

Map 2

★ FAIRMONT PITTSBURGH $$$

When celebrities are in town filming a movie or performing a concert, they often stay at the Fairmont, located in the Cultural District. The sleek interior is a shout-out to Pittsburgh's history, featuring steel and glass accents and local artwork. The Fairmont, one of Pittsburgh's top luxury hotels, boasts Gold level LEED certification. The 185 rooms are what you would expect from a luxury hotel: modern design, lush linens, and top-notch technology.

MAP 2: 510 Market St., 412/773-8800 or 888/270-6647, www.fairmont.com/pittsburgh

★ KIMPTON HOTEL MONACO PITTSBURGH $$

The international Kimpton Hotel brand is known for its boldly designed boutique hotels that stand apart. Kimpton Hotel Monaco Pittsburgh, housed in the Beaux Arts-style James H. Reed building in the Cultural

District, is full of unexpected touches and bold design elements that will make anyone's stay memorable. Whimsical details like birdcage chandeliers, turquoise doors, and tufted kelly-green headboards appeal to travelers with an eye for design. The hotel also features bonus amenities, like luxury bath soaps, daily evening wine hours, and even yoga mats in every one of the nearly 250 rooms.

MAP 2: 620 William Penn Place, 412/471-1170 (hotel) or 855/338-3837 (reservations), www.monaco-pittsburgh.com

COURTYARD BY MARRIOTT PITTSBURGH DOWNTOWN ⑤⑤

If you like the predictability of a chain hotel but also appreciate the charm of a historic building, the Courtyard in downtown is a perfect compromise. This Marriott brand hotel is right in the Cultural District and close to the convention center, so whether you're in town for business or pleasure, you're close to some of the best restaurants, bars, and entertainment in the city. The nine-floor hotel is housed inside four renovated historical buildings but still provides top-notch comfort and modern amenities in its 172 rooms and 10 suites.

MAP 2: 945 Penn Ave., 412/434-5551, www.marriott.com/pitcy

DRURY PLAZA HOTEL PITTSBURGH DOWNTOWN ⑤⑤

One of downtown's newest lodging options is the Drury Plaza Hotel, right in the heart of the city in the historic Federal Reserve Bank building. The hotel, which opened in 2017, features an art-deco style and has more than 200 comfortable and modern rooms on its 12 floors. Many of the original features of the federal building have been integrated into the hotel's design: The vaults have been converted into meeting rooms, and a former firing range (used for training the Federal Reserve Bank's guards) is now an indoor pool. The Drury brand is known for its extras, like the free "5:30 Kickback" happy hour with complimentary hot food and cocktails.

MAP 2: 745 Grant St., 412/281-2900, www.druryhotels.com

OMNI WILLIAM PENN HOTEL ⑤⑤

Since opening in 1916, the 17-story, 596-room Omni William Penn had been the premier luxury downtown hotel in Pittsburgh until the Fairmont Pittsburgh came onto the scene in 2010. Even still, the opulent decor (think a grand lobby decorated with lush silk curtains, chandeliers, tufted couches, and gold accents) makes a stay here feel like you're stepping back in history. And speaking of history, this hotel has a rich one, with a guest log of movie stars, politicians, and heads of state in its century-plus run. The rooms are modern and feature luxurious touches like crown molding and plush furniture. Even if you're not staying here, don't miss a chance to walk through the impressive lobby, as many downtown workers do during the day.

MAP 2: 530 William Penn Pl., 412/281-7100 (hotel) or 888/444-6664 (reservations), www.omnihotels.com/pittsburgh

Clockwise from top left: Fairmont Pittsburgh; Renaissance Fulton Pittsburgh Downtown Hotel; the trendy Kimpton Hotel Monaco Pittsburgh.

PITTSBURGH MARRIOTT CITY CENTER 💲💲

The Pittsburgh Marriott City Center is a good option for those attending a hockey game, concert, or other event at the PPG Paints Arena, due to its proximity. The 11-floor hotel features 400 spacious rooms, luxury linens, marble bathrooms, and up-to-date technology. You might even catch a glimpse of your favorite star, as many performers crash here after shows at the arena. The hotel also has a fitness center and indoor pool.

MAP 2: 112 Washington Pl., 412/471-4000 or 888/456-6600, www.marriott.com/pitdt

RENAISSANCE FULTON PITTSBURGH DOWNTOWN HOTEL 💲💲

The Renaissance, though owned by Marriott, has the distinct vibe of a historical hotel and is one of the few places to stay downtown that don't have a cookie cutter feel. Housed in the Fulton Building in the Cultural District, the hotel mixes historical architecture with sleek modern design, giving visitors a truly luxurious experience. The 296 rooms of this 14-floor hotel are decorated in a chic urban style, with cool features like Pittsburgh-themed artwork and custom-designed duvets. The gorgeous courtyard of the hotel is a popular place for photography shoots, and you'll often see wedding parties posing underneath the copper rotunda.

MAP 2: 107 6th St., 412/562-1200, www.renaissancepittsburghpa.com

WESTIN CONVENTION CENTER PITTSBURGH 💲💲

If you're in town for an event at the convention center, the 26-floor Westin is the obvious place to stay. Guests don't even have to step outside to enter the convention center, as an enclosed skywalk connects the two buildings (ideal during Pittsburgh's unpredictable winters). The hotel's 616 rooms are simply and elegantly decorated with neutral colors and crisp white linens. The hotel includes a large fitness center, sauna, lap pool, and fitness class offerings. Inside the building is gourmet burger spot **Bill's Bar & Burger.**

MAP 2: 1000 Penn Ave., 412/281-3700 or 888/627-7053, www.westinpittsburgh.com

WYNDHAM GRAND PITTSBURGH DOWNTOWN 💲💲

The Wyndham Grand affords a stunning view of Point State Park and Pittsburgh's three rivers. The modern rooms are decorated in neutral colors and feature pillow-top mattresses, complimentary wireless Internet, and designer toiletries. This is one of the largest hotels in the city and is within walking distance of both downtown attractions and North Shore destinations. Be sure to specify when you make your reservation if you want a room with a view of the rivers.

MAP 2: 600 Commonwealth Pl., 412/391-4600 or 866/238-4218, www.wyndham.com/pittsburgh

CAMBRIA SUITES PITTSBURGH AT PPG PAINTS ARENA 💲

Adjacent to PPG Paints Arena, Cambria Suites is the official hotel of the Pittsburgh Penguins and has an ideal location if you're in town for a hockey game or other big event at the arena. The all-suites hotel features nearly 150 spacious and luxurious rooms with modern amenities like luxury linens and up-to-date technology. Other bonuses include indoor and outdoor lounge areas, a bistro-style restaurant, a fitness center, and a pool.

MAP 2: 1320 Centre Ave., 412/381-6687, www.cambriasuitespittsburgh.com

Oakland

Map 3

HILTON GARDEN INN PITTSBURGH UNIVERSITY PLACE 💲💲

Located right on Forbes Avenue, the 13-story Hilton Garden Inn Pittsburgh University Place is in the ideal spot if you're visiting the University of Pittsburgh—or any part of the city, really. The 202 spacious, up-to-date rooms come with microwaves, refrigerators, Keurig coffeemakers, premium linens, and free Wi-Fi. Parking is an extra $20, but the hotel provides free shuttle service within a three-mile radius.

MAP 3: 3454 Forbes Ave., 412/683-2040, www.hiltongardeninn.hilton.com

HAMPTON INN UNIVERSITY CENTER 💲

If you're visiting one of Oakland's universities, the Hampton Inn University Center is conveniently located in South Oakland. The hotel includes Hampton Inn's usual amenities, like up-to-date decor in its 130-plus rooms, crisp linens, free Wi-Fi, a complimentary hot breakfast, and a fitness center. A free shuttle service will take you anywhere within a three-mile radius of the hotel. Its location can be hard to find, so out-of-town guests may want to plug the address into a GPS.

MAP 3: 3315 Hamlet St., 412/329-4969, http://hamptoninn.hilton.com

RESIDENCE INN PITTSBURGH UNIVERSITY/MEDICAL CENTER 💲

The Residence Inn is Marriott's extended-stay hotel, but it's also a great option if you're only staying for a night or two. The hotel is located on Bigelow Boulevard and is one of the few places to stay close to North Oakland. Choose from a studio, a one-bedroom suite, or a two-bedroom suite. Amenities include free breakfast, a kitchenette, and pet-friendly rooms. There's also a complimentary shuttle to help you get around Oakland. As with most Oakland hotels, parking is extra and will run you $15 a day.

MAP 3: 3896 Bigelow Blvd., 412/621-2200 or 800/513-8766, www.residenceinn. marriott.com

WYNDHAM PITTSBURGH UNIVERSITY CENTER 💲

The Wyndham Pittsburgh University Center is on a side street across 5th Avenue from the University of Pittsburgh Campus Center. This out-of-the-way location gets you within walking distance of Pitt and Carnegie Mellon (and very close to the stunning Cathedral of Learning) but will still keep you mostly out of the way of partying college students. The hotel has 251 guest rooms that feature contemporary decor, gourmet coffee, and

luxury bath products. The Wyndham also offers free Wi-Fi, an indoor pool
and fitness center, a casual restaurant, and complimentary shuttle service.
MAP 3: 100 Lytton Ave., 412/682-6200, www.wyndham.com

South Side

Map 4

★ SHERATON HOTEL STATION SQUARE ⓢⓢ

If you want an amazing view of the city skyline, the 15-story Sheraton Hotel
Station Square is one of the best spots to stay in town. Its location in Station
Square is directly across the Monongahela River from downtown, accessible
via a walk across the Smithfield Street Bridge. You'll also have access to the
Monongahela Incline and Mount Washington, and you're only minutes
away from the South Side and East Carson Street. The 399 rooms are clean
and modern. Amenities include a fitness room, pool, restaurant, and bar.
MAP 4: 300 W. Station Square Dr., 412/261-2000, www.sheratonstationsquare.com

HOLIDAY INN EXPRESS HOTEL & SUITES ⓢⓢ

If you want to stay at the Holiday Inn Express Hotel & Suites in the South
Side, make your reservations early. With only 125 rooms across six floors,
this place books up quickly, especially during special events like football
games and the St. Patrick's Day parade. The hotel is fine; its popularity is
due to its great location. It's within walking distance of the East Carson
Street bars and restaurants but also close to SouthSide Works. The hotel
is clean and modern, with amenities like free Wi-Fi and a free shuttle that
will take you around town. Parking is $18 per day.
MAP 4: 20 S. 10th St., 412/488-1130, www.hiexpress.com/pittsburghpa

HYATT HOUSE PITTSBURGH SOUTH SIDE ⓢⓢ

The five-floor Hyatt House in the South Side is an extended-stay hotel with
an amazing location and even better amenities. Right in the SouthSide
Works shopping and entertainment district, the 136 roomy and modern
suites will make you feel right at home. Though you can always stay for just
a night or two, extra amenities (like an outdoor grilling area with a view of
the Monongahela River) make this hotel a perfect choice for longer term
guests. Other amenities include a free breakfast buffet, an indoor pool, free
Wi-Fi, and even a complimentary grocery shopping service.
MAP 4: 2795 S. Water St., 412/390-2477, www.pittsburghsouthside.house.hyatt.com

MORNING GLORY INN ⓢⓢ

For a change of pace from chain hotels, the Morning Glory Inn is a sweet
and cozy bed-and-breakfast in the heart of the South Side. This Victorian
townhouse was built in the 1860s and features Italianate decor and five
uniquely decorated guest rooms. You'll find traditional touches like fireplaces and claw-foot tubs, as well as modern amenities. Guests enjoy a
gourmet cooked breakfast each morning. The Morning Glory Inn is also
very popular for weddings. (Fun fact: The home's builder constructed an

Staying Green in Pittsburgh

It may come as a surprise to some that Pittsburgh, the city that was once so affected by pollution from the steel industry, is at the forefront of sustainability and green initiatives. The city has several organizations that push for better energy efficiency, such as the Western Pennsylvania Energy Consortium, the Green Building Alliance (which helps building owners cut energy usage), and Sustainable Pittsburgh (who push for sustainable practices by businesses and government).

For visitors who wish to limit their carbon footprint, Pittsburgh has several accommodations that are taking sustainability seriously. Though many hotel brands have integrated some green practices into their day-to-day operations, like encouraging guests to reuse towels, the places listed here have gone above and beyond.

Fairmont Pittsburgh

One of Pittsburgh's newest luxury hotels, located right smack in the middle of downtown, the Fairmont Pittsburgh stands apart from the pack with Gold level LEED (Leadership in Energy and Environmental Design) certification. This is the city's first LEED-certified hotel. Through building practices and operating initiatives, the Fairmont has demonstrated dedication to reducing energy usage and waste. During construction, 99 percent of the waste created was diverted from landfills and recycled for use in other projects. The hotel also employed energy-efficient lighting, like LED and CFL bulbs; reduced water consumption with low-flow toilets and aerators; improved indoor air quality with low-VOC paints, carpeting, and other materials; and also used as much green building materials as possible, from organic bedding to wood flooring from sustainably harvested forests. In day-to-day operations they use low-toxicity cleaning products, encourage guests to recycle, and recycle fryer oil into biodiesel.

Kimpton Hotel Monaco Pittsburgh

You don't have to sacrifice style to stay at an environmentally friendly hotel.

underground brick-walled room connected to the house by a tunnel. It's thought that this may have been intended for use as a safe house on the Underground Railroad.)

MAP 4: 2119 Sarah St., 412/431-1707, www.gloryinn.com

SPRINGHILL SUITES PITTSBURGH SOUTHSIDE WORKS ⑤⑤

The SpringHill Suites in SouthSide Works is an all-suites hotel right in the center of the popular SouthSide Works, a modern shopping, dining, and entertainment district. It's also within walking distance of the (much rowdier) East Carson Street bars and restaurants. The six-story hotel has a modern design and decor that makes it feel more like a boutique hotel. Each of the 115 suites has its own microwave, fridge, and wet bar. There's also free Wi-Fi and a fitness center.

MAP 4: 2950 S. Water St., 412/488-8003, www.springhillsuites.marriott.com

The notably trendy Kimpton Hotel Monaco Pittsburgh downtown is mostly known for its bold design, quirky decor touches, and boutique hotel feel. But the Kimpton brand doesn't mess around when it comes to keeping it green. Kimpton was the first hotel brand to become 100 percent certified by the Green Key Eco-Rating Program. It's also won a slew of awards, like the National Geographic Geo Tourism Award and Condé Nast World Savers Award. Besides having many LEED-certified hotels (Pittsburgh isn't one of them, but they still participate in many of the brand's green initiatives), Kimpton keeps their hotels eco-friendly by using non-toxic cleaners, extensively recycling, and minimizing water consumption. They have partnered with the Clean the World program to collect soap and hygiene products to be recycled and distributed to impoverished people throughout the world. The program helps prevent disease and improve hygiene education globally.

Hyatt House Pittsburgh South Side

Another LEED-certified hotel can be found in the city's bustling South Side neighborhood. Besides providing a stylish and comfortable place to stay near tons of restaurants, bars and shops, the Hyatt House Pittsburgh South Side is a LEED-certified Silver level hotel. This hotel brand also has its own green initiative, called Hyatt Thrive. It's a corporate responsibility program that ensures the brand does all it can to be environmentally responsible, among other goals. Their 2020 Environmental Sustainability Program aims to reduce energy, emissions, and water usage. They divert waste by recycling old materials when renovating hotels, and their goal is to divert 40 percent of each hotel's waste from landfills by the year 2020. They follow enhanced sustainable design guidelines for all new hotels and aim to achieve LEED certification for most of their hotels in the future. The hotel brand has also enacted procedures to reduce food waste, use suppliers with sustainability practices in place, and source only sustainable seafood for their restaurants.

Shadyside

Map 5

★ MANSIONS ON FIFTH ⑤⑤⑤

This luxury hotel, located right on 5th Avenue in Shadyside, is one of the most elegant lodging options in Pittsburgh. The grand mansion was once the home of a powerful Pittsburgh lawyer, Willis F. McCook. The hotel features 22 historical rooms ranging in price and grandeur. The hotel also boasts an art gallery, a wine cellar, and a beautiful veranda. They offer frequent events, with musical performances often taking place in the Oak Room Pub. There's also a shuttle service.

MAP 5: 5105 5th Ave., 412/381-5105, www.mansionsonfifth.com

THE INN ON NEGLEY $$

The Inn on Negley describes itself as having "the charm of a bed and break-fast with the comfort of a luxury hotel." This description is spot on, as the inn is a beautifully restored 19th-century house with eight guest rooms that are decorated with period furnishings. They come with private luxury baths, free Wi-Fi, Bose radios, and cable television. Upscale amenities like L'Occitane bath products and plush robes set the inn apart from the competition. Guests also receive a custom gourmet breakfast cooked by the inn's professional chef, plus wine and cheese in the evening.

MAP 5: 714 S. Negley Ave., 412/661-0631, www.innonnegley.com

THE MANSION AT MAPLE HEIGHTS $$

The Mansion at Maple Heights is a 1903 English manor house and the former home of Ted Berger, who was a prominent Pittsburgh businessman. The house features rich wood details, a grand staircase, and stained-glass windows. The six suites are a bit more modern and spacious than other historical bed-and-breakfasts in the city, and some of them have amenities like Jacuzzi tubs and separate living areas (there's even a steam room in the Executive Suite). The Mansion at Maple Heights is also a popular location for weddings and events.

MAP 5: 5516 Maple Heights Rd., 412/586-7940, www.shadysidemansion.com

SHADYSIDE INN ALL SUITES HOTEL $$

This four-story all-suites hotel looks like a modest apartment building from the outside. But inside are 106 clean and modern suites, many with hardwood floors, full kitchens, and living areas. There's even free on-site parking. Amenities include charging stations, pillow-top mattresses, free Wi-Fi, laundry facilities, and bike rentals. Some of the suites are even pet friendly.

MAP 5: 5405 5th Ave., 412/441-4444, www.shadysideinn.com

Bloomfield and East Liberty

Map 7

★ ACE HOTEL PITTSBURGH $$

The Ace Hotel brand has a philosophy of creating a community within its hotels. This is certainly true of its five-story, 63-room Pittsburgh location, which is housed in a century-old former YMCA and hosts events like dodgeball games and concerts in its 4,500-square-foot gymnasium. Choose between four room types: small, medium, large, and suite. The rooms and public spaces have a decidedly hip, midcentury minimalist appeal. All rooms come with flat-screen televisions, a stocked minibar, free Wi-Fi, and designer bath products. The hotel also has a lobby bar, coffee bar, and a popular restaurant, Whitfield.

MAP 7: 120 S. Whitfield St., 412/361-3300, www.acehotel.com/pittsburgh

Clockwise from top left: The Inn on Negley; the Ace Hotel; the Mansions on Fifth.

COURTYARD PITTSBURGH SHADYSIDE ❸❸

This member of the Courtyard Marriott chain claims to be in Shadyside, but its Liberty Avenue address places it in Bloomfield. Nevertheless, the six-story, 126-room hotel is conveniently located on the border of Shadyside and Bloomfield, close to Oakland's universities. The guest rooms are your standard fare and are clean and modern. The hotel features free Wi-Fi, a fitness center, indoor pool, and meeting spaces. Room service is available in the evening, and a free hot breakfast is included with your stay.

MAP 7: 5308 Liberty Ave., 412/683-3113, www.courtyardshadyside.com

SPRINGHILL SUITES PITTSBURGH BAKERY SQUARE ❸❸

Located in the middle of the Bakery Square area of East Liberty, this six-floor, 110-room hotel is within easy walking distance of upscale shops and great restaurants. It's also near the restaurants, art galleries, and shops of East Liberty and Shadyside. This all-suites hotel offers plush linens, clean and modern rooms, and all the amenities you expect from the Marriott brand.

MAP 7: 134 Bakery Square Blvd., 412/362-8600, www.springhillsuites.marriott.com

HOTEL INDIGO PITTSBURGH EAST LIBERTY ❸

Though the Indigo brand is owned by the same group as Hampton Inn and Holiday Inn, this six-story hotel's common spaces and 135 rooms have a hip, boutique feel that sets them apart from the big-name chain hotels. Guests will enjoy spa-like bathrooms, plush linens, and Wi-Fi. The hotel's restaurant, Wallace's TapRoom, features tavern-style dining with a nod to the Prohibition era. Hotel Indigo is conveniently located near the restaurants, bars, and art museums in East Liberty and nearby Shadyside and Oakland.

MAP 7: 123 N. Highland Ave., 412/665-0555, www.ihg.com/hotelindigo

NOT ANOTHER HOSTEL ❸

As its name suggests, Not Another Hostel isn't really a hostel in the traditional sense. While it does have the expected communal areas, bunk beds, and international vibe, it's inside a private home, making the experience of staying there more akin to couch-surfing. What's more, the hostel operates on a donation-only model: Pay the owners what you think your stay is worth. The only catch: NAH doesn't publicly share its address; however, it's within easy walking distance of Children's Hospital. To secure a spot on a hammock, air mattress, or couch in one of the two bedrooms, you'll need to call or email (using a contact form on the hostel's website) 24 hours or less in advance of your stay to receive confirmation. Please call only between the hours of 9am and 9pm. The owners operate a second NAH location in Cincinnati, Ohio.

MAP 7: Near Penn Ave. and Main St., Lawrenceville, 412/667-8362, www. notanotherhostel.org

Greater Pittsburgh

Map 9

DOONE'S INN AT OAKMONT $$$

If you want to stay close to Pittsburgh but away from the urban sprawl, Doone's Inn, in the charming village of Oakmont, is the place to be. Guests can roam the tree-lined streets and check out the various shops and restaurants. The two-story, eight-room inn is popular with golfers who come to play at the world-famous Oakmont Country Club, site of several U.S. Open championships. The inn itself features traditionally appointed rooms with private baths, some with fireplaces or private porches. Enjoy complimentary breakfast each morning, an exercise room, and even a putting green.
MAP 9: 300 Rte. 909, Verona, 412/828-0410, www.theinnatoakmont.com

ARBORS BED & BREAKFAST $$

Just outside the city, in a little-known area of the North Side, Arbors Bed & Breakfast will give you the distinct feeling that you're staying on a quiet farm rather than just minutes from downtown. The farmhouse that is Arbors was once the home of a Civil War lieutenant. The rooms convey a traditional bed-and-breakfast style, but with modern amenities like central air conditioning, private baths, and cable TV. The sunroom features a hot tub and large deck for guest use. Breakfast is served each morning. There are two rooms and one larger suite here; these can be rented by the night or weekend, or you can rent out the entire house ($425 per night).
MAP 9: 745 Maginn Ave., Pittsburgh, 412/231-4643, www.arborsbnb.com

HYATT REGENCY PITTSBURGH
INTERNATIONAL AIRPORT $$

If you're in town for business and want to stay close to the airport, this is the most convenient hotel available. You don't even need to go outside to reach your room; an enclosed walkway connects the airport to the hotel. The 11-floor hotel features a sleek modern design with stylish and 336 comfortable rooms, which are stocked with luxury linens, a large flat-screen television, and upscale bath products. The hotel restaurant, Bellfarm Kitchen, provides travelers with locally sourced seasonal cuisine.
MAP 9: 1111 Airport Blvd., 724/899-1234 or 800/233-1234, https://pittsburghairport.hyatt.com

HOTELS
GREATER PITTSBURGH

Excursions

Sometimes you gain a new perspective on a city after waving goodbye. You've got to gain some distance. Exploring the area surrounding Pittsburgh gives you a new appreciation for the city itself.

Globetrotters the world over have long been visiting the Laurel Highlands, and for good reason: Not only does world-famous architecture coexist with the quiet beauty of wooded nature, but regular ol' fun can be had as well, especially along the banks of the Youghiogheny (pronounced yaw-ki-GAY-nee) River, where some of Pennsylvania's wildest tubing and rafting takes place.

And while art, history, and railroad museums seem to exist in every last nook and cranny of this corner of the world, it's quite likely that you'll experience much more in locales with less institutional flavor: In a booth at a backwoods diner, for instance, where the apple pie and the eccentric locals remind you more of *Twin Peaks* than "America the Beautiful." In central Pennsylvania, you'll find Johnstown and Altoona, both of which offer a variety of historical sites and picturesque rural views. Then there's State College, a town pretty much run by Pennsylvania State University (Penn State to those in the know).

Beaver and Butler Counties offer a respite from the bustle of the city with their largely rural landscapes, antique shops, farms, and even parts of the Underground Railroad that you can visit.

But ultimately, it doesn't much matter which way you explore the outer reaches of Pittsburgh or how you decide to have fun. What matters is that you've simply gotten out there.

Previous: Fallingwater; McConnells Mill State Park.

Highlights

★ **Boldest Ode to Local Ingenuity:** The Big Mac sandwich was invented by a McDonald's franchise owner in the mid-1960s. The **Big Mac Museum Restaurant** is, naturally, the place to show your due respect (page 200).

★ **Best Residential Architecture:** Still regarded as one of the finest examples of American residential architecture, **Fallingwater** is quite possibly the most gorgeous—and the most photogenic—of Frank Lloyd Wright's works of utilitarian art (page 201).

★ **Best Retro Amusement Park: Idlewild Park** isn't necessarily the place to visit for death-defying roller coasters. But for a fun weekend afternoon, it can't be beat. Bring your "bathing costume" for a trip to **SoakZone,** the on-site water park (page 204).

★ **Best River Rafting:** Whether you're looking to master some of the country's most vicious Class V white-water rapids or would prefer to float lazily in a giant inner tube, you'll find outfitters along the banks of the Youghiogheny in **Ohiopyle State Park** (page 206).

★ **Best Landmark:** A must-see sight for rail fans the world over, the **Horseshoe Curve National Historic Landmark** is a 220-degree curve outside Altoona at the Kittanning Gap. Even today, it's considered an absolutely masterful feat of modern engineering (page 211).

★ **Classiest Tribute to a Local Tragedy:** No matter what's on your itinerary, an afternoon at the somber but impressive **Johnstown Flood Museum** is a must. The flood is still considered one of the country's worst natural disasters (page 212).

★ **Best State Park:** With its Old Mill and its covered bridge, the forested **McConnells Mill State Park** in Portersville is as picturesque as it is welcoming to adventurists (page 217).

★ **Best Blast from the Past:** Just a short drive from downtown Pittsburgh, **Old Economy Village** is the former home of the fiscally ingenious Harmony Society. The village gives some of the best clues as to how the society lived and worked (page 217).

Excursions

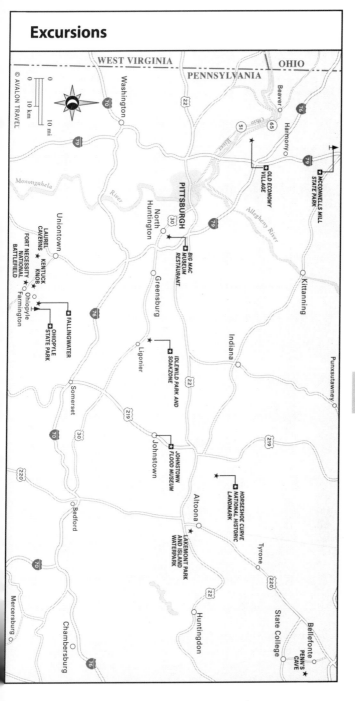

PLANNING YOUR TIME

Visitors without a lot of time to spare should consider heading toward the nearby Laurel Highlands. Not only can the area be reached quickly by car from Pittsburgh (about an hour's drive), but it also offers a wide variety of popular activities, from protected wilderness areas to amusement parks to world-famous works of architecture. This trip could be stretched out to a long weekend, particularly if you plan on camping and boating.

You may want to devote a day to Johnstown, Altoona, and State College to visit the various railroad museums and historical sites. Hardcore Penn State fans may want to add an extra day.

Laurel Highlands

The Laurel Highlands region contains a wealth of diverse activities. A family of four with differing interests may need to visit four separate sites to keep everyone happy, but for what it's worth, you'll probably find all four of them here. The area's most popular tourist attraction is Frank Lloyd Wright's Fallingwater, but if you're planning to visit the house during a quick day trip, consider leaving a little earlier and mixing in a few side activities along the way.

The highlands encompass a large area. Some of the most popular towns to visit are Ligonier, historic Brownsville, and Uniontown, but many of the region's attractions exist in the less settled areas.

A massive archive of area activities can be found on the website of the **Laurel Highlands Visitors Bureau** (120 E. Main St., Ligonier, 724/238-5661 or 800/333-5661, www.laurelhighlands.org).

SIGHTS
★ Big Mac Museum Restaurant

Pittsburgh boosters are quite fond of reminding out-of-towners that McDonald's iconic Big Mac sandwich was invented in the region (by franchise owner Jim Delligatti in 1965). The **Big Mac Museum Restaurant** (9061 US-30, North Huntingdon, 724/863-9837, 5am-midnight Sun.-Thurs., 5am-1pm Fri.-Sat.) is positive proof of that very fact. And aside from bowing down at the altar of the famous sandwich, you can also sink your teeth into one, as this site actually is a working McDonald's restaurant. You'll find a life-sized bust of Delligatti himself, a ridiculously huge (and unnervingly lifelike) Big Mac statue, and classic McDonald's memorabilia. Whether you're a junk food junkie or a pop culture obsessive, you'll get a kick out of this over-the-top homage to the two all-beef patties. (Take exit 67 off the Pennsylvania Turnpike.)

Bushy Run Battlefield

The events that took place in the summer of 1763 at **Bushy Run Battlefield** (1253 Bushy Run Rd., Jeannette, 724/527-5584, www.bushyrunbattlefield.com; 9am-5pm Wed.-Sat., noon-5pm Sun.; $5 adults, $3 children), named

The Jimmy Stewart Museum

The city of Indiana is a pretty good distance to travel for just one museum (about 60 miles and a little over an hour from Pittsburgh), but for hard-core Jimmy Stewart fans, the pilgrimage will be more than worth your while. The star of the silver screen (1908-1997) grew up in Indiana, and the town boasts a statue of his likeness as well as the **Jimmy Stewart Museum** (835 Philadelphia St., Indiana, 724/349-6112, www.jimmy.org, 10am-4pm Mon.-Sat., noon-4pm Sun., $8 adults, $7 seniors, $6 children), which can be found inside the Indiana library and next to its city hall.

The museum contains all manner of movie memorabilia pertaining to Stewart's life, including posters and film clips. There's also a decent gift shop. Don't miss the separate room dedicated to the Stewart family history in Western Pennsylvania—Jimmy Stewart's kin, apparently, have lived in and around the Indiana area since the time of the Civil War.

While at the museum, ask for directions to Jimmy's boyhood home, which remains a private residence. Also ask for directions to the former location of J. M. Stewart & Sons Hardware, Jimmy's father's store, where he worked as a boy.

after a small area stream of the same name, were certainly nothing fun. While pressing west in an effort to relieve the soldiers who'd been defending Fort Pitt (the present-day Point State Park), a British army was ambushed by Native Americans. As is always the case with turf wars, much blood was spilled on both sides.

The 250th anniversary of the battle at Bushy Run occurred in 2013, so what better time than now—especially given our own country's current conflicts—to remind yourself and perhaps your family that history always repeats itself? Aside from being the Keystone State's only recognized Native American battlefield, Bushy Run offers live battle reenactments, troop encampments, a visitors center, and guided tours of the battlefield itself.

Compass Inn Museum

At **Compass Inn Museum** (1382 US-30 E., Laughlintown, 724/238-4983, www.compassinn.com; 11am-4pm Tues.-Sat., 1pm-5pm Sun.; $9 adults, $6 children), a restored 1799 stagecoach stop, guided tours given by docents in period costume share the story of how life was lived in the early 1800s, with a specific focus on transportation. This particular stagecoach stop was an inn, and on the grounds are three reconstructed outbuildings, including a blacksmith shop and a barn. Inside the barn visitors will see and learn about the Conestoga wagon and the standard stagecoach. The 90-minute tour also includes a stop at a reconstructed cookhouse, complete with a beehive oven. Gifts and period reproductions are available at the on-site country store, and hour-long candlelight tours are offered November through mid-December.

★ Fallingwater

Declared by architects and critics worldwide as one of the most stunning

EXCURSIONS
LAUREL HIGHLANDS

private structures ever built in the United States, Frank Lloyd Wright's **Fallingwater** (1491 Mill Run Rd., 724/329-8501, www.fallingwater.org; 8am-4pm Thurs.-Tues.; $30 adults, $18 children) is an absolute must-see for anyone visiting Pittsburgh who also has access to a car. Considering that a mere 90-minute drive from downtown Pittsburgh will get you there, this makes for a fantastic day trip no matter what the season.

Designed in 1935 for the Kaufmann family, who at the time owned one of Pittsburgh's most profitable department store companies, Fallingwater is quite possibly the finest example of Wright's praiseworthy architectural philosophy, which he referred to as "organic architecture": Wright was a staunch believer in the concept that art and nature could coexist peacefully, so when Edgar J. Kaufmann asked for his house to be built next to a favorite waterfall in Mill Run, Wright instead designed it to rest *above* the falls. To see the house from its left or right side is equally stunning; Wright cleverly built the boxy sandstone shapes and cantilevered levels directly into the sloping earth.

After serving its initial purpose for 26 years (the house was used as a weekend getaway), Fallingwater opened to the public in 1963. Notably, it remains the only important Wright structure in the area open to the public with both its furniture and artwork intact. (Wright was legendary for wishing to control the interior look and layout of the homes he designed.)

Besides regular tours, visitors may choose from a variety of special tours, such as an in-depth tour ($80 pp), dinner tours, brunch tours, and hikes. Adjacent to the Fallingwater grounds is the 5,000-acre **Bear Run Nature Reserve**—great for hiking and bird-watching. And Frank Lloyd Wright's **Kentuck Knob** (www.kentuckknob.com)—another innovatively designed residence—is only seven miles away.

Flight 93 National Memorial

On September 11, 2001, a great many innocent people lost their lives. And while the World Trade Center in New York City was certainly the most tragic of the three sites affected, there were victims in Southwestern Pennsylvania as well: the 40 passengers and crew members who were traveling aboard United Airlines Flight 93, which crashed into an open field in Somerset County. The permanent **Flight 93 National Memorial** (6424 Lincoln Hwy., Stoystown, 814/893-6322, www.nps.gov/flni, www.honorflight93.org; sunrise-sunset daily, visitors center 9am-5pm daily; free) pays homage to them all.

A 2.5-mile access road leads to a one-mile ring road, which itself encircles a field adjacent to the crash site, where the passengers and crew now rest in peace. The memorial includes a tasteful and minimalistic white marble wall, on which all 40 names are engraved. Thousands of personal items left behind by visitors as tributes can be viewed along a 40-foot fence, which was erected specifically to display the mementos. The 150-acre Field of Honor, meanwhile, which covers one-half mile of land in diameter, links the entire site. The Tower of Voices monument, at the park entrance, contains 40 wind chimes to represent the voices of the passengers and crew members aboard the flight.

Clockwise from top left: Frank Lloyd Wright's Fallingwater; Big Mac Museum Restaurant; waterfall at Ohiopyle State Park.

Fort Ligonier

Built by the British for protection during the French and Indian War, **Fort Ligonier** (200 S. Market St., intersection of US-30 and PA-711, Ligonier, 724/238-9701, www.fortligonier.org; 10am-4:30pm Mon.-Sat., noon-4:30pm Sun. mid-Apr.-mid-Nov.; $10 adults, $6 children) hold historical interest largely due to its seeming impenetrability: During its eight years of existence, the fort's walls were somehow never penetrated.

A full eight acres of the original fort site have been preserved and can be toured today. There's also an impressive museum featuring a French and Indian War art gallery and a rare collection of pistols once owned by George Washington.

Fort Necessity National Battlefield

If you've already visited the Fort Pitt Museum in Pittsburgh's Point State Park, you may be encouraged to stop by **Fort Necessity National Battlefield** (1 Washington Pkwy., Farmington, 724/329-5512, www.nps.gov/fone; 9am-5pm daily; free), where the French and Indian War of 1754 first rang out. To start, stop by the battlefield's **visitors center** for a current schedule of activities and to view a short film, *Road to Necessity,* which summarizes the bloody events that took place here. Interactive museum exhibits briefly explain the war as well.

Next, follow a short path to an area known as the **Great Meadow.** Nestled into the shadow of the Allegheny Mountains, this is a site of serious historical proportions, as the war actually began here. Visitors feeling a bit restless may want to explore the five miles of hiking trails that surround the site, while history buffs might prefer the seven-mile side trip to **Jumonville Glen** (9am-4pm daily, free with paid admission to Fort Necessity National Battlefield), where George Washington met the French face to face for the very first time.

Ohiopyle State Park, Fallingwater, and Laurel Caverns are all nearby.

★ Idlewild Park and SoakZone

Originally constructed in 1878, **Idlewild Park** (US-30 E., Ligonier, 724/238-3666, www.idlewild.com; 10:30am-8pm daily June-Aug.; $44 general admission, $35 seniors, free for children 2 and under) during its salad days wasn't much more than a recreational campground with picnic tables and an artificially constructed lake. As the mid-20th century approached, however, Idlewild began attempting to transform itself into an honest-to-goodness amusement park. That plan didn't fully come to fruition until 1983, when the Kennywood Park Corporation bought the company out.

Today, the park consists of seven theme areas, including Olde Idlewild, where the Ferris wheel, the merry-go-round, and other similarly quaint attractions are located, and **SoakZone,** a water park with various slides and pools. The five remaining areas, including Daniel Tiger's Neighborhood and Story Book Forest, are considerably tame, and aimed toward the youngest of guests.

Steelers Training Camp

Serious football fans passing through the Laurel Highlands in midsummer should absolutely visit the **Pittsburgh Steelers Training Camp,** which has been held at **Saint Vincent College** (300 Fraser Purchase Rd., Latrobe, 724/537-4560, www.stvincent.edu, free) since 1968.

The six-time Super Bowl champs show up at some point in mid-July, and the camp, one of the most fan-friendly in the NFL, lasts for roughly one month. Practices open to the public tend to run 3pm-5pm daily. (Morning practices are off-limits.) The training schedule is neither finalized nor made public until a few weeks prior to the camp's start, so keep an eye on the Steelers website (www.steelers.com) for details.

If you're planning on bringing little ones, consider enrolling them in **The Steelers Experience,** a kid-friendly program that takes place during the afternoon practices, on a field adjacent to the Steelers themselves. Players, coaches, and other team employees host games, exhibits, and simulated practice sessions for kids. Check the website or call the college for more information.

Saint Vincent is also home to the **Fred Rogers Center** (300 Fraser Purchase Rd., Latrobe, 724/805-2750, www.fredrogerscenter.org), where visitors can stop by the multimedia **Fred Rogers Exhibit,** an interactive display designed for both adults and children.

Kentuck Knob

Although it's certainly less visited than Fallingwater, **Kentuck Knob** (723 Kentuck Rd., Chalk Hill, 724/329-1901, www.kentuckknob.com; 9am-5pm Sun.-Tues. and Thurs.-Sat., noon-5pm Wed. Mar.-Oct., 9am-3pm Sun.-Tues. and Thurs.-Sat., noon-3pm Wed. Nov., 10am-3pm Sun.-Tues. and Thurs.-Sat. Dec.; tours $25 adults, $18 children) is nonetheless a fascinating and truly unique example of Frank Lloyd Wright's architectural genius. Exploring both structures during a day trip from Pittsburgh is definitely possible. Aside from the standard admission tour, brunch tours, sculpture garden tours, and in-depth tours are also available.

Wright was 86 years old when he designed Kentuck Knob for a family who'd visited Fallingwater a number of times and greatly admired it. Alternatively known as "Hagan House" and "The Child of Fallingwater," Kentuck Knob was constructed according to the specifications of a style Wright referred to as "Usonian," which had no attics or basements and was intended to keep building and utility costs low. Derived partly from Wright's Prairie-style homes, the Usonians were relatively small, one-story structures with flat roofs. Kentuck fits that descriptor well, although it also features a number of surprising 60-degree angles; the house was built on a hexagonal grid. Pay attention while wandering around the house, as the hexagonal theme is repeated throughout.

Laurel Caverns

Fifty miles south of Pittsburgh near Uniontown, 435-acre **Laurel Caverns Geological Park** (200 Caverns Park Rd., Farmington, 724/438-3003 or

800/515-4150, www.laurelcaverns.com; 9am-5pm daily May-Oct.; tours $12 adults, $10 children) offers a wealth of family-style activities, including 55-minute guided tours of the sandstone caverns, as well as much more strenuous caving exploration tours lasting as long as three hours. Before or after taking a tour of the caverns, visitors can pay $35 to rappel three times off a 45-foot-high cliff. And for a mere $7 per person there's Kavernputt, an 18-hole miniature golf course inside a 10,000-square-foot artificial cave. Gemstone panning will set you back $7.

Originally called Laurel Hill Cave, and then Dulaney's Cave, Laurel Caverns is the largest cave in the state of Pennsylvania. It's also the 16th-longest developed cave in the United States; there are 2.8 miles of passages for visitors to safely explore. According to local historians and anthropologists, the caverns have been explored since the late 1700s and were once used by Native Americans as protection from enemies and the natural elements.

Because the temperature inside the caverns remains steady at about 55°F year-round, visitors are encouraged to bring sweaters or light jackets even on warm summer days.

Lincoln Highway Experience Museum

Any serious aficionado of roadside Americana knows that the Lincoln Highway, which was formally dedicated on Halloween, 1913, was our country's first coast-to-coast highway. Most visitors to the Laurel Highlands, however, aren't aware that the historic highway traverses the area. Those who'd care to educate themselves should pay a visit to the **Lincoln Highway Experience Museum** (3435 US-30 E., Latrobe, 724/879-4241, www.lhhc. org, 9am-4pm Mon.-Fri., 9am-1pm Sat., $7 adults), perhaps the kitschiest tourist attraction in all of Southwestern Pennsylvania.

A brief documentary about the highway is one of the museum's highlights, but don't miss the gift shop, where crafts by area artisans mix with books, collectible items, and goofy pop-culture trinkets. Best of all, the price of admission includes a copy of the 60-page *Lincoln Highway Driving Guide*. But if you'd prefer to simply tour the highway on your lonesome, explore the website at www.lhhc.org (click the "LH Tour" tab), where self-guided trip suggestions abound.

★ Ohiopyle State Park

Encompassing just over 19,000 forested acres, **Ohiopyle State Park** (124 Main St., Ohiopyle, 724/329-8591, www.dcnr.pa.gov, sunrise-sunset daily, free) provides standard state park activities: biking, trekking, horseback riding, fishing, and even hunting. But without a doubt, the vast majority of Pittsburghers who come here have something else in mind: a white-water boating or white-water rafting trip on the ever-popular Youghiogheny (pronounced "yaw-ki-GAY-nee") River.

There are all sorts of reasons why Pennsylvanians love the Yough (pronounced "yock"), but the diversity of the river is certainly at the top of the list. Beginners can easily float down the Lower Yough's Class II rapids, while at the same time, some of the country's most experienced rafters

Soar Like a Bird

Visitors to the Laurel Highlands who happen to have an adventurous streak will likely be pleased to learn that the quickly growing trend of **ziplining** has reached the area. At the **Adventure Center at Nemacolin Woodlands Resort** (1001 Lafayette Dr., Farmington, 866/344-6957, www.nemacolin.com), a high-altitude obstacle course known as the **Fatbird Canopy Tour** ($45 pp) is your destination. The three ziplines are some of the longest in the state.

The **Ohiopyle Zip Line Adventure Park** (4 Sherman St., Ohiopyle, 724/329-8531, www.laurelhighlands.com; $20-44 pp) is another option. Two levels of difficulty allow children as young as four to participate. While not nearly as death-defying as the aforementioned Fatbird Canopy, the 200-foot Ohiopyle zipline experience involves a similar up-in-the-air jungle gym complete with spider-web netting, wooden logs, and rickety bridges.

Finally, there's the **Canopy Tour & Zip Line Course** at **Seven Springs Mountain Resort** (777 Waterwheel Dr., Seven Springs, 814/352-7777, www.7springs.com; $51-89 pp). The nearly 2,000 feet of ziplines include the **Screaming Hawk Zipline,** which allows adrenaline junkies to pause briefly on a series of swaying wooden towers, some of them standing 350 feet in the air. This one ain't for the squeamish, folks.

can challenge themselves in the Class IV and V rapids of the Upper Yough, where some of the finest white-water rafting on the entire East Coast takes place. Numerous outfitters in the area rent equipment and offer tours for all levels.

Camping at Ohiopyle is a possibility—visit the park's website for detailed information and a campground map. Wooden camping cottages that sleep five people are also available.

What's more, Ohiopyle doesn't empty out during the winter months. Snowmobiling, cross-country skiing, and sledding all take place.

Saint Vincent Gristmill

Built in 1854 by the same community of Benedictine monks who continue to grind grain here today, **Saint Vincent Gristmill** (300 Fraser Purchase Rd., Latrobe, 724/537-0304, www.saintvincentgristmill.com; 9am-4pm Mon.-Sat.; free) offers a rare opportunity to experience a religious tradition that isn't often made public. The Gristmill General Store sells hard-crusted breads baked by the monks, jams, flour, bread mix, and more. An on-site museum contains exhibits and screens a video of the milling process. A viewing area offers the opportunity to watch the monks at work, but because the grinding schedule varies, it's not always possible to catch the brothers in action.

Westmoreland Museum of American Art

One of only three museums in the state that focus exclusively on American art, the **Westmoreland Museum of American Art** (221 N. Main St., Greensburg, 724/837-1500, www.wmuseumaa.org; 11am-5pm Tues. and

Thurs.-Sun., 11am-7pm Wed.; $15 suggested donation) has been welcoming visitors to Greensburg ever since 1959. Especially in its first two decades, the curatorial team managed to build a rather impressive collection of work by American masters, including paintings by Winslow Homer, Mary Cassatt, and John Singer Sargent.

Along with various paintings and portraiture, items kept in the permanent collection include sculpture, toys, works on paper (such as lithographs and etchings), and decorative arts, which include jugs, cupboards, and other largely utilitarian pieces.

Families visiting the museum might enjoy spending time at the Center for Creative Connections, a hands-on interactive room where children can make their own creations.

RESTAURANTS

Located in downtown Ligonier, the **Ligonier Tavern** (139 W. Main St., Ligonier, 724/238-7788, www.ligoniertavern.com; 11am-9pm Sun.-Thurs., 11am-10pm Fri.-Sat.; $17-24) has three separately designed dining rooms inside a beautifully detailed turn-of-the-20th-century Victorian house. Cuisine is fairly casual and leans toward American and seafood. Sandwiches, salads, pasta, and chicken entrées are all popular. If the weather is nice, diners can choose to sit outside on the house's second-floor patio. A bakery offers a wide selection of fantastic cakes.

With a name like **Ruthie's Diner** (1850 US-30, Ligonier, 724/238-9930; 6am-9pm daily; $7-11), you can probably guess the sort of food that's on offer: burgers, sandwiches, and cups of black coffee, for the most part. This is the perfect place to make a pit stop if you're in the midst of road-tripping and searching for the heart of America, or some such romantic notion. And as any local will surely tell you, Ruthie's also serves one of the finest breakfasts in town. Not terribly healthy, of course, but delicious and protein-packed just the same.

Adjacent to the Great Allegheny Passage (GAP) at the West Newton trailhead is **The Trailside** (108 W. Main St., West Newtown, 724/872-5171, www.thetrailside.com; 11am-11pm Mon.-Thurs., 11am-midnight Fri.-Sat., 11am-10pm Sun.; $6-10), a casual American-bistro-style eatery serving sandwiches, burgers, and salads. Ask for a table on the outdoor deck, which overlooks the GAP trail and the Youghiogheny River. Free Wi-Fi is available, and a pub offers a decent selection of craft beers.

HOTELS

Home to one of only six Frank Lloyd Wright homes in the country in which visitors can actually stay the night, the most sought-after accommodation at **Polymath Park Resort** (187 Evergreen Ln., Acme, 877/833-7829, www.polymathpark.com) is known as **Duncan House** ($399). It's a minimalist Usonian-style structure, and visitors must rent the entire home, which is actually a bargain when you consider it sleeps six. Other structures on the resort that can be rented include the **Blum House** ($299), with its geometric windows and roof lines, and the **Balter House** ($299); both were designed by Wright's apprentice, Peter Berndtson. For those who'd rather bunk elsewhere, tours of the resort ($24 pp) take place daily except Wednesday at 11am, noon, 1pm, 2pm, and 3pm.

Roughly a 20-minute drive from Fallingwater is the **Lodge at Chalk Hill** (2920 National Pike/US-40, Chalk Hill, 724/438-8880, www.thelodgeatchalkhill.com; $70-200), a recently renovated lakeside lodge and mountain retreat situated on 37 acres of land. Visitors to Ohiopyle, Fort Necessity, and Laurel Caverns will all find their destinations within an easy drive of the lodge.

Along US-40 in Farmington, the historical **Stone House Inn** (3023 National Pike/US-40, Farmington, 724/329-8876, www.stonehouseinn.com; $159-200) sits a mere two miles from the Fort Necessity National Battlefield. Fallingwater, Kentuck Knob, and Ohiopyle are also close. One of the first inns to open along the National Road, Stone House Inn has been lodging and feeding travelers since 1822. There are seven Victorian-style bed-and-breakfast suites on-site, as well as six modern rooms in the New Zeigler Wing that come complete with whirlpool tub, contemporary furnishings, and other modern conveniences.

A four-star luxury resort, **Nemacolin Woodlands Resort** (1001 Lafayette Dr., Farmington, 724/329-8555 or 866/344-6957, www.nemacolin.com; $420-3,500) is so lovely that you may decide not to leave the grounds at all. Visitors and guests can indulge in golfing, luxurious spa packages, casual or fine dining, and a wide variety of adventure or cultural-recreation activities. Lodgers have a choice of six different accommodation options, including a boutique hotel, a classic European-style hotel, a lodge, and a townhouse. Nightly rates are steep but well worth the unique experience.

Not far from Seven Springs Mountain Resort (page 151) is the **Historic Log Cabin Inn** (191 Main St., Donegal, 724/771-9131, www.historiclogcabininn.com; $149-349), which was built sometime around 1750 and truly is just as fun as it sounds. It's said to have the largest logs in the county, and you'll even find a potbelly stove and a natural log staircase. Supposedly, George Washington once spent the night.

Backpackers and Great Allegheny Passage cyclists requiring affordable lodging will be pleased to learn of **The Hostel on Main** (506 Main St., Rockwood, 814/926-4546, www.hostelonmain.com; $27.50-65), in a historical building that was renovated in 2009. It offers three private rooms, a standard dorm with bunk beds, and bicycle storage and racks.

PRACTICALITIES
Visitor Information
The **Laurel Highlands Visitors Bureau** is in Ligonier (120 E. Main St., 724/238-5661 or 800/333-5661, www.laurelhighlands.org; 8:30am-4:30pm Mon.-Fri.). Information for Fayette, Somerset, and Westmoreland Counties can be collected at the bureau, or you can simply gather the info online.

Getting There
The majority of the Laurel Highlands' major attractions can be accessed by heading east out of the city on US-30.

Greyhound buses (800/231-2222, www.greyhound.com) regularly travel to cities within the Laurel Highlands region.

A one-way **Amtrak** (800/872-7245, www.amtrak.com) ride from Pittsburgh to Greensburg (Harrison Ave. and Seton Hill Dr., 724/542-4354) will set you back $11-26.

The **Arnold Palmer Regional Airport** (LBE, Latrobe, www.palmerair-port.com) serves the greater Greensburg area.

Getting Around

For the most part, visitors to Laurel Highlands should arrive with a car or other private vehicle. Contact information for travel and transportation options can be found on the website of the **Laurel Highlands Visitors Bureau** (www.laurelhighlands.org), including companies that offer organized tours of the area.

Visitors to Greensburg can visit the website of the **Westmoreland County Transit Authority** (www.westmorelandtransit.com) for schedule and fare information.

Altoona, State College, and Johnstown

Johnstown offers a fairly large number of activities and sights. And it's a simple drive from Pittsburgh: If you're headed east toward the Westmoreland Museum of Art or Idlewild, you're halfway there.

Not much farther northeast is Altoona, which is something of an international meeting point for rail fans: The Railroaders Memorial Museum and the Horseshoe Curve Historic Landmark are both here. Continue onward to State College, the home of Penn State. It's a perfectly quaint college town and also home to small museums and interesting cave sites, many of which can be explored via guided tours.

SIGHTS
Frank & Sylvia Pasquerilla Heritage Discovery Center

Included with the price of admission to the Johnstown Flood Museum is admission to the **Frank & Sylvia Pasquerilla Heritage Discovery Center** (201 6th Ave., Johnstown, 814/539-1889 or 888/222-1889, www.jaha.org; 10am-5pm Tues.-Sat., noon-5pm Sun.; $9 adults, $7 seniors and children). It tells the stories of the thousands of southern and eastern European immigrants who flocked to Johnstown during the last two decades of the 1800s and the first decade of the 1900s.

You'll learn what life was like in Johnstown for a Slovakian butcher, a Russian shopkeeper, and a Hungarian goose farmer, to name just a few. Through an interactive video display, visitors will also view the experience of immigrants being questioned at Ellis Island, and they'll learn about

Flood City Music Festival

Should you happen to find yourself in the Pittsburgh area over Labor Day weekend, and should you happen to be a fan of Americana and roots music—blues, zydeco, folk, jazz, and R&B, for instance—you're in luck. That's when the **Flood City Music Festival** (www.floodcitymusic.com, $20-60) takes place at **People's Natural Gas Park** (90 Johns St., Johnstown), which can be found just across the river from Point Stadium and beside the Cambria Iron Company National Historic Landmark.

Throughout the three days of the festival, which was formerly known as the Johnstown FolkFest, concertgoers can expect to hear roughly 70 hours of live music by bands both world-famous and nearly unknown. Past performers have included Los Lobos, Sleepy LaBeef, The Smithereens, Sharon Jones and the Dap-Kings, Brave Combo, Robert Cray Band, Big Sandy & His Fly-Rite Boys, Robbie Fulks, Southern Culture on the Skids, Buckwheat Zydeco, and R. L. Burnside. Check the festival's webpage for information about accommodations and driving directions. Free parking is generally available—signs will be posted—and free shuttle buses frequently travel back and forth between parking lots and the festival grounds.

Insider tip: The legendary **Johnstown Inclined Plane** operates free of charge throughout the festival's three days.

the conditions in Europe that led many to seek a new life elsewhere in the first place.

Other exhibits at the museum show what life was like in the steel mills where many immigrants toiled, while a theater exhibition includes interviews with the children and grandchildren of the immigrants.

★ Horseshoe Curve National Historic Landmark

A longtime favorite of hard-core rail fans who journey to Altoona to visit the Railroaders Memorial Museum is the **Horseshoe Curve National Historic Landmark** (visitors center 1300 9th Ave., Altoona, 814/946-0834, www.railroadcity.com; 10am-4pm Mon.-Sat., 11am-5pm Sun.; admission $8, free with admission to Railroaders Memorial Museum). A legendary railroad curve located about six miles west of Altoona at the Kittanning Gap, the rail's extreme bend is, in fact, shaped like a horseshoe. Its 220-degree arc was designed by J. Edgar Thomson; it opened to trains in 1854 as a way to significantly reduce the travel time from one end of Pennsylvania to the other. The arc was necessary because of the summit of the Allegheny Mountains, which the track was designed to skirt. Designated as a National Historic Landmark in 1966, the curve has been a successful tourist attraction for decades.

Stop by the visitors center first, where displays illustrate the construction of the curve. The center also features a gift shop packed with items of interest to the rail fan. From there, guests can ride a funicular railway up to the train tracks or hike up a stairway instead.

★ Johnstown Flood Museum

The **Johnstown Flood Museum** (304 Washington St., Johnstown, 814/539-1889 or 888/222-1889, www.jaha.org; 10am-5pm Tues.-Sat., noon-5pm Sun.; $9 adults, $7 seniors and children) documents a massive flooding catastrophe that took place in that city on May 31, 1889, and in which 2,209 people perished. The causes of the disaster were a neglected dam and a massive storm.

Those who stop at this especially well-developed museum will have the chance to view artifacts and documents relating to the greatest tragedy ever to befall the city of Johnstown, including a 26-minute Academy Award-winning documentary film that recreates the flood by using archival photos. Also on-site is a relief-map model that uses lights and sound effects to illustrate the flood's path through the Conemaugh Valley. Particularly moving—even disturbing—is the museum's collection of personal artifacts that were recovered after the flood, including a set of keys belonging to a telegraph operator who warned of the dam's impending danger. Also part of the permanent exhibit is an original, renovated "Oklahoma House." Although they were originally designed for Oklahoma Territory homesteaders, the prefab houses, which measured either 10 by 20 feet or 16 by 24 feet, were also used to shelter refugees of the Johnstown flood.

Visitors can also request information about a downtown Johnstown walking tour, on which many historical buildings that survived the flood can be seen. More information about the tour and a map of the downtown area can be found on the museum's website.

Johnstown Inclined Plane

The cable cars of the **Johnstown Incline** (711 Edgehill Dr., Johnstown, 814/536-1816, www.inclinedplane.org, 11am-9pm Sun.-Thurs., 11am-11pm Fri.-Sat. Apr.-Dec., tickets $3 one way, $5 round-trip) travel 896.5 feet up the side of Yoder Hill—which has a grade of 70.9 percent—to reach an elevation of 1,693.5 feet. Built by the Cambria Iron Company in 1890 and 1891, the incline, known as the world's steepest vehicular inclined plane, was designed specifically so that residents of the hilltop community known as Westmont could easily transport their horses and wagons from ground level to home and back again.

However, on March 1, 1936, the incline served a distinctly different role when, once again, the city suffered a flood. Nearly 4,000 area residents were lifted to dry, higher ground via the incline. The cable cars served the same emergency purpose again on June 20, 1977, during the city's most recent flood.

Visitors to the incline, which was built by Samuel Diescher, the engineer also responsible for building Pittsburgh's Duquesne and Monongahela Inclines, can walk out onto an extended observation deck that offers a rather lovely view of the Johnstown area. A visitors center displays archival photographs of the city and its numerous floods, and from the center's lobby it's possible to view the massive machinery of the incline in action. The **James Wolfe Sculpture Trail** (3.3 miles) is directly behind the incline.

Penn State Campus

State College (aka Happy Valley) is home to the renowned **Pennsylvania State University** (www.psu.edu). The sprawling college campus is a great destination not just for prospective college students, but also for anyone looking for an academically focused day trip. Penn State's campus features an art museum, gorgeous campus buildings, an arboretum, and the famous **Berkey Creamery** (Curtin Rd. and Bigler Rd., 814/865-7535, 7am-9pm Mon.-Fri., 9am-9pm Sat.-Sun.), where it's almost required that you get ice cream. Die-hard fans won't want to miss a visit to **Beaver Stadium,** where the school's football games are played, or the **Nittany Lion Shrine,** the large sculpture of the school's mountain lion mascot on the center of campus.

Penn's Cave

Known as the country's only all-water cavern, **Penn's Cave** (222 Penns Cave Rd., Centre Hall, 814/364-1664, www.pennscave.com; 11am-5pm Sat.-Sun. Feb. and Dec., 10am-5pm daily Mar. and Nov., 9am-5pm daily Apr.-May and Sept.-Oct., 9am-7pm daily June-Aug., tours $18.50 adults, $10.50 children) is a particularly unique local site. Because the caverns are literally flooded, guided one-hour tours are given by motorboat. Along the way, visitors will see stalagmites, stalactites, and limestone corridors, and trout can often be seen jumping high above the water. (Look out for the stalagmite that bears a striking resemblance to the Statue of Liberty.)

Penn's Cave also offers a 90-minute wildlife, farm, and nature tour ($21.50 adults, $13 children), during which safari buses shuttle visitors throughout the area's 1,500 acres of preserved forests and fields. Mountain lions, wolves, bison, black bears, and wild mustangs are just some of the animals you may encounter. The **Prospector Pete's Miners Maze** ($6 adults, $3 children) is a 4,800-square-foot maze full of twists and turns; it's especially popular with kids.

Railroaders Memorial Museum

One of Western Pennsylvania's most popular railroading attractions, the **Railroaders Memorial Museum** (1300 9th Ave., Altoona, 814/946-0834, www.railroadcity.com; 9am-5pm Mon.-Sat., 11am-5pm Sun.; $11 adults, $10 seniors, $9 children) was designed specifically to honor the American railroaders who have contributed significantly to the country's culture and industry. And it makes good sense that the site is located in Altoona: Not only has the city long been known as an important epicenter of rail activity, but the Horseshoe Curve National Historic Site and the Staple Bend Tunnel (the country's first railroad tunnel) are both nearby. (Admission to the Horseshoe Curve is included.)

The museum uses a mixture of interactive displays, video presentations, and exhibits to tell the cultural and social story of those who worked in the industry. In other words, the major emphasis is not on the wheels and tracks that moved the industry forward, but rather on the people who worked on and alongside the rails throughout the 1920s. And because the light-and-sound exhibits are fairly advanced, the museum feels much more like

Top: Johnstown Flood Museum. **Bottom:** McConnells Mill State Park.

a place to play than simply a place to drearily read placards and gaze at
dusty models.

RESTAURANTS

Conveniently located in Somerset, **The Summit Diner** (791 N. Center Ave., Somerset, 814/445-7154; 6am-4pm Sat.-Thurs., 6am-9pm Fri.; $7-14) is a greasy spoon with surprisingly good food. You'll find it open for business literally every day of the year. The menu is filled with American standards, and the hotcakes are a local favorite. All the meat is cut and served right in the restaurant's own kitchen.

A third-generation family-owned and -operated establishment, **Mel's Restaurant and Bar** (127 W. Patriot St., Somerset, 814/445-9841; 9am-2am Mon.-Sat., noon-11pm Sun.; $3-11) is the sort of honky-tonk café where one might expect to find a preponderance of gentlemen sporting cowboy hats and chewing tobacco. The menu is a low-budget selection of cheeseburgers, hot dogs, and sloppy joes, and don't be surprised if yours is served on a paper plate. Mel's also boasts a 240-square-foot dance floor, live music on the weekend, and a pool table.

HOTELS

Tucked away in the Allegheny Mountains near Blue Knob is the **Majestic World Lodge and Retreat** (679 Memory Ln., Portage, 814/693-0189 or 877/365-6972, www.majesticworldlodge.com; $400/night for up to 8 people, $200 each additional night), a family-owned and -operated lodge 3,000 feet up in the Alleghenies—one of the highest elevations in the state. The lodge itself is a converted, historical barn where guests can gaze out at an elk herd from the comfort of a covered wooden deck. The grounds are absolutely gorgeous, and incidentally, the snowy winter season is a particularly picturesque time of the year to visit. In spring, the grounds are covered with a carpet of lovely wildflowers. All rooms are uniquely designed; rustic types will feel especially at home amongst the patchwork quilts and incredibly creative headboards fashioned from antler horns and cedar logs. The inn offers hunts for elk, red stags, whitetails, buffalo, fallow deer, and rams.

Bunking at **Schantz Haus** (687 E. Campus Ave., Davidsville, 814/479-2494; $65-80), a bed-and-breakfast on 120 acres of farm land, is a good call for visitors who'd like to add a little rural adventure to their accommodations. It sits on a working dairy farm, and guests can milk cows or bottle-feed a calf.

PRACTICALITIES
Visitor Information

The **Central Pennsylvania Convention & Visitors Bureau** (800 E. Park Ave., State College, 814/231-1400 or 800/358-5466, www.visitpennstate. org; 7:30am-6pm Mon.-Fri., 9am-6pm Sat.-Sun.) services State College and offers resources for outdoor adventures and cultural and sporting events.

The Altoona section of the **Official Tourism Website of the State of Pennsylvania** (www.visitpa.com) is a good resource, along with the **Altoona Visitors Bureau** website (www.explorealtoona.com).

Those headed to Johnstown should check out the **Greater Johnstown/Cambria County Convention & Visitors Bureau** (111 Roosevelt Blvd., Ste. A, Johnstown, 814/536-7993 or 800/237-8590, www.visitjohnstownpa.com, 9am-5pm Mon.-Fri.), in particular for information on seasonal events, such as the city's annual **PolkaFest** (www.visitjohnstownpa.com/polkafest).

Getting There

From Pittsburgh, a drive to either Altoona, State College, or Johnstown will require a trip on US-22. Those headed to Johnstown will eventually go south on PA-403, while explorers venturing up to Altoona or State College will use US-220/I-99.

Greyhound (800/231-2222, www.greyhound.com) buses leave the downtown Pittsburgh depot multiple times a day for the station in **State College** (152 N. Atherton St., 814/238-7971, $14-22). Buses leave twice a day each for the bus stop in **Johnstown** (47 Walnut St., $19-23) and the bus station in **Altoona** (1231 11th Ave., 814/944-8911, $19-23).

Amtrak trains (800/872-7245, www.amtrak.com) service **Altoona** (1231 11th Ave., no phone). A one-way ride from Pittsburgh will cost $21-28 for a coach seat.

University Park Airport (SCE, State College, www.universityparkairport.com) is right in State College and offers flights to major hubs, including Philadelphia, Detroit, and Washington/Dulles.

Getting Around

Public transport in the State College area is handled by CATA, the **Centre Area Transportation Authority** (www.catabus.com). The Campus Service routes are free, while the Community Service routes cost $2 per ride.

The **Cambria County Transit Authority** (www.camtranbus.com) is responsible for public transportation in Johnstown; when in Altoona use **AMTRAN** (www.amtran.org). For 24-hour **taxi service** in either Cambria or Somerset County, call 814/535-4584 or 814/539-1584.

Beaver County and Butler County

The counties of Beaver and Butler sit just north of the city of Pittsburgh and are quite often considered a part of Pittsburgh, especially by the counties' own residents. Old Economy Village and the Harmony Historic District are the big tourism draws—at both sites you can observe the unique and alternative ways of living practiced by the now-nonexistent Harmony Society.

For more extensive information, spend some time on the counties' official tourism sites, **Beaver County Tourism** (www.visitbeavercounty.com) and **Butler County Tourism** (www.visitbutlercounty.com).

Harmony Historic District and Harmony Museum

Founded in 1804 and now a National Landmark District, the **Harmony Historic District** is a relatively small but engaging area where examples of both Harmonist and Mennonite lifestyles can be seen and studied. This walkable area is where the **Harmony Museum** (218 Mercer St., Harmony, 724/452-7341, www.harmonymuseum.org; 1pm-4pm Tues.-Sun.; $7 adults, $6 seniors, $3 children) can be found. At the museum you'll see an example of a communal Harmonist room; also on-site is a Harmonist wine cellar, accessible by way of a stone-cut staircase. The museum also owns a small collection of Native American artifacts that were discovered in the area.

Other structures of interest in the district include the **Wagner-Bentel Haus,** which is a brick duplex that was constructed by the Harmonists for two sisters and their families, and the reconstructed **Henry Denis Ziegler log house,** which sits directly across the street from the museum and is made of hand-hewn oak logs.

★ McConnells Mill State Park

Encompassing 2,546 acres of the Slippery Rock Creek Gorge, **McConnells Mill State Park** (via I-79 near the intersection of US-19 and US-422, Portersville, 724/368-8811, www.dcnr.pa.gov; sunrise-sunset daily; free) is named after a logging mill built to channel the creek's water and the water's power. The park has long been a favorite day trip for those living in Pittsburgh's northern suburbs, but considering that it's less than 40 miles from downtown Pittsburgh, it also makes for a worthwhile excursion for city visitors in need of a quick wilderness break.

There are any number of activities to keep you occupied once inside the park. You're almost certain to see rock climbers, especially if you venture toward Rim Road's climbing area, which sits on the other side of the creek from the Old Mill (where an emergency phone is also located). Head to the intersection of Breakneck Bridge Road and Cheeseman Road to reach the advanced climbing area. White-water rafting and kayaking are also big, and with seven miles of trails, it would be simple to pass half a day simply exploring the pristine, forested splendor of the region.

The **McConnells Mill Heritage Festival** takes place during the third or fourth weekend of September. The operational era of the Old Mill (1852-1928) is celebrated during the festival, and visitors can enjoy activities such as corn-grinding demonstrations and old-time musical entertainment.

To reach the park from downtown, take I-79 to US-19 (Exit 28). Look for signs pointing toward McConnells Mill Road, where you'll find the park sitting roughly 1,000 feet north of the US-19 and US-422 intersection. From mid-May through the end of October, 45-minute interpretive tours of the **Historic Gristmill** (1761 McConnells Mill Rd., Portersville, 724/368-8811; 10:30am-3:30pm Wed.-Sun.; free) take place.

★ Old Economy Village

Formerly the home of the 19th-century communal Christian group known as the Harmony Society, the village of Economy, known in its current restored form as **Old Economy Village** (270 16th St., Ambridge, 724/266-4500, www.oldeconomyvillage.org; 10am-5pm Wed.-Sat., noon-5pm Sun.; $10 adults, $9 seniors, $6 children), was in its day widely recognized as a God-fearing and stoically hard-working place.

The Harmonists fled Germany in the late 1700s due to persecution from the Lutheran Church and went on to purchase 3,000 acres of land in Pennsylvania's Butler County. After moving to Indiana and then returning to Pennsylvania, they settled here; their curious sect is today regarded as one of the country's most successful experiments in economics and alternative living. Completely regardless of gender, the Harmonists shared all manner of village tasks; they also produced everything needed for survival within the confines of the village. And although the society lasted for more than a century, no Harmonists remain today. Why not? The society's members were all unmarried, and none believed in the concept of procreation.

Nonetheless, the Harmony Society's history and the Old Economy Village site both make for fascinating studies. Village visitors will have the opportunity to see the society's community kitchen, its cabinet shop and blacksmith shop, a granary, the Economy Post Office, and more.

Grove City Premium Outlets

About an hour's drive from downtown Pittsburgh, **Premium Outlets** (1911 Leesburg Grove City Rd., Grove City, 724/748-4770, www.premiumoutlets.com; 10am-9pm Mon.-Sat., 10am-7pm Sun.) is an almost ridiculously large outlet mall—it covers so much ground, in fact, you may have to return for a second visit in order to see it all. There are 130 brand-name outlet stores, including Banana Republic, Brooks Brothers, Coach, J.Crew, and Nike. Also available are housewares, home furnishings, children's apparel, lingerie, and luggage.

RESTAURANTS

A self-described beanery, eatery, brewery, and community center, the **North Country Brewing Company** (141 S. Main St., Slippery Rock, 724/794-2337, www.northcountrybrewing.com; 11am-11pm Mon.-Thurs., 11am-midnight Fri.-Sat., 11am-10pm Sun.; $8-23) is close to McConnells Mill State Park. The on-site brewery is phenomenal, the weekly specials often include wild game, and the creatively built sandwiches and burgers are exactly what you'd expect to find in a college town: mouthwatering and especially large. Check the website for live music schedules.

If your itinerary includes a quick side trip to the Mars town square in Butler County, where a **flying saucer** (Brickyard Rd., Mars) makes for a fantastic photo-op, you might also want to pop into the **Breakneck Tavern** (273 Mars Valencia Rd., Mars, 724/625-9150, www.breaknecktavern.com; 11am-10pm Mon.-Thurs., 11am-11pm Fri.-Sat.; $11-28) for a quick pick-me-up. No, the Breakneck Tavern isn't an alien abduction site; it's a Southern- and Cajun-style restaurant with a seriously talented chef.

Particularly popular with golfers, **Conley Resort** (740 Pittsburgh Rd., Butler, 724/586-7711, www.conleyresort.com; $89 and up) offers all guests a complimentary breakfast as well as use of the on-site water park, which consists of two slides, a pool, a sauna, a hot tub, and a replica of a pirate ship with its own water cannon. Guests also receive a discount at the resort's golf course. Rooms are nothing to shout about but are certainly clean and comfy enough. And since Conley is such a spacious place, it's also a popular spot for business meetings and conferences.

Located on a 175-acre farm in the Butler County town of Renfrew is the **Heather Hill Bed and Breakfast** (268 Rader Scholl Rd., Renfrew, 724/538-5168, www.heatherhillbnb.com; $116-145), where the farm animals range from Peruvian Paso Fino horses to Hereford cattle. The renovated 1821 farmhouse includes four bedrooms, a game room, three wood-burning stoves, and a large country-style kitchen.

PRACTICALITIES
Visitor Information
The **Beaver County Recreation & Tourism Department** (121 Bradys Run Rd., Beaver Falls, 800/342-8192, www.visitbeavercounty.com; 8:30am-4:30pm Mon.-Fri.), in the Bradys Run Recreation Facility, offers information on attractions, seasonal events, lodging, and other amenities.

The **Butler County Tourism & Convention Bureau** (310 E. Grandview Ave., Zelienople, 724/234-4619 or 866/856-8444, www.visitbutlercounty. com; 8:30am-4:30pm Mon.-Fri.) provides information on cultural events, sports, local history, and much more.

Getting There
Driving to both Beaver and Butler Counties from downtown Pittsburgh is a breeze: Simply take US-22 West to US-30 West to reach Beaver County. For Butler County, head out of the city on I-279 North, which turns into I-79 North. Pittsburgh's Yellow Cab drivers will be all too happy to shuttle you anywhere within the two counties, but be sure to ask about any extra fees you might accrue by traveling outside Allegheny County.

Getting Around
The **Beaver County Transit Authority** (724/728-8600, www.bcta.com) is responsible for operating the region's bus service. For information about travels in and around Butler County, visit the website of **The Bus** (www.butlertransitauthority.com), or call 724/283-1783. Information about various **limousine and taxi services** in Butler County can be found at www.visitbutlercounty.com. Or call the **National Taxi Directory** (www.1800taxicab.com) toll-free at 800/829-4222. The NTD offers telephone numbers of the nearest taxi companies based on the phone number you're calling from.

EXCURSIONS
BEAVER COUNTY AND BUTLER COUNTY

Background

The Landscape

Because of the three rivers that wind and wend their way throughout all stretches of the city, and also because of the small hills and deep valleys that seem to appear out of nowhere in this region, Pittsburgh is well known as an often difficult-to-traverse part of the country. Yet it's also known as a deeply beautiful place. Much of Southwestern Pennsylvania, as well as much of suburban Pittsburgh, is heavily forested; many regions are blanketed with strong trees and wildlife.

Within Pittsburgh's inner-city limits, the story is much different. The majority of the neighborhoods where tourists will find themselves are quite urban, and many of the most interesting eastern areas are surrounded by low-income neighborhoods.

GEOGRAPHY AND CLIMATE

Pittsburgh is located in the southwest corner of the state of Pennsylvania, where it sits near the foothills of the Allegheny Mountains. The city sits 696 feet above sea level.

In total, Pittsburgh consists of 58.3 square miles, with 55.6 square miles consisting of landmass and 2.7 square miles consisting of water. In other words, approximately 4.75 percent of the City of Pittsburgh is water.

The city sits on a landmass known as the Allegheny Plateau; this is the area where the city's three rivers—the Allegheny, the Monongahela, and the Ohio—come together at the westernmost tip of the downtown Pittsburgh area, which is also known as the Golden Triangle.

Pittsburgh is an especially hilly city, and while it has a continental climate with four seasons, it's also a relatively rainy and snowy place, with approximately 35 inches of rain annually and 43 inches of snow annually.

Pittsburgh's temperature varies widely throughout the year, with the winter months of December, January, and February averaging a low temperature of a chilly 22°F and the summer months of June, July, and August averaging a high temperature of a rather steamy (and often humid) 82.6°F.

ENVIRONMENTAL ISSUES

Because of the many industrial factories and steel-producing mills that dotted the Pittsburgh cityscape for roughly 150 years, it was inevitable that the town would eventually suffer from the effects of environmental pollution. In fact, during much of the 20th century, the entirety of Pittsburgh was so smoke- and soot-covered that visitors nicknamed it "The Smoky City"; still very much a part of Steel City lore are stories of businessmen leaving the confines of their downtown offices during the lunch break and returning an hour later to find their white shirts turned dark gray. As a result of the pollution, an alarmingly large number of Pittsburghers living within the city limits at the time suffered from respiratory illnesses. But thanks to the

Previous: Allegheny County Courthouse; Duquense Incline and Pittsburgh skyline.

steadfast efforts of one of the city's most popular mayors, David Lawrence, things began to change for the better during the 1950s, as smoke control became a leading local issue.

And although Pittsburgh has a good distance to travel before it becomes a leading national light in the area of environmental pollution control, many changes have been made for the better. The Port Authority public buses that have been a source of emissions are being at least partially replaced with electric and natural gas-fueled versions. The locally based Green Building Alliance (www.gbapgh.org) is a nonprofit organization concerned with integrating environmentally responsible design into new area construction. Pittsburgh can now claim the world's first LEED-certified convention center, the David L. Lawrence Convention Center, and the country's first LEED-certified dormitory, Carnegie Mellon University's Stever House (formerly New House Residence Hall). In fact, Western Pennsylvania today is home to some 500 professionals with LEED credentials.

History

It's something of a little-known fact that Pittsburgh's history is very much intertwined with that of our nation's first president, George Washington, who first visited the area in 1753. Then a 21-year-old major, Washington surveyed the land at the junction of the Allegheny and Monongahela Rivers (the current location of Point State Park) and wrote that it was "extremely well suited for a Fort; as it has the absolute Command of both Rivers."

Perhaps not surprisingly, the French were also impressed by the city's strategic location at the fork of the three rivers. In 1754, they managed to drive Washington's Virginia militia away, and then built a fort on the site themselves. It was named Fort Duquesne. Four years passed, and the British, led by General John Forbes, defeated the French and reclaimed the fort, which was first rebuilt and then renamed. (The wily French had burned the fort to the ground before fleeing.) The new site became known as Fort Pitt, after William Pitt, the English prime minister. On the first day of December, General Forbes named the camp at Fort Duquesne "Pittsburgh."

In 1787, roughly a decade after a heated dispute between the states of Virginia and Pennsylvania, both of whom wanted to claim Pittsburgh as their own, the Pittsburgh Academy was founded in a small log cabin; it would eventually become the University of Pittsburgh. (The cabin can still be visited on Pitt's campus; it sits near the corner of Forbes Avenue and Bigelow Boulevard.)

Clearly, the Pittsburgh of the late 18th century was becoming an outpost to reckon with; the weekly *Pittsburgh Gazette,* the first newspaper to exist west of the Alleghenies, had seen its first issue in 1786. In 1816, Pittsburgh was finally incorporated as a city. By 1820, Pittsburgh's population was just north of 7,000 souls. A decade later, it had grown to more than 12,500.

Pittsburgh had its first experience with major tragedy in 1845, when a fire destroyed roughly a third of the city and left about 12,000 people homeless. Less than a decade later, Pittsburgh's reputation as the "Smoky City" began to grow: The Jones & Laughlin Steel Corporation was founded in 1853. The Clinton iron furnace opened in 1859. And then in 1864, at the age of 29, Andrew Carnegie decided to join the iron business. A Scotsman, he soon became known as the richest man in America. In 1889 he dedicated the region's first Carnegie Library, which still operates in Braddock, and in 1900 he founded the Carnegie Technical School, now known as Carnegie Mellon University.

A true city of industry, Pittsburgh continued cranking through a series of milestones for the next 50 years: The first World Series was played here in 1903; the first motion picture house opened here in 1905; the country's first commercial radio station broadcast from here in 1920. For all its successes, however, Pittsburgh's reputation as an unpleasant place to visit managed to precede it. At the time, the town was known as one of the most polluted cities in America; streetlights were often kept on throughout the day. That all began to change in 1946, though, when Mayor David Lawrence kicked off the city's first official renaissance, an urban renewal plan that eventually stripped Pittsburgh of its Smoky City image and transformed it into the epicenter of medicine, education, technology, and culture that it is today. One of the city's biggest triumphs came in 1953, when Dr. Jonas Salk discovered the polio vaccine at the University of Pittsburgh.

Although its population has been in steady decline for decades, Pittsburgh continues to march on as a top-ranked metropolis, and in both 1985 and 2007 it was named "America's Most Livable City" by Rand-McNally's *Places Rated Almanac.* That honor was repeated in 2009 and 2014 by *The Economist,* and in 2010 by *Forbes.*

In 1989, the city elected its first female mayor, the much-loved Sophie Masloff. And then in 2006, another victory: The Pittsburgh Steelers, whose successful 1970s franchise resulted in the town becoming known as the City of Champions, managed to regain a touch of their former glory by winning a fifth Super Bowl. Just three years later, the Steelers tumbled into the history books by grabbing an unprecedented sixth Super Bowl win. After winning the Stanley Cup in 2016 and 2017, the Pittsburgh Penguins hockey team became the first team to win the cup in back-to-back seasons in 19 years.

In 2014, Democrat Bill Peduto was inaugurated as the 60th mayor of Pittsburgh; he won re-election in 2017. Of his notable accomplishments, Peduto allowed ride-hailing services like Uber and Lyft to operate in the city. Peduto was in the national spotlight in 2017, when he spoke out against President Donald's Trump's mentioning of Pittsburgh in his defense of withdrawing from the Paris Climate Agreement. The mayor spoke about Pittsburgh's commitment to fight climate change.

The Best, the Worst, and Everything in Between

You may have heard of Pittsburgh's notable civic commendation, which, interestingly enough, came in the form of a 2012 article in *National Geographic Traveler* magazine.

The article in question was the magazine's annual roundup known as "Top 25 Places"—the 25 locales across the globe considered by *Nat Geo*'s editors to be the year's most desirable and of-the-moment travel destinations. Tucked in between such exotic destinations as Sri Lanka and Croatia was the Steel City itself. To say that local hearts were aflutter would be putting it mildly.

In fact, for a midsized town that most outsiders—and even some locals—tend to think of as unremarkable at best, Pittsburgh seems to have quite an uncanny knack for popping up on such lists. Then again, the city has also had more than its fair share of egg-on-face moments where the mainstream media is concerned. Here's a brief list of some of the other national yardsticks by which Pittsburgh has been measured.

· **America's worst drivers (tied with New York City):** EverQuote, 2017

· **Most livable city in America:** Rand-McNally's *Places Rated Almanac,* 2007

· **America's 25th fittest city:** *Men's Health,* 2009

· **America's third-worst hair city:** TotalBeauty.com, 2009

· **Most underrated city:** *Harper's Bazaar,* 2017

· **Most livable city in America:** *Forbes,* 2010

Government and Economy

GOVERNMENT

Although Pittsburgh was a serious Republican stronghold in the years prior to the Great Depression, the city and its surrounding Allegheny County have largely supported Democratic politicians and ideals in the decades since. The city's support of Democrats initially came about in the 1930s, when immigration to the area was in full bloom, largely due to the huge need for unskilled laborers to populate the area's mills. Indeed, President Franklin Delano Roosevelt's Works Progress Administration proved so popular with the city's largely Eastern European immigrant population that voting Democrat essentially became expected of members of Pittsburgh's working class. Today, that tradition continues, and in Allegheny County there are roughly 2.07 registered Democratic voters for every registered Republican.

- **America's 10th dirtiest city:** *Forbes,* 2010

- **Twentieth prettiest city in the world:** *Huffington Post,* 2010

- **America's 28th best bicycling city:** *Bicycling Magazine,* 2010

- **Third worst-dressed city in America:** *GQ,* 2011

- **America's second-best city for moms:** *The Daily Beast,* 2011

- **America's second best city for millennials:** *CNBC,* 2017

- **America's eighth-best city for single mothers:** *Zillow.com,* 2011

- **America's sixth vainest city:** *Men's Health,* 2012

- **America's fourth most-literate city:** *Central Connecticut State University,* 2012

- **One of the country's 10 best cities for older singles:** *AARP,* 2012

- **America's eighth most-polluted city:** *American Lung Association,* 2013

- **America's best city for retirement:** *NerdWallet.com,* 2013

- **America's number 1 city to buy your first home:** *Business Insider,* 2017

ECONOMY

Pittsburgh first became an economic powerhouse in the mid-1800s, thanks to the efforts of Scottish immigrant Andrew Carnegie and others involved in the city's iron, steel, and glass industries. The American steel industry suffered a massive collapse in the early 1980s, however, as production began moving to more affordable plants overseas. Displaying the most admirable side of its entrepreneurial and hardworking nature, Pittsburgh steadfastly refused to wither away and took immediate and massive strides to reinvent itself. The city today owes its economic strength to a diverse mixture of health care, education, technology, and biotechnology. Finance and tourism also play important roles.

The University of Pittsburgh Medical Center (UPMC) is by far the region's largest employer, with 46,500 employees in Allegheny County alone. Highmark Health employs 20,000, while the University of Pittsburgh employs approximately 12,000 area residents. Nonetheless, Pittsburgh continues to lead the country in population decline. Although the city claimed

677,000 residents in 1950, today fewer than 304,000 remain. This likely has much to do with Allegheny County's current per capita income, which rests at $54,090.

A number of Fortune 500 and Fortune 1,000 companies continue to be headquartered in Pittsburgh, including Alcoa, PPG Industries, and Allegheny Technologies. Other well-known mega-companies headquartered in Pittsburgh include American Eagle Outfitters, Bayer Corporation, Westinghouse Electric, and 84 Lumber. Pittsburgh is also home of the beloved H. J. Heinz Company. In 2013, the company was purchased by Berkshire Hathaway and 3G Capital, and in 2015 Heinz merged with Kraft, forming Kraft Heinz Company.

Health Care

It simply isn't possible to overstate the contribution of the University of Pittsburgh Medical Center to the local economy. Easily the largest employer in Western Pennsylvania, UPMC is also responsible for much of the area's construction boom; the organization spends roughly $250 million annually on construction activity. UPMC's annual economic impact is estimated at $26.5 billion, including a $412 million investment in state-of-the-art facilities and technology, $1.4 billion of revenue in taxes and 130,000 direct and indirect employees in the region.

West Penn Allegheny Health System, the region's second-most important economic leader in the health-care industry, consists of Allegheny General Hospital, West Penn Hospital, Canonsburg General Hospital, and other regional hospitals.

Education

Referred to by some civic boosters as the College City, the greater Pittsburgh area is home to 33 colleges and universities, the most prominent being the University of Pittsburgh, Carnegie Mellon University, and Duquesne University. Economically, Pitt is the area's powerhouse; the school pours out $3.9 billion in total economic impact. Pitt is responsible for roughly $187 million in government revenues, such as real estate and sales taxes, each year. Pitt faculty, staff, and students generate $74.3 million annually in charitable donations and volunteer services.

More than 135,000 college and university students matriculate at a Pittsburgh area school each year. Some schools, such as Carlow University, Chatham College, the Art Institute of Pittsburgh, Point Park University, and Robert Morris University, sit right within the city limits. Other schools, such as Seton Hill University, Slippery Rock University, Indiana University of Pennsylvania, and Washington & Jefferson College, are spread throughout the southwestern region of the state.

More information can be found on the website of the Pittsburgh Council on Higher Education (www.pchepa.org).

Technology and Biotechnology

Pittsburgh's tech and biotech industries are much larger and more developed than even most locals realize. Carnegie Mellon University continues to take giant strides in the fields of robotics and software engineering; the school's Software Engineering Institute (a federally funded research and development center) spent upward of $43 million in 2003.

Organizations such as the Pittsburgh Lifesciences Greenhouses (a joint venture between Pitt and CMU) have been instrumental in positioning Southwestern Pennsylvania as a bioscience, nanobiotechnology, and robotics leader. Researchers study neurological disorders, tissue engineering, and drug discovery, among other biotechnology developments.

To stay abreast of local tech news and information, check out the website of the Pittsburgh Technology Council (www.pghtech.org).

Local Culture

POPULATION

In 2016, the U.S. Census Bureau listed the population of Pittsburgh as 303,625. That figure represents a whopping population decline from 2000, when the census counted a total of 334,563 Pittsburgh residents. Currently, women and senior citizens are well represented in Pittsburgh; the population is nearly 52 percent female, and persons over the age of 65 make up 13.8 percent of the population. Twenty-six percent of Pittsburgh's population is black or African American, while the local population of Hawaiians and other Pacific Islanders is so small that the group failed to rate on the census report. Just over 66 percent of all Pittsburghers are white or Caucasian.

Historically, Pittsburgh has welcomed immigrants since the mid-1700s, the majority being from southern and eastern European countries such as Italy and Poland. Pittsburgh saw its largest influx of European immigration during the end of the 19th century and the beginning of the 20th. The majority came in search of work, having heard of Pittsburgh's reputation as an industrial powerhouse. Many of the smaller row houses (or "mill houses") that still stand today in Lawrenceville, the South Side Slopes, and other riverside neighborhoods were first occupied by these eastern European laborers.

A good number of early immigrants also came to Pittsburgh from Germany and Ireland. The North Side of Pittsburgh, originally a separate city known as Allegheny, is the region where the majority of the city's German immigrants settled, and in the eastern neighborhood of Squirrel Hill, Hebrew and Yiddish are still widely spoken on the streets today.

THE ARTS

Probably because Pittsburgh has for so long been an industrial town with a deeply woven blue-collar temperament, many of the fine arts, performing arts, and visual arts haven't caught on here as quickly or successfully as in other metropolitan cities of equivalent size. And although Pittsburghers tend to vote Democratic, ours is something of a rural-influenced backwoods culture. Professional sports are hugely popular; a citywide passion for the Pittsburgh Steelers in particular seems to be the one cultural quirk that unites all Pittsburghers.

For the most part, Pittsburghers are a very proud people; regional pride is something you're likely to encounter over and over again during your stay. Unlike on the more recently developed West Coast, a large number of Pittsburgh residents have lived in the area their entire lives. In many cases, their parents have as well; grandparents of Pittsburghers in their late 20s and early 30s were quite often European immigrants. Many of those life-long Pittsburghers, especially those who grew up within the city limits and speak with an accent known as "Pittsburghese" (technically North Midland U.S. English), are referred to as "yinzers." This is generally considered a derogatory term and shouldn't be used outside of familiar company. To learn about the unique Southwestern Pennsylvania accent, visit www.pitts-burghspeech.com and www.pittsburghese.com.

Today, Pittsburgh's arts scene is slowly gaining both traction and national attention. The Pittsburgh Symphony Orchestra has long been noted as one of the nation's best. And due in large part to the city's extremely low cost of living, young artists and other creative types have been relocating to Pittsburgh—generally in the eastern neighborhoods—from bigger and more expensive urban areas.

Literature

Pittsburgh has long had a strong literary history, and, in fact, the University of Pittsburgh was the first institution of higher learning in the United States to offer a Master of Fine Arts degree in Creative Nonfiction. Pittsburgh author Lee Gutkind spearheads the program; he's also the founding editor of the literary journal *Creative Nonfiction,* which is headquartered in Shadyside.

Pitt's nationally regarded writing program has seen scores of well-known and widely published instructors; writers of note who've recently taught in the program include the hard-living fiction writer Chuck Kinder, who was one of Raymond Carver's best friends and, according to rumor, was the Pitt professor that the character in Michael Chabon's *Wonder Boys* is based on. (The street that Kinder's character lives on in the *Wonder Boys* film is South Atlantic Street in Friendship.) The poet Toi Derricotte was also a Pitt instructor, as was Faith Adiele, a nonfiction writer and the author of *Meeting Faith: The Forest Journals of a Black Buddhist Nun.* Current instructors of note include the poet Lynn Emanuel and the National Book Award winner Terrance Hayes.

Renowned poet Jack Gilbert (*Views of Jeopardy, Monolithos*) was born in Pittsburgh in 1925. Author David McCullough, who won the Pulitzer Prize for the masterful biography *John Adams,* is also a Pittsburgh native. And although he has since left town, author John Edgar Wideman (*Brothers and Keepers*) wrote highly regarded novels about African American life in the Pittsburgh neighborhood of Homewood. Pittsburgher Stewart O'Nan's novel *Everyday People* explored the hardscrabble life of African Americans living in the neighborhood of East Liberty.

Possibly better known than all the above combined are Pittsburghers

Annie Dillard and Gertrude Stein. Dillard's *An American Childhood*
examines the events of her childhood in 1950s Pittsburgh. Stein (*The Autobiography of Alice B. Toklas*) was a legendary feminist novelist and playwright who grew up on the city's North Side and eventually settled in Paris.

Music

Possibly Pittsburgh's most famous musician, historically speaking, was Stephen Collins Foster, who lived in Lawrenceville and is buried in Allegheny Cemetery. Foster was a singer, a song leader, and a composer whose first major success was "Oh! Susanna."

Pittsburgh has also produced its share of jazz legends. Although he was a native of Dayton, Ohio, Billy Strayhorn's music career officially began in Pittsburgh; today he's best known for composing the jazz staple "Take the A Train." The jazz pianist and composer Erroll Garner was born here in 1921; he went on to play with Charlie Parker, among others. Like Gertrude Stein, jazz drummer Kenny Clarke was born here but chose to settle in Paris. He's known as an important innovator of the bebop drumming style. Earl Hines was another well-known jazz pianist also born in Pittsburgh, as was Mary Lou Williams, who worked with Duke Ellington and Thelonious Monk.

Pittsburgh's most legendary jazz venue was the Hill District's Crawford Grill, which still stands today at 2141 Wylie Avenue. Throughout the 1930s, '40s, and '50s, Pittsburgh's Hill District (then known as "Little Harlem") and the Crawford Grill were both well known and respected in prominent African American social circles. The jazz guitarist George Benson, in fact, was born and raised in the Hill District and later graduated from Schenley High School. The midcentury American doo-wop group known as the Del-Vikings, meanwhile, consisted of U.S. Air Force members who were stationed in Pittsburgh at the time of the group's founding.

Since the late 1970s, rock 'n' roll—especially the brand of rock now known as "classic rock"—has been favored in Pittsburgh. One of the area's most famous rockers is Joe Grushecky. As a longtime friend of Bruce Springsteen's, Grushecky has been known to bring the Boss to town—unannounced—to perform secret concerts at small clubs. Local musician Donny Iris was a pop and R&B superstar in his own right throughout the 1970s, and the rock group the Clarks, which still performs and records today, has managed to achieve national and even some international success. Bret Michaels, who fronted the world-famous hair-metal band Poison in the 1980s and early '90s and then went on to become something of a reality TV star, is also originally from the Pittsburgh area.

Of the city's more recent musical talent, the young rappers Mac Miller and Wiz Khalifa, along with electronic musician Girl Talk (Gregg Gillis), have seen the widest recognition outside Pittsburgh's borders. That is, unless you count Christina Aguilera, who grew up in Wexford. Other Pittsburgh-based bands of note include legendary punk outfits Aus-Rotten and Anti-Flag, the math-rock band Don Caballero, and the jam-band Rusted Root.

Pittsburgh's Famous Faces

Regardless of its plain and simple "jus' folks" facade, the Steel City has cranked out an impressive roster of iconic celebrities in fields ranging from music and the visual arts to literature and theater. This is a list of superstars who were either born in the Pittsburgh area or lived and worked here for a significant length of time.

- **Actors and Hollywood players:** F. Murray Abraham, Steven Bochco, Dan Cortese, Ann B. Davis, Jeff Goldblum, Michael Keaton, Gene Kelly, Dennis Miller, Fred Rogers, George Romero, Tom Savini, Jimmy Stewart, Sharon Stone

- **Artists and writers:** Nellie Bly, Rachel Carson, Mary Cassatt, Willa Cather, Michael Chabon, Annie Dillard, Teeny Harris, Philip Pearlstein, Gertrude Stein, Bunny Yeager, Andy Warhol, August Wilson

- **Singers and musicians:** Christina Aguilera, Perry Como, Billy Eckstine, Stephen Foster, Erroll Garner, Wiz Khalifa, Henry Mancini, Bret Michaels, Mac Miller, Trent Reznor

Television and Film

Certainly the city's proudest television accomplishment was the airing of *Mister Rogers' Neighborhood*, a genuine broadcasting treasure hosted by a true American icon, Fred Rogers, who passed away in February 2003. Produced for 33 years, it was the longest-running program ever aired by PBS.

Pittsburgh's film history has been long and varied. Aside from the 1980s classic *Flashdance,* probably the most important movie filmed in the city remains George Romero's *Night of the Living Dead.* Much of the film, which Romero co-wrote with fellow Pittsburgher John Russo, was filmed in Evans City, which sits about 30 miles north of Pittsburgh in Butler County. Romero has since relocated to Toronto, although the famed makeup artist Tom Savini, who worked on Romero's *Dawn of the Dead* (a *Night of the Living Dead* sequel that was filmed inside the Monroeville Mall), still resides in the city.

Hollywood classics filmed in and around the Pittsburgh area in years past include *The Deer Hunter; Lorenzo's Oil;* and *The Silence of the Lambs,* a few scenes of which were shot in the Carnegie Museum of Natural History. More recent productions that have taken place locally include *The Dark Knight Rises; The Fault in Our Stars; Southpaw; The Perks of Being a Wallflower;* and *Fences,* based on the screenplay of Pulitzer Prize winning playwright August Wilson.

Essentials

Transportation

GETTING THERE

Pittsburgh is an easily accessible city, with a major airport within 25 minutes of the city center, a convenient location on I-76, and plenty of bus and train depots.

Air

Pittsburgh International Airport (PIT, 412/472-5510 or 412/472-3525, Pittsburgh, www.flypittsburgh.com) is the busiest airport in Western Pennsylvania and the second busiest in the state, after Philadelphia International Airport. Over eight million passengers are served each year, flying to and from 68 nonstop destinations across the United States, Europe, Canada, and the Caribbean, including Reykjavik, Iceland; Paris, France; and Frankfurt, Germany. Pittsburgh International Airport has been consistently ranked as one of the world's best airports by several different publications.

Commercial airlines serving the airport include American Airlines, Delta, United Airlines, and Air Canada, among others. Budget airlines serving the airport include JetBlue, Frontier, Southwest, Spirit, and WOW. For domestic flights, allow about 90 minutes for check-in and to get through security, two hours for an international flight.

AIRPORT TRANSPORTATION

Getting to and from the airport is relatively easy. The **28X Airport Flyer** (412/442-2000, www.portauthority.org) is your best bet for cheap transportation: It's just $2.75 from the airport to downtown or Oakland. Allow about 45 minutes from Oakland and 30 minutes from downtown for travel time. During the week, the first drop-off at the airport is at 4:15am and the last drop-off is at 11:44pm.

You can also utilize a taxi service, like **zTrip** (412/777-7777, www.ztrip. com), by calling on demand or reserving a trip in advance. There's also an app for your convenience. However, be forewarned that taxis in Pittsburgh don't have the best reputation for showing up on time, so book at your own risk.

The airport has a designated pickup location for **ride-hailing services** like Uber and Lyft. Meet your ride at the designated pickup point right outside the baggage claim exit. Pittsburgh also has several customer courtesy **shuttles** that run regularly from most downtown hotels. Inquire at your hotel about this service.

Train

Pittsburgh's **Amtrak station** (1100 Liberty Ave., 412/471-6170, www.am-trak.com) is downtown, near the Strip District. Trains arrive daily from destinations throughout the United States and Canada. Major origin cities include Washington DC (7.5 hours, $42-87), Philadelphia (7.5 hours, $48-81), and New York (9 hours, $59-93).

Bus

The **Greyhound station** (55 11th St., 800/231-2222, www.greyhound.com) is directly across from the Amtrak station and near the David L. Lawrence Convention Center. The station is easy to spot with its cylindrical glass facade and giant sign.

The popular **Megabus** (www.megabus.com) is a double-decker coach bus operated by a British company that offers cheap fares. These are arguably nicer and more comfortable than Greyhound buses. The coaches feature electrical outlets, free Wi-Fi, and onboard restrooms. The bus drops off passengers at the **David L. Lawrence Convention Center** (10th St. and Penn Ave.). Major origin cities include Philadelphia ($5-35 one-way), New York City ($20-49 one-way), Cleveland, Detroit, and Washington DC.

GETTING AROUND
Public Transportation

Port Authority Transit (412/422-2000, www.portauthority.org) operates buses, trains, and two inclines within Allegheny County. Bus, train, and incline rides are $2.50 with a ConnectCard or $2.75 with cash. Transfers cost an extra $1 and are only available on the ConnectCard; they're generally good for 3-4 hours and can be used for one ride going in any direction. You can get a ConnectCard at the **Port Authority Downtown Service Center** (534 Smithfield St., 412/442-2000, www.connectcard.org) or at many retailers in the area, including grocery store Giant Eagle.

Pittsburgh has a somewhat limited **light rail system,** known as **the T,** which can take you around town or out to the South Hills suburbs. The rail system has four stops in downtown, two on the North Shore and another one at **Station Square**. There is a Free Fare Zone that includes the four downtown stops and two North Shore stops. All rides outside of the Free Fare Zone cost $2.50 with a ConnectCard or $2.75 cash.

Another popular way to get around town is to take one of the **inclines.** Of course, this is only convenient if you are traveling from the city to Mount Washington, but it's a great way to get to the top of the mountain and take in the amazing views. The Monongahela Incline starts across the street from Station Square and takes passengers up to its station on Grandview Avenue. The Duquesne Incline will take you to another location on Grandview Avenue, about a mile down the road in the Duquesne Height area. This is where some of Mount Washington's best restaurants are located. Fares for adults are $2.50 one way with a ConnectCard ($2.75 cash). Port Authority passes are also accepted.

Driving

If you plan to stay within the city limits, you can get by just fine without a car. However, if you want to explore the outlying neighborhoods and more rural areas surrounding the city, you'll be better off renting a vehicle. Driving in Pittsburgh can be confusing, with short merges and lots of bridges and tunnels, so you might want to make sure that your GPS or phone navigation system is up to date.

Rental cars are available at various locations throughout the city. At the Pittsburgh International Airport, you'll find rental counters for **Budget** (800/527-0700, www.budget.com), **Dollar** (800/800-4000, www.dollarrentacar.com), **Hertz** (800/654-3131, www.hertz.com), and **Avis** (412/472-5200, www.avis.com) on the same level as baggage claim.

Most of the neighborhoods within the city have designated residential parking, so make sure to pay attention to the posted time limit and other signage. Pittsburgh has replaced most of its cash meters with multi-space meters that allow you to just punch in your car's license plate number and pay with cash or credit card. There's also an app called **Go Mobile Pittsburgh** that allows you to pay for parking with your phone, even adding time to the meter remotely. Parking downtown can be hard to come by, particularly during the weekday when commuters are parked for the day. Another app, **ParkPGH,** will show you real-time parking availability for downtown's parking garages.

Taxis and Ride-Hailing Services

The city's main taxi company is **zTrip** (www.ztrip.com), which offers service via phone, website, or smartphone app. The company is notoriously unreliable, however. You can still hail a cab, but only in certain parts of town like the South Side, Station Square, and downtown, and usually only at busy times of day. **Uber** and **Lyft** are quickly becoming the preferred mode of transportation for quick, fast, and convenient rides. There is no shortage of Lyft and Uber drivers in Pittsburgh.

Bicycling

Pittsburgh used to be ranked as one of the worst cities for cyclists. However, this reputation has been changing in recent years as Pittsburgh has become increasingly bike friendly. This is in large part due to organizations like **Bike Pittsburgh** (188 43rd St., 412/325-4334, www.bike-pgh.org), which advocate for better biking routes and increased safety for cyclists. In fact, Pittsburgh has added bike lanes to parts of downtown and is planning on adding bike routes to Forbes Avenue in Oakland as well.

There are lots of options for off-road cycling on Pittsburgh's extensive trail systems. **Bike Pittsburgh** has several great maps available for download on their website that will give you all the best bike routes in the city and surrounding areas, including the **Three Rivers Heritage Trail** and **Great Allegheny Passage.**

Accessibility

The Pittsburgh International Airport offers services for travelers with disabilities, including reserved parking spaces, visual paging services on flight information screens, and wheelchair or porter service throughout the airport.

Port Authority of Allegheny County buses, light rail cars, and

Veteran-owned and -operated taxi service **VETaxi** (412/481-8387) has
vehicles that are equipped to provide transportation for those with wheel-
chairs or scooters.

For more information about access in and around the city, check out official tourism site **VisitPittsburgh** (www.visitpittsburgh.com).

Travel Tips

WEATHER

The weather in Pittsburgh is quite seasonal, with warm humid weather
in the summer and a cold and somewhat snowy and cloudy climate in the
winter. Fall and spring in Pittsburgh bring moderate sunshine and mild
temperatures. The average high is 37°F in January, 62°F in April, 83°F in
July, and 64°F in October. Pittsburgh is known for its wildly unpredictable
weather, partly due to its hilly topography and lake effect weather coming
from Lake Erie to the north. The record lowest temperature in January
was a chilly -22°F. The temperatures may climb near the triple digits in
the summer.

The average annual rainfall in Pittsburgh is around 35 inches, and many
people are surprised to find out that the city's precipitation levels rival those
of notoriously rainy Seattle. According to data from 2015, the city is tied
for second place with Portland, Oregon, for the title of dreariest city in the
United States. If you're looking for sunshine, visit in the summer, when the
city gets more sunny days.

HOURS

Pittsburgh tends to call it a night somewhat early. Pennsylvania liquor
laws mandate that restaurants that serve alcohol and bars close at 2am;
private clubs must close by 3am. A handful of restaurants stay open late
or 24 hours. The busiest time for most fine Pittsburgh restaurants on a
weekend is around 8pm. Some spots stop serving as early as 10 or 10:30pm,
even on weekends.

SMOKING

In 2008, Pennsylvania put the Clean Indoor Air Act into place, which led
to the banning of smoking in most public, retail, and community buildings across the state (there are some exceptions for the city of Philadelphia,
which generally has tighter anti-smoking regulations). Despite this, a few
loopholes in the regulations allow private clubs and casinos to permit smoking, along with taverns that make up less than 20 percent of their total gross
sales on food. Most hotels are either smoke free or have designated rooms
where smoking is allowed.

The law requires that designated smoking areas be located away from
building entrances and windows. The law doesn't specify a minimum

distance for smoking areas, but the Department of Health recommends that these areas be at least 20 feet away from doorways.

In 2017, Allegheny County Council decided to ban the use of electronic vapor devices in public indoor spaces. The council voted to hold e-cigarettes and handheld vapor devices to the same regulations as cigarettes.

MEDIA AND COMMUNICATION
Phones and Area Codes

Most Allegheny County phone numbers (including those within Pittsburgh) use the 412 area code. In 1998, Pittsburgh gained a 724 area code for numbers outside city limits, which changed around 1.5 million phone numbers for land lines. Most of these are outside of Allegheny County. Other counties using the 724 area code include Armstrong, Beaver, Butler, Fayette, Greene, Indiana, Lawrence, Mercer, Washington, and Westmoreland Counties, as well as parts of Clarion, Crawford, and Venango Counties.

Magazines and Newspapers

Pittsburgh has two daily newspapers: the **Pittsburgh Post-Gazette** (www.post-gazette.com) and the **Pittsburgh Tribune-Review** (www.triblive.com). The *Post-Gazette* tends to be more politically left-leaning while the *Tribune* is more conservative. There is also the weekly alternative **Pittsburgh City Paper** (www.pghcitypaper.com).

For business news, check out the **Pittsburgh Business Times** (www.bizjournals.com). **The New Pittsburgh Courier** (www.newpittsburghcourieronline.com) focuses mostly on news and events in the African American community, while **Pittsburgh Catholic** (www.pittsburghcatholic.org) is the city's Catholic publication. **Out** (www.out.com) offers LGBTQ news. **The Jewish Chronicle of Pittsburgh** is published weekly for the Jewish community by the Jewish Publication and Education Foundation.

The well-written and informative **Pittsburgh Magazine** (www.pittsburghmagazine) is a monthly publication featuring stories about local arts, food, entertainment, and travel. **Pittsburgh Quarterly** (www.pittsburghquarterly.com) features stories about Pittsburgh culture, commerce, science, and education. If you're more interested in Pittsburgh society and local celebrity goings-on, check out **Whirl** (www.whirlmagazine.com).

Foodies will enjoy flipping through a copy of **Table Magazine** (www.tablemagazine) or **Edible Allegheny** (www.ediblecommunities.com/allegheny), both of which cover the Greater Pittsburgh and Southwestern Pennsylvania food and restaurant scene.

Pittsburgh Technology Council puts out **Pittsburgh teQ** magazine, the go-to publication for Pittsburgh's entrepreneurial tech community. **Dirt Rag** (www.dirtragmag.com), **Bicycle Times** (www.bicycletimesmag.com), and **Urban Velo** (www.urbanvelo.org) are all national bicycle magazines that are published in the Pittsburgh area.

Radio and TV

You'll find affiliates of all the major television networks in Pittsburgh, including CBS, ABC, and NBC. Pittsburgh's PBS station, **WQED** (www.wqed.org) was the first community-owned station in the country. **PCTV21** (www.pctv21.org) is that city's public access station.

The most popular radio stations are **WESA 90.5 FM,** Pittsburgh's NPR affiliate; **WQED 89.3 FM** (classical and public radio); **WYEP 91.3 FM** (community-supported adult alternative); **WDVE 102.5 FM** (hard rock and classic rock); **WXDX 105.9** (rock and alternative); **WBZZ Star 100.7** (pop); **WKST-FM 96.1 Kiss FM** (pop); **3WS 94.5 FM** (oldies and classics); **WTAE 1250 AM** (local news and sports); **Y108FM** (country); **KDKA 1020AM** (news and talk); and **WRCT 88.3 FM** (free-form independent music from Carnegie Mellon).

Health and Safety

HOSPITALS AND PHARMACIES

Pittsburgh has an exceptionally high number of major hospitals and health-care centers, most within the Oakland neighborhood. The **University of Pittsburgh Medical Center** (www.upmc.com) operates many of the hospitals in this area. Oakland hospitals include **UPMC Presbyterian, UPMC Montefiore, Magee-Womens Hospital of UPMC,** and **Western Psychiatric Institute and Clinic of UPMC.** Patients from all over the world come to receive treatment at **The Hillman Cancer Center of UPMC.** The **Children's Hospital of Pittsburgh of UPMC,** located in Lawrenceville, is one of the top 10 pediatric hospitals in the country. **UPMC Mercy** is located between Oakland and downtown.

Allegheny General Hospital, in the North Side, and **Western Pennsylvania Hospital,** in Bloomfield, are part of **West Penn Allegheny Health System** (www.wpahs.org).

For nonemergency care, there are plenty of quick-care clinics available in Pittsburgh, including **MedExpress** (www.medexpress.com) and **UPMC Urgent Care** (www.upmc.com).

EMERGENCY SERVICES

To call the police, or for fire or medical emergencies, dial 911. For an electrical emergency, dial 412/393-7000. If you have a gas emergency in Pittsburgh, dial 412/442-3095. The Poison Information Center can be contacted at 412/681-6669 or 412/390-3300. For water and sewer emergencies in Pittsburgh, dial 412/255-2409. The toll-free number for PA Crime Stoppers is 800/472-8477. Dial Pittsburgh's nonemergency services phone number, 311, to access information about city government services and to report nonemergencies such as potholes.

CRIME

Pittsburgh is a relatively safe city that has seen a lot of gentrification in recent years, and many of the neighborhoods are in transition. Be aware of your surroundings and safety, especially at night. The North Side sees a higher crime rate, but there are distinct areas that are more dangerous, like parts north of the Andy Warhol Museum. In general, the North Shore area, where PNC Park, Heinz Field, and the Carnegie Science Center are located, is safer. East Liberty is slowly being gentrified but has rougher sections. Try to avoid the residential streets on the side of Penn Avenue that sits opposite the Bloomfield and Friendship neighborhoods. Other areas to avoid after dark include the Hill District and Uptown.

Resources

Suggested Reading

Bell, Thomas. *Out of this Furnace*. University of Pittsburgh Press, 1976. An emotionally wrenching story that tells of the trials and tribulations of three generations of a Slovakian family who immigrated to America and ended up working in the Braddock steel mills.

Chabon, Michael. *The Mysteries of Pittsburgh*. Harper Perennial, 1989. Chabon is a graduate of the University of Pittsburgh and a former employee of the long-lived but now shuttered Jay's Bookstall; *Mysteries* was his first novel and also the book that was meant to catapult his rising star into the stratosphere. It didn't happen exactly that way, but this is nonetheless an incredible read about the existential and sexual dilemmas of a group of young adults passing their first summer after college.

Creative Nonfiction Foundation. *Pittsburgh in Words*. Creative Nonfiction, 2008. Published in celebration of the city's 250th anniversary, this magazine-like publication (which was produced by *Creative Nonfiction,* a local literary journal) features true stories by writers attempting to share and explain the true essence of the Steel City.

Dillard, Annie. *An American Childhood*. Harper Perennial, 1988. Dillard ponders her 1950s Pittsburgh childhood in this classic book about growing up, seeing the world anew, and the unavoidable pain of slowly becoming an adult.

Lorant, Stefan. *Pittsburgh: The Story of an American City*. The Derrydale Press, 1999. Based on decades of tireless research, this heavy, hardcover coffee-table book tells nearly every last facet of the city's story, from the battles of the mid-1750s to the 1990s. Incredibly detailed and packed with dozens of gorgeous photos, *Pittsburgh* reset the standard for historical and cultural books about cities when it was first published in the 1970s.

Musson, Robert A. *Brewing in Greater Pittsburgh*. Arcadia Publishing, 2012. As part of the *Images of America* series, Musson's volume documents Pittsburgh's surprisingly active 250-year history as a beer-brewing town. The book features more than 200 historical photographs.

O'Nan, Stewart. *Everyday People.* Grove Press, 2001. A fictional tale about gangs, drugs, and the life of hard knocks in East Liberty, a still economically disadvantaged neighborhood that is nevertheless growing more gentrified each year.

Orr, C. Prentiss, Abby Mendelson, and Tripp Clarke. *Pittsburgh Born, Pittsburgh Bred.* Senator John Heinz History Center, 2008. Experience a touch of Steel City pride as you thumb through this engaging coffee-table book, which contains the stories of "500 of the more famous people who have called Pittsburgh home."

Toker, Franklin. *Pittsburgh: A New Portrait.* University of Pittsburgh Press, 2009. A stunningly ambitious look at Pittsburgh as a timeless American city, this heavy volume has now replaced Stefan Lorant's legendary *Pittsburgh* book as the definitive final word on the Steel City, from its earliest days to modern times.

Wideman, John Edgar. *Brothers and Keepers.* Holt, Rinehart, and Winston, 1984. One of the most popular books from this Pittsburgh-based writer, who long chronicled life in the Homewood ghetto. In *Brothers and Keepers,* Wideman waxes poetic about the differences between his life, heavy with learning and culture, and the life of his brother, who is serving a life sentence in jail.

Wilson, August. *Fences.* Samuel French, Inc., 1986. Probably the most legendary play ever penned by Hill District native August Wilson. The story, for which Wilson was awarded the Pulitzer Prize, concerns the struggle of Troy Maxson, a proud black man who can't quite get a grasp on the quickly changing world of the 1960s.

Internet Resources

INFORMATION AND EVENTS
About.com
www.pittsburgh.about.com
A solid online destination for keeping abreast of upcoming events and local news, About's Pittsburgh site also boasts info about finding a job, finding a home, and finding fun things to do with the family.

Carnegie Library of Pittsburgh
www.carnegielibrary.org
The Carnegie Library's website is an absolutely indispensable research site for scholars of all things Pittsburgh. Click the Tools & Research tab at the top of the homepage, and then choose the Pittsburgh link. There, you'll be directed to a wonderfully detailed collection of Pittsburgh data, be it cultural, historical, or just about anything else.

City of Pittsburgh
www.pittsburghpa.gov
The official City of Pittsburgh site provides information about city parks, tourism, road closures, and city-sponsored events. New residents in particular should explore the site's Resources and City Directory pages.

The College City
www.thecollegecity.com
Particularly useful for its fantastic collection of local links, this site should also be the first stop for any college student interested in area schools. It's also a useful site for new residents and tourists looking to discover the city's youthful and active opportunities.

Global Pittsburgh
www.globalpittsburgh.org
This wonderfully useful site is concerned with connecting Pittsburgh's various international communities. Visitors or new residents from abroad can search for job opportunities, new friends and activities, and information about immigration.

Imagine Pittsburgh
www.imaginepittsburgh.com
Launched as part of a three-year, $3 million marketing campaign to increase awareness of the Pittsburgh area's numerous achievements and its nearly unlimited possibility for growth, this site does a wonderful job of explaining why Pittsburgh is such a unique place. You'll also find links to the helpful tourism sites of 11 surrounding counties.

Pittsburghese
www.pittsburghese.com
This is a hilariously good-natured guide to one of North America's most curious regional dialects, Pittsburghese. It includes a glossary, a translator, an audio quiz—even Pittsburghese calisthenics. (Believe me, yinz are gonna need it.)

Venture Outdoors
www.ventureoutdoors.org
Local nonprofit organization Venture Outdoors is responsible for a surprisingly large percentage of the activities that take place on Pittsburgh's rivers. Check this site for a bevy of outdoorsy recreation opportunities.

VisitPittsburgh
www.visitpittsburgh.com
The Greater Pittsburgh Convention & Visitors Bureau site is where you'll find all the necessary information to plan a vacation or business trip to the Steel City. Essentially a mini online guidebook, VisitPittsburgh also allows visitors to book hotel and vacation packages. Particularly useful are the

suggested itineraries for those interested in taking day trips to the nearby counties and countryside.

NEWS

New Pittsburgh Courier
www.newpittsburghcourieronline.com
The online version of the weekly newspaper geared toward the city's African American community.

Pittsburgh Business Times
www.bizjournals.com/pittsburgh
This local edition of the nationwide *Business Times,* a weekly newspaper, is a must-read for local entrepreneurs and corporate types.

Pittsburgh Catholic
www.pittsburghcatholic.org
This widely read weekly newspaper is published by the Diocese of Pittsburgh. It boasts the largest circulation of any paper in the region.

Pittsburgh City Paper
www.pghcitypaper.com
The city's solitary alternative newsweekly maintains a huge online archive of feature stories. The website is also indispensable for its comprehensive event listings and many restaurant reviews.

Pittsburgh Indymedia
www.pittsburgh.indymedia.org
This community-based media site is filled with regional news, most with a heavily liberal bias. Pittsburgh's activism community is surprisingly large, and this is where many of them congregate. Information about upcoming protests and antiwar marches can be found here.

Pittsburgh Magazine
www.pittsburghmagazine.com
The website of Pittsburgh's regional monthly magazine offers a wealth of feature stories, an extensive events calendar, thoughtful dining reviews, and more.

Pittsburgh Post-Gazette and Pittsburgh Tribune-Review
www.post-gazette.com
www.triblive.com
Find up-to-the-minute local and national news at the websites of Pittsburgh's two daily newspapers, the liberal and more critically acclaimed *Post-Gazette* and the conservative *Tribune-Review,* which publishes a handful of smaller community papers under its Trib Total Media banner.

Pop City
www.popcitymedia.com

This weekly online magazine documents the Pittsburgh experience primarily for the young and active crowd. Tech, lifestyle, and entrepreneurial news is featured.

BLOGS

Behind the Steel Curtain
www.behindthesteelcurtain.com
Pittsburgh is home to an untold number of Steelers fan blogs, and this is one of the very finest.

Boring Pittsburgh
www.boringpittsburgh.com
In its role as an enthusiastic cheerleader for the city, Boring Pittsburgh covers cool and quirky happenings and other events.

I Heart Pgh
www.iheartpgh.com
This is a quirky, well-edited, and frequently updated listing of events, especially those with a focus on the arts.

Pittsburgh Bloggers
www.pghbloggers.org
A blog about local blogs, it's useful largely because of its incredibly extensive collection of links.

Steeltown Anthem
www.steeltownanthem.com
This is an art, design, and architecture blog with a distinctive *Dwell* magazine sensibility.

Yinzperation
www.yinzperation.com
Inspired by a challenge to meet new Pittsburghers, Yinzperation is a clever interview-style blog that introduces readers to some of the city's unique personalities.

Index

Nightlife Index

Shops Index

Hotels Index

Photo Credits

Title page photo: © F11photo | Dreamstime.com; page 2 (top) © Mike Reiss, (bottom) © Haveseen | Dreamstime; page 22 (top left) © Jeff Greenberg / VisitPittsburgh, (top right) © Emily King, (bottom) © 00_SkylineNight_H; page 23 © Cjorgens | Dreamstime; page 25 © Sean Pavone | Dreamstime.com; page 26 © VisitPittsburgh/Denise Giangiulio; page 27 © Kurt Miller; page 29 © Sean Pavone | Dreamstime; page 30 © Chris Rokitski | Dreamstime; page 31 © christianhinkle/123RF; page 33 (top) © Christian Hinkle | Dreamstime.com, (bottom) © Maria Feklistova | Dreamstime.com; page 36 (top left) © National Aviary / VisitPittsburgh, (top right) © Anna Lee Fields, (bottom) © Emily King; page 43 (top left) © Emily King, (top right) © Philip Scalia / VisitPittsburgh, (bottom) © Phil Scalia/Visit Pittsburgh; page 46 (top) © Emily King, (bottom) © Joahua Franzos / Carnegie Museum of Natural History; page 54 (top) © Laura Petrilla, (bottom) © Sohail Khwaja; page 59 (top left) © Jose Luis de Solar, (top right) © Adam Milliron, (bottom) © Emily King; page 64 (top left) © Emily King, (top right) © Emily King, (bottom) © Laura Petrilla; page 78 (top left) © Emily King, (top right) © Laura Petrilla, (bottom) © Emily King; page 89 (top) © Pittsburgh Cultural Trust / Jason Cohn, (bottom) © Omni William Penn Hotel; page 95 (top) © Adam Milliron, (bottom) © Club Café; page 103 (top) © Hidden Harbor, (bottom) © Kurt Miller; page 107 (top left) © Jody O'Donnell, (top right) © Emily King, (bottom) © Mixtape; page 113 (top) © Joey Kennedy, (bottom) © Emily King; page 118 (top left) © Emily King, (top right) © Mattress Factory/Visit Pittsburgh, (bottom) © Emily King; page 121 (top left) © Emily King, (top right) © Emily King, (bottom) © Pittsburgh Cultural Trust ; page 124 (top left) © Michael Rubino, (top right) © Emily King, (bottom) © Rachellynn Schoen; page 132 (top left) © Ron Rankin/VisitPittsburgh, (top right) © Pittsburgh Cultural Trust, (bottom) © Adam Isovitsch; page 135 (top) © Laura Petrilla, (bottom) © Dave DiCello; page 140 (top) © Emily King, (bottom) © Emily King; page 143 (top) © Dave DiCello, (bottom) © Just Ducky / VisitPittsburgh; page 147 (top) © Emily King, (bottom) © Emily King; page 152 (top) © Martha Rial, (bottom) © VisitPittsburgh; page 158 (top left) © Emily King, (top right) © Emily King, (bottom) © Social Status; page 162 (top left) © Emily King, (top right) © Emily King, (bottom) © SouthSide Works / VisitPittsburgh; page 167 (top left) © Emily King, (top right) © Emily King, (bottom) © Emily King; page 179 (top) © Jeff Greenberg / VisitPittsburgh, (bottom) © Emily King; page 183 (top) © Linda Morland | Dreamstime, (bottom) © Emily King; page 186 (top left) © Fairmont Pittsburgh, (top right) © Renaissance Pittsburgh Hotel, (bottom) © Cris Molina for Kimpton Hotels; page 193 (top left) © Inn on Negley, (top right) © Emily King, (bottom) © Emily King; page 196 (top) © VisitPittsburgh, (bottom) © Kurt Miller/ VisitPittsburgh; page 203 (top left) © VisitPittsburgh, (top right) © VisitPittsburgh, (bottom) © Kenneth Keifer | Dreamstime; page 214 (top) © Johnstown Area Heritage Association, (bottom) © Tina Patterson | Dreamstime; page 220 (top) © Mike D. Tankosich | Dreamstime.com, (bottom) © Richard Nowitz; page 231 (top) © Roy Engelbrecht, (bottom) © Allegheny County Airport Authority

Acknowledgments

I'd like to thank my friends, family and husband, Frank, for their ongoing support, encouragement, and coffee and restaurant dates to help me with the process of researching and writing this guide. I'd also like to thank the team at Avalon Travel who made the writing and editing process so smooth and enjoyable.

MOON PITTSBURGH

Avalon Travel
Hachette Book Group
1700 Fourth Street
Berkeley, CA 94710, USA
www.moon.com

Editor and Series Manager: Leah Gordon
Copy Editor: Deana Shields
Graphics Coordinator: Krista Anderson
Production Coordinator: Krista Anderson
Cover Design: Faceout Studios, Charles Brock
Moon Logo: Tim McGrath
Map Editor: Albert Angulo
Cartographer: Brian Shotwell
Indexer: Rachel Kuhn

ISBN-13: 9781631215551

Printing History
1st Edition — 2007
4th Edition — July 2018
5 4 3 2 1

Front cover photo: Mount Washington, © Kord.com/Getty Images
Back cover photo: Andy Warhol Bridge, © Jonathan Steele/Dreamstime.com

Printed in Canada by Friesens